21 世纪高职高专电子信息系列技能型规划教材

U0369891

电子信息专业英语

主　编　高金玉

副主编　王维利　王立亚

参　编　于宏伟　韩学尧　姜　明

北京大学出版社
PEKING UNIVERSITY PRESS

内 容 简 介

本书为"21世纪全国高职高专电子信息系列技能型规划教材"之一,以培养学生阅读和理解机电类专业英语的能力为目标,内容丰富,涵盖了电子技术、机电一体化技术、单片机技术、可编程控制器、电气控制技术、现代通信技术等方面的专业英语知识。每篇课文后都配有词汇、短语、注释、课后练习及参考译文,每个单元后配有专业英语的词法、语法及翻译技巧,以便读者学习。

本书旨在扩大学生的专业词汇量,提高学生英文专业文章的阅读能力,同时使学生获得更多机电类专业方面的新知识,并了解新的发展动态。

本书可作为高职高专院校机电类、电子信息类、自动化类专业的专业英语教学用书,也可供相应水平的读者与技术人员参考使用。

图书在版编目(CIP)数据

电子信息专业英语/高金玉主编. —北京:北京大学出版社,2010.10

(21世纪高职高专电子信息系列技能型规划教材)

ISBN 978-7-301-17877-5

Ⅰ. ①电… Ⅱ. ①高… Ⅲ. ①电子技术—英语—高等学校:技术学校—教材②信息技术—英语—高等学校:技术学校—教材 Ⅳ. ①H31

中国版本图书馆CIP数据核字(2010)第192798号

书 名:	**电子信息专业英语**
著作责任者:	高金玉 主编
策 划 编 辑:	赖 青 张永见
责 任 编 辑:	李娉婷
标 准 书 号:	ISBN 978-7-301-17877-5/TN·0062
出 版 者:	北京大学出版社
地 址:	北京市海淀区成府路205号 100871
网 址:	http://www.pup.cn http://www.pup6.com
电 话:	邮购部 010-62752015 发行部 010-62750672 编辑部 010-62750667
电 子 邮 箱:	pup_6@163.com
印 刷 者:	北京虎彩文化传播有限公司
发 行 者:	北京大学出版社
经 销 者:	新华书店
	787mm×1092mm 16开本 14.5印张 333千字
	2010年10月第1版 2022年1月第7次印刷
定 价:	36.00元

前　言

通过学习专业英语，可以扩大专业词汇量，提高英文专业资料的阅读能力，同时获得更多机电类专业方面的新知识和新的发展动态。

本书为"21世纪全国高职高专电子信息系列技能型规划教材"之一。本书具有如下特点。

(1) 立足于高等职业教育，面向高职高专教育对象，以能力培养为本位，以训练为手段，旨在切实提高读者阅读和理解电子信息类专业英语的能力。每个单元模块目标明确，并将科技英语的词法、语法及阅读翻译技巧贯穿于专业英语的教学中，有针对性地加以训练，使学生掌握阅读技巧，提高阅读科技英语资料的能力。

(2) 在内容安排上，根据高职高专机电类专业所涉及的专业课程分为电子技术基础、自动化技术及应用、通信技术三大部分。本书共12个单元，每个单元3篇课文，前两篇为精读课文，第3篇为阅读材料。每个单元突出一个领域的技术与应用，是机电类专业通用的专业英语教材。

(3) 每篇课文后都提供了课后练习题，具有较强的针对性，有利于检验学生掌握课文的程度，便于教师更好地组织教学活动；每个单元中的阅读材料可作为学生自学内容，学生通过阅读，可以了解更多的专业知识。

(4) 选材新颖，许多内容选自英、美等国外文献原著；点面结合，注重各专业、学科间知识的相关性；选材不仅能体现专业性，还能体现趣味性；贴近实际，选取了大量的新知识和新的应用实例。

(5) 为便于提高学生阅读英文专业资料的能力，本书还系统介绍了专业英语的词法、语法特点与翻译技巧，对学生掌握和理解专业词汇会有很大的帮助。

本书由高金玉担任主编，王维利、王立亚担任副主编，于宏伟、韩学尧、姜明参与编写；由高金玉、王维利、于宏伟、姜明统稿。本书具体编写分工如下：韩学尧编写了第1~3单元；姜明编写了第4单元；王维利和王立亚编写了第5~8单元，并汇总、整理常用专业英语词汇和短语；于宏伟编写了第9~12单元；于宏伟、韩学尧整理编写了专业英语的词法、语法及翻译技巧。

本书在编写时参考了大量的文献资料及一些专业网站，在此对这些文献资料的作者深表谢意，并对各位参与编写工作的老师一并致以诚挚的谢意。

本书建议总课时为72学时，各章节建议课时分配见下表。

章　节	建议课时
Part Ⅰ　Electronics	24
Part Ⅱ　Automatic Control Technology	24
Part Ⅲ　Communications	24

由于编者水平有限，加之时间仓促，书中难免有不足、疏漏之外，敬请广大读者不吝赐教，以便对本书进行进一步修订与完善。

编　者

2010年8月

Contents

Part I
Electronics

Unit One　Basic Knowledge of Electronics

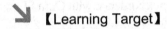 【Learning Target】

In this Unit, our target is to train your reading comprehension. Try to grasp the main idea of these passages and learn the speciality vocabularies.

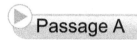
Passage A

Resistors, Capacitors and Inductors

Questions for passage discussion

What is a resistor? And what are the characteristics of a resistor?
What is a capacitor? And what is the capacitance? What can capacitors be applied to?
What can inductors be used to do?

Text

A resistor(Fig. 1.1) is a two-terminal electronic component that produces a voltage across its terminals that is proportional to the electric current through it in accordance with Ohm's Law: $V = IR$.

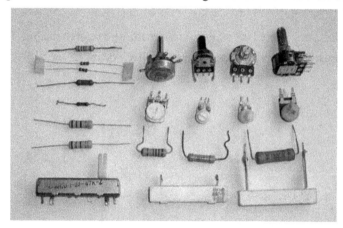

Fig. 1.1   Resistors

Resistors are elements of electrical networks and electronic circuits and are ubiquitous in most electronic equipment. Practical resistors can be made of various compounds and films, as well as resistance wire (wire made of a high-resistivity alloy, such as nickel/chrome). The primary characteristics of a resistor are the resistance, the tolerance, maximum working voltage and the power rating. Other characteristics include temperature coefficient, noise, inductance and critical resistance. The ohm (symbol: Ω) is a unit of electrical resistance. Commonly used in electrical and electronic usage are the kilohm and megohm.

Capacitors(Fig. 1.2) store electric charge. They are used with resistors in timing circuits because it takes time for a capacitor to fill with charge. They are used to smooth DC supplies by acting as a reservoir of charge. They are also used in filter circuits because capacitors easily pass AC (changing) signals but they block DC (constant) signals.

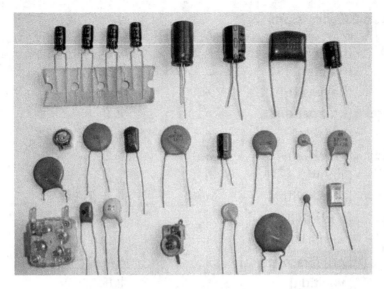

Fig. 1.2   Capacitors

Capacitance is a measure of a capacitor's ability to store charge. A larger capacitance means that more charge can be stored. Capacitance is measured in farads, symbol F. However 1F is very large, so prefixes are used to show the smaller values. Three prefixes are used, μ (micro), n (nano) and p (pico).

An inductor (Fig. 1.3) is formed by winding wire around a suitable mold to form a coil. Its electrical property is called inductance and the unit for it is the henry, symbol H. 1H is very large so mH(milli-henry) and μH(micro-henry) are used, 1000μH = 1mH and 1000mH = 1H. Iron and ferrite cores increase the inductance. Inductors are mainly used in tuned circuits and to block high frequency AC signals. They pass DC easily, but block AC signals, this is the opposite of capacitors. Inductors are rarely found in simple projects, but one exception is the tuning coil of a radio receiver. This is an inductor which you may have to make yourself by neatly winding enamelled copper wire around a ferrite rod.

Fig. 1.3   Inductors

New Words and Expressions

resistance	[ri'zistəns]	*n.*	电阻
resistor	[ri'zistə]	*n.*	电阻器
capacitor	[kə'pæsitə]	*n.*	电容器
capacitance	[kə'pæsitəns]	*n.*	电容
inductor	[in'dʌktə]	*n.*	电感器
inductance	[in'dʌktəns]	*n.*	电感
unit	['juːnit]	*n.*	单位
ubiquitous	[juː'bikwitəs]	*adj*	普遍存在的
resistivity	[ˌriːzis'tiviti, riˌz-]	*n.*	电阻系数
alloy	['æləi,ə'ləi]	*n.*	合金
prefix	[ˌpriː'fiks,'priːfiks]	*n.*	前缀
voltage	['vəultidʒ]	*n.*	电压
constant	['kɔnstənt]	*n.*	常数，常量
AC			交流
DC			直流
charge	[tʃɑːdʒ]	*n.*	电荷
mold	[məuld]	*n.*	模子，模型
coil	[kɔil]	*n.*	线圈
frequency	['frikwənsɪ]	*n.*	频率
Ohm's Law			欧姆定律
electronic circuits			电子电路
timing circuits			定时电路
critical resistance			临界电阻
power rating			额定功率
enamelled copper wire			漆包线
ferrite cores			铁氧体磁芯
filter circuits			滤波电路
ferrite rod			铁磁棒

Notes

1. A resistor is a two-terminal electronic component that produces a voltage across its terminals that is proportional to the electric current through it in accordance with Ohm's Law: $V = IR$.

电阻器是一个二端电子元件。根据欧姆定律 $V=IR$，电阻两端的电压正比于通过它的电流。

be proportional to：正比于……

2. The ohm (symbol: Ω) is a unit of electrical resistance.

电阻的单位是欧姆。unit，单位

3. They are also used in filter circuits because capacitors easily pass AC (changing) signals but they block DC (constant) signals.

AC (changing) signals 交流信号；DC (constant) signals 直流信号

4. An inductor is formed by winding wire around a suitable mold to form a coil.

be formed by ： 由……组成(形成)

Exercises

Ⅰ. **Try to match the following columns.**

1. two-terminal component   电子电路

2. Ohm's Law   额定功率

3. electronic circuits   二端元件

4. power rating   欧姆定律

5. critical resistance   滤波电路

6. electric charge   漆包线

7. enamelled copper wire   电荷

8. filter circuits   临界电阻

Ⅱ. **Fill in the blanks in each of the following sentences.**

1. _____is proportional to the electric current through the resistor.

2. Practical resistors can be made of various compounds and _____, as well as _____.

3. Capacitance is a measure of a capacitor's ability to store _____.

4. An inductor is formed by winding wire around a suitable _____ to form a _____.

5. Inductors are mainly used in _____ and to block high frequency AC signals.

Passage B

Direct and Alternating Current

Questions for passage discussion

What is direct circuit? What is alternating circuit?

How can we convert alternating current into direct current?

And how can we convert direct current into alternating current?

What can alternating circuit be used to do and what is the advantage of it?

Text

Circuits consisting of just one battery and one load resistance are very simple to analyze, but they are not often found in practical applications. Usually, we find circuits where more than two components are connected together. And there are two basic ways in which to connect more than two circuit components: series and parallel. Series circuit is a circuit in which two or more pieces of apparatus are connected end to end or in tandem where the current is not divided at any point. Parallel circuit, a closed circuit in which the current divides into two or more paths before recombining to complete the circuit, is the opposite of series circuit.

And we know that if two resistors were connected in series, to get the total resistance of two resistors, R1 and R2, you add them together. On the other hand, to find total resistance of two in parallel circuits, you have to add the reciprocals of the resistances and take the reciprocal of the result. Capacitors and inductors in series circuits or in parallel circuits have the similar characters.

It's one of the main classification methods about circuits in electronics. Not by connecting methods of components in circuit , it is well known that electric circuit is usually divided into two classes: direct circuit and alternating circuit, by the signal or current flowing through direct current, abbreviation, DC, is a current that always flows in the same direction (i.e., the polarity never reverses). The current might be constant, as from a battery or a regulated power supply; it might be pulsating, as from an unfiltered rectifier. And these systems are usually called direct current circuit. The first utility systems installed by Edison used DC technology. Not long after Edison installed his direct current system, others realized that the use of an alternating current system had advantages over the DC.

Every time we turn on a television set, a radio, or any of other electrical appliances, we are calling on alternating currents to provide the power to operate them. But, what is the alternating current? Different from direct current moving through a conductor or circuit in one direction only, alternating current, abbreviation, AC, is a current that periodically reverses its direction of flow. As Fig. 1.4 showing, in one cycle, an alternation starts at zero, rises to a maximum positive level at 90 degrees, returns to zero at 180 degrees, rises to a maximum negative level at 270 degrees, and again returns to zero at 360 degrees. The number of such cycles completed per second is termed the AC frequency. In the United States and many other areas of the world, the frequency is 60 hertz or cycles per second. And in our country the current used for the transmission of electrical energy and the operation of common machines has a frequency of 50 hertz.

AC is widely used for the operation of the vast majority of circuits, which can be transmitted over long distances, even without using connecting wires between source and receiver, provided the change rate of current is fast enough, transformed to various voltages and easily to larger or smaller values using a device known as a transformer, but DC cannot. However, in many circuit applications such as general purpose lighting and heating, either AC or DC can be used. We can convert DC to AC by using a DC-AC converter, a circuit that converts a DC input voltage into an AC output voltage, with or without step-up or step-down, and AC to DC by rectification circuit formed by the diode, resistor and capacitor.

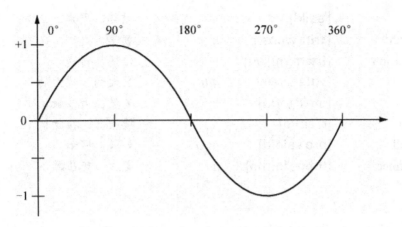

Fig. 1.4 Alternating current

New Words and Expressions

battery	['bætəri]	n.	电源
application	[ˌæpli'keiʃən]	n.	应用
component	[kəm'pəunənt]	n.	器件，元件
series	['siəriz]	n.	串联
parallel	['pærəlel]	n.	并联
apparatus	[ˌæpə'reitəs]	n.	器件，仪器
tandem	['tændəm]	adv.	串联式，双人的
divide	[di'vaid]	v.	分离，隔开
recombine	[ri:kəm'bain]	vt.	合并，汇合
opposite	['ɔpəzit]	adj.	相反，不同
reciprocal	[ri'siprəkəl]	n.	倒数
classification	[ˌklæsifi'keiʃən]	n.	分类，类别
direct	[di'rekt]	adj.	直流，直接
alternating			交流，交变
current	['kʌrənt]	n.	电流
abbreviation	[əˌbri:vi'eiʃən]	n.	缩写，简写
polarity	[pəu'læriti]	n.	极性
reverse	[ri'və:s]	v.	反转，倒相
constant	['kɔnstənt]	n.	恒定，不变，常量
regulate	['regjuleit]	v.	控制，调节
pulsate	['pʌlseit]	v.	波动的，脉动的
unfilter	[ʌn'filtə]	adj.	未滤波的
rectifier	['rektifaiə]	n.	整流，整流器
utility	[ju(:)"tiliti]	n.	应用程序，功用
periodically	[ˌpiəri'ɔdikəli]	adv.	周期性地

cycle	['saikl]	*n.*	循环，周期
frequency	['friːkwənsi]	*n.*	频率
transmission	[trænz'miʃən]	*v.*	传播，传送
vast	[vɑːst, væst]	*adj.*	巨大的，广大的
majority	[mə'dʒɔriti]	*n.*	多数，大多数
receiver	[ri'siːvə]	*n.*	接收器，接收机
provided	[prə'vaidid]	*conj.*	如果，假如
transformer	[træns'fɔːmə]	*n.*	变压，变压器

Notes

1. Series circuit is a circuit in which two or more pieces of apparatus are connected end to end or in tandem where the current is not divided at any point.

end to end: 首尾相连

2. On the other hand, to find total resistance of two in parallel circuits, you add the reciprocals of the resistances and take the reciprocal of the result.

on the other hand: 另一方面

the reciprocal of …: ……的倒数

3. Not by connecting methods of components in circuit, it is well known that electric circuit is usually divided into two classes: direct circuit and alternating circuit, by the signal or current flowing through.

it is well known that: 众所周知

be divided into … : 被分成……

4. Direct current, abbreviation, DC, is a current that always flows in the same direction (i.e., the polarity never reverses).

in the same direction: 相同的方向

5. Not long after Edison installed his direct current system, others realized that the use of an alternating current system had advantages over the DC.

not long after … : 在……后不久

have an advantage over … : 比……有优势

Exercises

I. Try to match the following columns.

1. step-up	负载
2. step-down	直流电路
3. DC-AC converter	交流电路
4. regulated power	整流电路
5. load resistance	直流-交流转换器
6. series circuit	降压
7. parallel circuit	稳压电源

8. direct circuit   升压
9. alternating circuit   并联电路
10. rectification circuit   串联电路

II. Translate the following sentences into Chinese.

1. Circuits consisting of just one battery and one load resistance are very simple to analyze, but they are not often found in practical applications.

2. And there are two basic ways in which to connect more than two circuit components: series and parallel.

3. On the other hand, to find total resistance of two in parallel circuits, you add the reciprocals of the resistances and take the reciprocal of the result.

4. Not by connecting methods of components in circuit, it is well known that electric circuit is usually divided into two classes: direct circuit and alternating circuit, by the signal or current flowing through.

5. Direct current, abbreviation, DC, is a current that always flows in the same direction (i.e., the polarity never reverses).

6. AC is widely used for the operation of the vast majority of circuits., which can be transmitted over long distances, even without using connecting wires between source and receiver , provided the change rate of current is fast enough, transformed to various voltages and easily to larger or smaller values using a device known as a transformer, but DC cannot.

Integrated Circuits

Questions for passage discussion

What is the integrated circuit? Which components can be included in a integrated circuit?
Which systems can IC be applied to?
What benefits using the IC can bring?

Text

In 1958, an extremely important device was invented independently by Jack Kilby, working at Texas Instruments, and by Noyce and Moore at Fairchild Semiconductor: the integrated circuit (IC, see Fig. 1.5), which combines BJTs, MOSFETs, resistors, and capacitors, as well as their interconnections, into a functional circuit on a single chip.

Fig. 1.5   Integrated circuits

Integrated circuits are usually called ICs or chips. They are complex circuits which are combination of a few interconnected circuit elements such as transistors, diodes, capacitors and resistors produced in a single manufacturing process on one and the same bearing structure, called the substrate, and intended to perform a definite function involved in converting information.

In the early 1960s, ICs contained perhaps 100 devices, and the smallest features were about 25 micrometers (μm). Realizing that the cost of complex electronic systems could be reduced dramatically by the use of more complex ICs, process engineers have worked diligently to increase the practical dimensions of chips and to reduce the sizes of the devices. Today's most advanced ICs contain in excess of 10 million devices and have features as small as $0.25\,\mu m$ (A human hair is about $25\,\mu m$ in diameter). The trend toward smaller devices is expected to continue. In addition to the increased number of devices, the reduction in the size of features results in higher performance (i.e., faster) digital circuits. Thus, we can anticipate even greater advances in the field of electronics.

The manufacturing techniques used for ICs can be divided into two main types: film technique and monolithic technique. And ICs can be classified by function into two: circuits to be applied in digital systems and those to be applied in linear systems. The digital ICs are employed mostly in computers, electronic counters, frequency synthesizers and digital instruments. And the analog or linear ICs operate over a continuous range, and include such devices as operational amplifiers.

These advances will result from teamwork by physical electronics scientists, process engineers, circuit designers, and systems designers. Although this book primarily considers circuit design, it provides useful background information for all engineers in the electronics industry.

The invention of IC is a great revolution in the electronic industry. Sharp size, weight reductions are possible with these techniques; and more importantly, high reliability, excellent functional performance, low cost and low power dissipation can be achieved. ICs are widely used in the electronic industry.

Exercises

Ⅰ. Answer the following questions.

1. When did the integrated circuits be invented?

2. How many methods did manufacturing techniques use for ICs?

Ⅱ. Translate the following sentences into Chinese.

1. In the early 1960s, ICs contained perhaps 100 devices, and the smallest features were about 25 micrometers (μm).

2. In addition to the increased number of devices, the reduction in the size of features results in higher performance (i.e., faster) digital circuits.

3. The manufacturing techniques used for ICs can be divided into two main types: film technique and monolithic technique.

4.   ICs can be classified by function into two: circuits to be applied in digital systems and those to be applied in linear systems.

Translating Skills

专业英语的语法特点

专业英语作为一种揭示客观外部世界的本质和规律的信息传递工具，具有准确、简明扼要和客观正式等特点。科技文章文体的特点是：语言简练、结构严谨、逻辑性强、原理概念清楚、重点突出、段落章节分明。具体而言，专业英语在用词、语法结构及表达方式上有其自身的特点，下面分别予以介绍。

1. 词汇

(1) 大量使用专业词汇和半专业词汇，例如，calculus(微积分学)、bandwidth(带宽)、flip-flop(触发器)等是专业词汇，而 series、work 等是半专业词汇，在不同的学科领域含义有所不同，例如 series 可翻译成"级数"(数学)，也可翻译成"串联"(电学)。

(2) 大量使用词缀和词根，例如，外语教学与研究出版社出版的《英汉双解信息技术词典》中以 tele-构成的单词有 30 个。

(3) 较多使用缩略词，常见的如 PCM(Pulse-Coded Modulation，脉冲编码调制)、CDMA(Code Division Multiple Access，码分多址)、DSP(Digital Signal Processing，数字信号处理)等。

(4) 词性变换多，例如 sound 一词作名词时，常译为"声音、语音"，作动词时，常译为"听起来"，作形容词时，以"合理的，健全的"较为多见。

2. 词法

(1) 常用一般现在时态，陈述真理或客观规律。

【例 1】 Vector and matrix techniques provide the framework for much of the developments in modem engineering.

矢量和矩阵方法为现代工程学的发展提供了框架。

(2) 广泛使用被动语态，强调所论述的客观事物。

【例 2】 Chapters 7 and 8 are devoted to the calculus of functions of one variable and，recognizing again the mixed background knowledge in mathematics of the students, the basic ideas and techniques of differentiation and integration are reviewed in Chapter 7.

第 7 章和第 8 章讨论单变量函数的微积分，考虑到学生数学基础参差不齐，第 7 章复习微分与积分的基本概念与方法。

(3) 普遍使用名词词组及名词化结构，强调客观存在的事实而非某一行为，故常使用表示动作或状态的抽象名词。

【例 3】 Television is the transmission and reception of images of moving objects by radio waves.

电视通过无线电波发射和接收移动物体的图像。

(4) 使用非限定动词，使句子简明。

【例 4】 The calculus, aided by analytic geometry, proved to be astonishingly powerful and capable of attacking hosts of problems that had been baffling and quite unassailable in earlier days.

微积分辅以解析几何是一个非常强大的工具，能够解决许多困扰人们已久甚至以前认为无法解决的问题。

3. 句法

(1) 较常使用"无生命主语+及物动词+宾语(+宾语补足语)"句型。

【例 5】 Chapter 6 provides a basic introduction to the ideas of sequences, series and limits.

第 6 章介绍序列、级数及极限等基本概念。

(2) 常用 it 作形式主语或形式宾语。

【例 6】 It has been proved that induced voltage causes a current to flow in opposition to the force producing it.

已经证明，感应电压使电流的方向与产生电流的磁场力方向相反。

【例 7】 The invention of radio has made it possible for mankind to communicate with each other over a long distance.

无线电的发明使人类有可能进行远距离通信。

(3) 尽量用紧缩型状语从句而不用完整句。

【例 8】 While designed primarily for use by engineering students, it is believed that the book is also highly suitable for students of the physical sciences and applied mathematics.

尽管本书主要为工科学生所用，我们相信，它也非常适合于修读物理与应用数学的学生。

(4) 割裂修饰比较普遍(包括短语或从句被分隔)。

【例 9】 It is hoped that this provision, together with the large number of worked examples and style of presentation, also makes the book suitable for private or directed study. (主谓分离)

希望这些练习，以及书中提供的大量实例及本书的写作风格也使本书适于自学和课堂教学。

(5) 较多使用祈使语气。

【例 10】 Let the forward-pass transfer function be given by the linear difference equation.

设前向传递函数由线性差分方程给出。

(6) 句中并列成分(各种并列短语、单词或从句)较多。

【例 11】 Radar has certain inherent advantages over detection systems employing light waves: (1) it has greater ranges, (2) it is usable in any weather and in day or night, and (3) the electronic circuitry and components for transmitting, receiving, amplifying, detecting and measuring are highly developed.

与光波检测系统相比，雷达具有如下优点：(1)检测范围广；(2)可全天候使用；(3)拥有先进的电子元器件与电子线路，可用于发射、接收、放大、检测和测量。

(7) 复杂长句多。科学技术要阐明事物之间错综复杂的关系，因而需要用复杂的语法关系来表达严密复杂的思维。长句所表达的科技内容的严密性、准确性和逻辑性较强。

【例 12】 Recognizing the increasing use of numerical methods in engineering practice, which often complement the use of analytical methods in analysis and design and are of ultimate relevance when solving complex engineering problems, there is wide agreement that they should be integrated within the mathematics curriculum.

本句是一个主从复合句，主句为 there is…，由 that 引导同位语从句对 agreement 进行补充说明；现在分词短语 recognizing…构成紧缩型状语从句表原因，which 引导的非限定性定语从句修饰 numerical methods，其谓语为两个并列的成分，该句中还嵌套了一个由 when 引导的紧缩型时间状语从句。

在分析与设计过程中常用数值计算方法来弥补解析法的不足，因此在求解复杂的工程问题时数值方法往往是最为恰当的。由于认识到数值方法在工程实践中的应用日趋增长，人们普遍认为它应该被整合到数学课程中来。

Unit Two   Analog Circuit

↘ 【Learning Target】

In this unit, our target is to introduce a nonlinear electrical device to you and improve your reading comprehension. Try to grasp the main idea of these passages quickly and learn the characters of the diode and transistor.

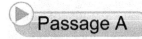

Diode

Questions for passage discussion

What is the diode? And what are the characteristics of a diode?

What can diode be used to do?

Is the diode a linear device or a nonlinear device? And what kinds of diodes are discussed in the passage?

Text

A diode is a nonlinear electrical device allowing current to move through it in one direction with far greater ease than in the other and usually acting as a one-way valve for current. The most common kind of diode in modern circuit design is the semiconductor diode, although other diode technologies exist. Semiconductor diodes are symbolized in schematic diagrams such as Fig. 2.1.

In Fig. 2.1, arrows indicate the direction of electroncurrent flow.

When placed in a simple battery-lamp circuit, the diode will either allow or prevent current through the lamp, depending on the polarity of the applied voltage (Fig. 2.2).

Fig. 2.2 (a) Current flow is permitted; the diode is forward biased.

Fig. 2.2 (b) Current flow is prohibited; the diode is reversed biased.

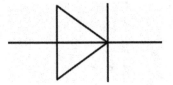   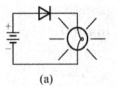

(a)   (b)

Fig. 2.1   Semiconductor diode schematic symbol   Fig. 2.2   Diode operation

When the polarity of the battery is such that electrons are allowed to flow through the diode, the diode is said to be forward-biased. Conversely, when the battery is "backward" and the diode blocks current, the diode is said to be reverse-biased. A diode may be thought of as like a switch: "closed" when forward-biased and "open" when reverse-biased. Oddly enough, the direction of the diode symbol's "arrowhead" points against the direction of electron flow. This is because the diode symbol was invented by engineers, who predominantly use conventional flow notation in their schematics, showing current as a flow of charge from the positive (+) side of the voltage source to the negative (−). This convention holds true for all semiconductor symbols possessing "arrowheads". The arrow points in the permitted direction of conventional flow, and against the permitted direction of electron flow.

One way to make a semiconductor diode is to metallurgically create a wafer of silicon containing N-type material adjoining P-type material. In an n-channel MOSFET, for example, the n-type drain juxtaposed to the p-type channel region forms a diode. An ohmmeter may be used to qualitatively check diode function. There should be low resistance measured one way and very high resistance measured the other way. When using an ohmmeter for this purpose, be sure you know which test lead is positive and which is negative! The actual polarity may not follow the colors of the leads as you might expect, depending on the particular design of meter.

The diode is popularly applied in electric equipment whether for military use or civilian use. For example: peak detector, clamper circuits, voltage multipliers and rectification which is the most popular application of the diode. And now LED(light emitting diode),a type of diode which can be directly change the electric signal into the photic signal, is popularly used for lighting, display, signal and decoration in our daily life.

New Words and Expressions

diode	['daiəud]	n.	二极管
nonlinear	['nɔn'liniə]	adj.	非线性
one-way			单向的
valve	[vælv]	n.	阀门
semiconductor	['semikən'dɔktə]	n.	半导体
schematic	[ski:'mætik]	n.	原理图
symbol	['simbəl]	n.	图表
arrow	['ærəu]	n.	箭头
battery	['bætəri]	n.	电源
lamp	[læmp]	n.	灯
permit	[pə'mit]	v.	准许
prohibit	[prə'hibit]	v.	禁止
polarity	[pəu'lærəti]	n.	极性
conversely	['kɔnvə:sli]	adv.	相反地
switch	[switʃ]	n.	开关
oddly	['ɔdli]	adv.	奇怪地
invent	[in'vent]	v.	发明
predominantly	[pri'dɔminəntli]	adv.	占主导地位地
conventional	[kən'venʃənl]	adj.	习惯的，传统的
notation	[nəu'teiʃən]	n.	符号，标记
metallurgically	[,metə'lə:dʒikəli]	adv.	冶金
silicon	['silikən]	n.	硅
N-type			N 型
P-type			P 型

juxtaposed	[ˌdʒʌkstəˈpəuad]	adj.	紧靠的
ohmmeter	[ˈəumˌmiːtə]	n.	欧姆表
qualitatively	[ˈkwɔlitətivli]	adv.	定性地
purpose	[ˈpəːpəs]	n.	目的
expect	[iksˈpekt]	v.	期望
military	[ˈmilitəri]	adj.	军用的
civilian	[siˈviljən]	adj.	民用的
peak	[piːk]	n.	峰值
clamper	[ˈklæmpə]	n.	钳子
rectification	[rektifikeiʃən]	n.	整流
photic	[ˈfəutik]	n.	光
decoration	[ˌdekəˈreiʃne]	v.	装潢，装饰

Notes

1. A diode is a nonlinear electrical device allowing current to move through it in one direction with far greater ease than in the other and usually acting as a one-way valve for current. 二极管是一种非线性器件，一个方向很容易通过电流，而另外一个方向却很难，因此，通常用做电流的单向阀门。

act as：作为……使用

2. When placed in a simple battery-lamp circuit, the diode will either allow or prevent current through the lamp, depending on the polarity of the applied voltage.

either … or …：或者……或者……

depend on：依赖于

3. When the polarity of the battery is such that electrons are allowed to flow through the diode, the diode is said to be forward-biase.

is said to be：被称为……

4. Oddly enough, the direction of the diode symbol's "arrowhead" points against the direction of electron flow.

oddly enough：稀奇的是

5. This convention holds true for all semiconductor symbols possessing "arrowheads".

hold true for：适用于

Exercises

Ⅰ. **Try to match the following columns.**

1. MOSFET   正向偏置

2. schematic diagrams   施加电压

3. forward-biased   高电阻

4. reverse-biased   电压倍增器

5. LED   原理图
6. voltage multipliers   反向偏置
7. high resistance   发光二极管
8. applied voltage   金属氧化物半导体场效应管

II. Translate the following sentences into Chinese.

1. Semiconductor diodes are symbolized in schematic diagrams such as Fig. 2.1.

2. A diode may be thought of as like a switch: "closed" when forward-biased and "open" when reverse-biased.

3. This is because the diode symbol was invented by engineers, who predominantly use conventional flow notation in their schematics, showing current as a flow of charge from the positive (+) side of the voltage source to the negative (−).

4. One way to make a semiconductor diode is to metallurgically create a wafer of silicon containing N-type material adjoining P-type material.

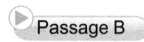

Passage B

Transistor

Questions for passage discussion

What is the transistor? And what are the characteristics of a transistor?

What can transistor be used to do?

Is the transistor a linear device or a nonlinear device? And what kinds of transistors are discussed in the passage?

Text

The transistor is a nonlinear semiconductor device being similar to the diode, commonly used as an amplifier or an electrically controlled switch. Because of its fast response and accuracy, the transistor may be used in a wide variety of digital and analog functions, including amplification, switching, voltage regulation, signal modulation, and oscillators. Transistors may be packaged individually or as part of an integrated circuit, which may hold a billion or more transistors in a very small area. So the transistor is becoming the fundamental building block of the circuitry that governs the operation of computers, cellular phones, and all other modern electronics.

There are two major transistor categories: The bipolar transistor, also called "the bipolar junction transistor" (BJT), and the field effect transistor (FET). The first type of solid-state electronic transistor was made by researchers William Shockley, John Bardeen and Walter Brattain at Bell Laboratories in December 1947. And bipolar junction transistor was invented by William Shockly in 1950 which is the common stander of the current transistor.

The bipolar junction transistor consists of three regions of semiconductor material. One type is called a NPN transistor, in which two regions of N-type material sandwich a very thin layer of P-type material. The two N-type material regions of the NPN transistor are called the emitter and collector and the P-type material is called the base. NPN transistors are symbolized in schematic diagrams such as Fig. 2.3.

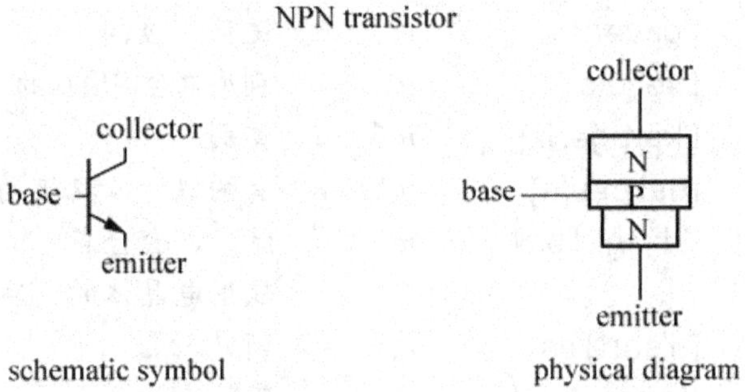

NPN transistor

schematic symbol　　　　　　　　physical diagram

Fig. 2.3　The schematic symbol and physical diagram of NPN transistor

When used as an amplifying element, the base to emitter junction is in a "forward-biased" (conducting) condition, and the base to collector junction is "reverse-biased" or non-conducting. Small changes in the base to emitter current (the input signal) cause either holes (for PNP devices) or free electrons (for NPN) to enter the base from the emitter. The attracting voltage of the collector causes the majority of these charges to cross into and be collected by the collector, resulting in amplification.

The only functional difference between a PNP transistor and an NPN transistor is the proper biasing (polarity) of the junctions when operating. For any given state of operation, the current directions and voltage polarities for each type of transistor are exactly opposite each other.

There are three ways of connecting a transistor, depending on the use to which it is being put. The ways are classified by the electrode that is common to both the input and the output. They are called: common-base configuration, common-emitter configuration, and common-collector configuration.

Although the first transistors and first silicon chips used bipolar transistors, most chips today are FET wired as CMOS logic, which consume less power.A FET has three terminals, a source, a drain and a gate. The semiconductor region between source and drain is called a channel and its conductivity is controlled by the potential of the gate terminal.

New Words and Expressions

transistor	[træn'zistə]	n.	三极管
amplifier	['æmpli‚faiə]	n.	放大器

response	[ris'pɔns]	n.	反应
accuracy	['ækjurəsi]	n.	精确，准确
semiconductor	[ˌsemikən'dʌktə]	n.	半导体
regulation	[ˌregju'leiʃən]	n.	管理，控制
oscillator	['ɔsileitə]	n.	振荡器
package	['pækidʒ]	v.	包装，封装
individually	[ˌindi'vidjuəli]	adv.	分别地，独立地
integrated	['intigreitid]	adj.	集成的
billion	['biljən]	adj.	十亿，数以十亿计的，大量
fundamental	[ˌfʌndə'mentəl]	adj.	基本的，必要的
govern	['gʌvən]	v.	统治，控制
cellular	['seljulə]	adj.	利用电台网通信的,蜂窝式无线通信系统的
categories	['kætigəriz]	n.	类别
bipolar	[bai'pəulə]	adj.	有两极的，双极的；两极世界的
junction	['dʒʌŋkʃən]	n.	结点，会合点
solid-state			使用电晶体的，不用真空管的
researchers	[ri'sə:tʃəs]	n.	研究人员
laboratory	[lə'bɔrətəri]	n.	实验室
consist	[kən'sist]	v.	包含，包括
sandwich	['sænwidʒ]	v.	把……夹在……之间
emitter	[i'mitə]	n.	发射极
collector	[kə'lektə]	n.	集电极
base	[beis]	n.	基极
element	['elimənt]	n.	原理，特性
conduct	[kən'dʌkt]	v.	传导
condition	[kən'diʃən]	n.	状态
hole	[həul]	n.	空穴
attract	[ə'trækt]	v.	吸引
operation	[ˌɔpə'reiʃən]	n.	工作，运行
opposite	['ɔpəzit]	adj.	相反的
connect	[kə'nekt]	v.	连接
common	['kɔmən]	adj.	共有的，公共的
electrode	[i'lektrəud]	n.	电极
configuration	[kənˌfigju'reiʃən]	n.	构造，接法
wire	['waiə]	v.	连线，以线加强
consume	[kən'sju:m]	v.	消耗
terminal	['tə:minl]	n.	端子
drain	[drein]	n.	漏极
channel	['tʃænl]	n.	沟道

| conductivity | [ˌkɔndʌk'tiviti] | n. | 导电性 |
| potential | [pəu'tenʃəl] | n. | 电压，电势 |

Notes

1. The transistor is a nonlinear semiconductor device being similar to the diode, commonly used as an amplifier or an electrically controlled switch.

be similar to … :　与……类似、相似

2. the transistor may be used in a wide variety of digital and analog functions, including amplification, switching, voltage regulation, signal modulation, and oscillators.

be used in: 被应用于……

a wide variety of: 多种多样的

3. The attracting voltage of the collector causes the majority of these charges to cross into and be collected by the collector, resulting in amplification.

result in: 导致……

4. The ways are classified by the electrode that is common to both the input and the output.

both … and … :　两者都……

5. The semiconductor region between source and drain is called a channel and its conductivity is controlled by the potential of the gate terminal.

between … and …:　在……和……之间

is controlled by ：　由……控制

Exercises

Ⅰ. **Try to match the following columns.**

1. signal modulation　　　　　模拟电路

2. analog functions　　　　　　信号调制

3. cellular phones　　　　　　　双极型晶体管

4. BJT　　　　　　　　　　　共基极

5. FET　　　　　　　　　　　手机、移动电话

6. cross into　　　　　　　　　场效应晶体管

7. proper biasing　　　　　　　共集电极

8. common-base　　　　　　　穿过

9. common-emitter　　　　　　正确偏置

10. common-collector　　　　　共发射极

Ⅱ. **Translate the following sentences into Chinese.**

1. Because of its fast response and accuracy, the transistor may be used in a wide variety of digital and analog functions, including amplification, switching, voltage regulation, signal modulation, and oscillators.

2. So the transistor is becoming the fundamental building block of the circuitry that governs

the operation of computers, cellular phones, and all other modern electronics.

3. When used as an amplifying element, the base to emitter junction is in a "forward-biased" (conducting) condition, and the base to collector junction is "reverse-biased" or non-conducting.

4. The only functional difference between a PNP transistor and an NPN transistor is the proper biasing (polarity) of the junctions when operating.

Reading

Amplifier

Questions for passage discussion

What is the amplifier? And what are the characteristics of an amplifier?
Is the amplifier a linear device or a nonlinear device?
What kinds of amplifiers are discussed in the passage?

Text

Much as the gate abstraction forms the foundation of most of digital electronics, the operational amplifier forms the basis of much of electronic circuit design. The operational amplifier is arguably the most useful single device in analog electronic circuitry. With only a handful of external components, it can be made to perform a wide variety of analog signal processing tasks. It is also quite affordable, most general-purpose amplifiers selling for under a dollar apiece. Modern designs have been engineered with durability in mind as well: several op-amps are manufactured that can sustain direct short-circuits on their outputs without damage.

The name operational amplifier originates from the bygone days of the analog computer (1940—1960), in which the constants in differential equations were represented by the gains of amplifiers. Thus these amplifiers, constructed from balanced pairs of specially manufactured vacuum tubes, had to have reliable, known, fixed gains. Because transistors are inherently more temperature-dependent than vacuum tubes, it was at first thought that satisfactory transistor Op Amps could not be built. But in 1964, it was discovered that by fabricating balanced transistor pairs close together on a single silicon chip to minimize thermal gradients, the temperature problems could be overcome. And thus were born in rapid succession the 703, the 709, and then the ubiquitous 741. Op Amps are rarely used for analog computers now, but instead have become universal building blocks in all aspects of analog circuitry.

The Op Amp is a multistage two-input differential amplifier that is designed to be an almost ideal control device, specifically, a voltage-controlled voltage source. An abstract representation of the operational amplifier shown in Fig. 2.4 suggests it is a four-port device. The four ports are an input port, an output port, and a pair of power ports. A+VS-voltage (for example, 15 volts) is applied at the plus power port and a −VS-voltage (for example, −15 volts) is applied at the minus power port. An input voltage (the control) applied across the non-inverting and inverting input terminals of the Op Amp is amplified by a large amount and appears at the output port. In the operational amplifier abstraction, the input impedance across the input port is infinity, and the output impedance is zero. The gain, or the factor by which the input voltage is amplified, is also infinity.

The symbol and standard labeling for the operational amplifier are shown in Fig. 2.4. The two required external power supplies have been explicitly shown in the diagram, although showing them is not the usual practice. All five currents have been labeled, in addition to appropriate node voltages, referred to the indicated common ground terminal. In this primitive circuit, the voltage vi is used to control the output voltage vo. Let us examine this control function in detail to find out both the extent of the control, and the cost of the control; that is, how much power must be applied from source vi to control a given amount of power at the vo terminal. To address the first problem, we set up the circuit exactly as in Fig. 2.5(a), and measure the output voltage vo, both as a function of time and as a function of vi, assuming vi is some low-frequency sinusoid. The results are shown in Fig. 2.5(b) and Fig. 2.5(c). Note the difference in scale of the voltage axes, indicating that the output voltage is perhaps 300,000 times as large as the input voltage. The plot of vo versus vi shows a region around the origin where vo is fairly linearly related to vi, but much beyond this range the control becomes ineffective, and vo stays at a fixed voltage, or saturates, at roughly either +12 volts or −12 volts, depending on the polarity of vi. The curves will also differ for different samples of the same Op Amp type.

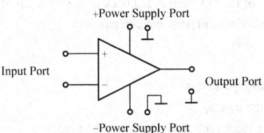

+Power Supply Port

Input Port

Output Port

−Power Supply Port

Fig. 2.4   The operational amplifier abstraction

Different devices of the same type might have different characteristics. The characteristics might also depend on temperature.

One key to the usefulness of these little circuits is in the engineering principle of feedback, particularly negative feedback, in which a portion of the output signal of the Op Amp is fed back to the v− input of the Op Amp. And it constitutes the foundation of almost all automatic control processes. Examples of Op Amp circuits built this way include inverting and non-inverting amplifiers, buffers, adders, integrators, and differentiators.

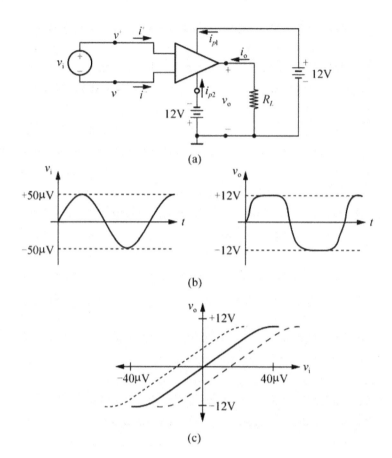

(a)

(b)

(c)

Fig. 2.5   The symbol and standard labeling (a) operational amplifier characteristics (b、c)

Op Amp circuits are sometimes built using the positive feedback connection, in which a portion of the output signal of the Op Amp is fed back to the v+ input of the Op Amp. Examples of such Op Amp circuits include oscillators and comparators.

Exercises

I. **Answer the following questions.**

1. What can amplifier be used to do?

2. What is the negative feedback? And what can it be used to?

II. **Translate the following sentences into Chinese.**

1. Thus these amplifiers, constructed from balanced pairs of specially manufactured vacuum tubes, had to have reliable, known, fixed gains.

2. The plot of vo versus vi shows a region around the origin where vo is fairly linearly related to vi, but much beyond this range the control becomes ineffective, and vo stays at a fixed voltage, or saturates, at roughly either +12 volts or −12 volts, depending on the polarity of vi.

3. Different devices of the same type might have different characteristics. The characteristics might also depend on temperature.

4. Op Amp circuits are sometimes built using the positive feedback connection, in which a portion of the output signal of the Op Amp is fed back to the v+ input of the Op Amp.

5. Op Amps are rarely used for analog computers now, but instead have become universal building blocks in all aspects of analog circuitry.

Translating Skills

专业英语翻译基本技巧

专业英语的翻译质量可用两个字概括，即"信"与"达"。所谓"信"，就是忠实，要求译文必须符合原意，正确传达原文的内容，不能随意增加、减少、歪曲或篡改；所谓"达"，也就是畅达，是指译文必须通顺流畅，符合语言规范，译文不能文理不通，结构紊乱，逻辑不清，晦涩难懂。

专业英语翻译分为直译与意译。直译是译文既忠实于原文的内容，又基本保留原文的语言形式；意译则是在正确理解原意的坚持上，重新遣词造句，用通顺的汉语表达出来。专业英语翻译一般的原则是能直译的尽量直译，直译不顺畅的才需要意译。意译时，必须把握分寸，务必把原文的意思完整而又准确地翻译出来。

进行专业英语翻译有 3 个重点，即英语理解、汉语表达、科技知识，三者缺一不可。常用的基本翻译技巧包括以下几个。

1. 词义选择

大多数英语单词都是多义词，但每个单词在特定句子中只能有一种含义，这样句意才不致模棱两可，莫衷一是。因此，应注意准确选定英语单词在句中应有的含义。

【例1】 Scientific discoveries and inventions have often been translated rapidly into practical devices.

科学的发现和发明，常常迅速变成实用器件。(translate 不能译为"翻译")

【例2】 Nanometer electronics is now in its infancy.

纳米电子学正处于发展的初级阶段。(词义引申)

【例3】 With transistors this equipment can be made much smaller and more lovely.

有了晶体管，这种设备可以制造得更加小巧玲珑。(借用成语)

2. 转换法

在忠实于原文、符合汉语习惯的前提下，将英语译成汉语时，词类、句子成分，以及修饰词等都可按需变更。

【例4】 Television is the transmission and reception of images of moving objects by radio waves.

电视是通过无线电波发送和接收移动物体图像的。(名词变动词)

【例5】 when the switch is off, the electric circuit is open.

打开开关，电路断开。(副词变动词，表语变谓语)

【例6】 Throughout the world come into use the same signs and symbols of mathematics.

全世界都采用同样的数学符号和记号。(状语作主语)

【例7】 There seem to be no other competitive techniques, which can measure range as well or as rapidly as can a laser.

就测量的精度和速度而论，似乎还没有其他技术能与激光相比。(副词变名词)

3. 增词法

所增补的词必须是在修辞上、语言结构上或语义上必不可少的，不可随心所欲地任意增补。

【例8】 The letter I stands for the current in amperes, E the electromotive force in volts, and R the resistance in ohms.

字母 I 代表电流的安培，E 代表电动势的伏特，R 代表电阻的欧姆。(增补原文中的省略成分)

【例9】 The signal-to-noise ratio is determined by the strength of the aerial signal and also by the amount of noise produced in the first stage of receiver.

信噪比取决于天线信号的强弱，也取决于接收机第一级噪声的大小。(补充省略的动词)

4. 省略法

翻译时，可省去冠词、代词、介词、连词或短语等。

【例10】 If you know the frequency, you can find the wavelength.

已知频率就可求出波长。(代词 you 省略翻译)

【例11】 As we know, electrons revolve about the nucleus, or center of an atom.

正如我们所知，电子围绕原子核旋转。(nucleus 与 center 的意思相同，所以省略翻译)

5. 次序调整

【例12】 Then came the development of the microcomputer.

后来，微型计算机发展起来了。

【例13】 In fact, technical English does differ from everyday English, because of the specialized contexts in which it is used and because of the specialized interests of scientists and engineers.

事实上，由于专业英语用于专业文章中，加上科学家和工程技术人员对专业的兴趣，因此，专业英语与日常英语有所不同。

注：表示条件、让步、原因、理由的状语从句或短语，尽管在英语中常常置于主句之后，但在译成汉语时，通常应置于主句之前。

6. 长句拆分翻译

专业英语中长句出现极为频繁，而汉语则习惯使用短句。造成长句的原因主要有 3 个：修饰语过多，并列成分多，以及语言结构层次多。因此，英译汉时，要特别注意英语和汉语之间的差异，将英语的长句分拆，翻译成汉语的短句。

分析长句时可以采用下面的方法。

(1) 分清主次，找出全句的主语、谓语和宾语，从整体上把握句子的结构。

(2) 化整为零，找出句中所有的谓语结构、非谓语动词、介词短语和从句的引导词。

(3) 弄清关系，分析从句和短语的功能，以及它们之间的相互关系。

(4) 注意特殊情况，如从句套从句，并列成分的判断，分裂结构，插入语等。

【例 14】   The progress made in recent years both at home and abroad in the development of apparatus capable of generating ultra high frequency electromagnetic waves whose wave length is a few centimeters has opened up a wholly new field of research in which for the first time the dimensions of one's apparatus are of the same order of magnitude as the wave length of the generated or received waves. (本句中 progress 作主语，谓语是 open up，宾语是 field)

近年来，国内外已制成能产生波长仅有数厘米的超高频电磁波的仪器，这一发展开辟了一个全新的研究领域，使仪器的尺寸第一次与它发出或接收的电磁波的波长处于同一个数量级。

Unit Three   Digital Circuit

【Learning Target】

In this Unit, our target is to train your reading comprehension. Try to grasp the main idea of these passages and learn the speciality vocabularies.

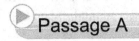 Passage A

Introduction of Digital Circuit

Questions for passage discussion

What is the digital circuit? Which components can be included in a digital circuit?
Which systems can digital be applied to?
What is the benefit of digital system compared with analogue system?

Text

Electronic circuit design has traditionally fallen into two main areas: analogue and digital. We have taught analogue circuit in the first unit. And in this topic, we will discuss the knowledge about digital circuit. Digital circuit is one of the fastest growing disciplines. And the extensive use of digital circuit has led to the development of integrated circuits. So some consumer electronics are becoming more and more intelligent which volume is becoming smaller and smaller. For example MP3 have almost entirely replaced analogue device for recording audio. And LCD-TV is invented to replace the CRT television. 3G is applied in communication to make a video conference and so on. And all of these are depending on the technique of digital and integrated circuits.

But what is digital circuit and what is digital system? And what are they made up of? Machines of all types, including computers, are designed to perform specific tasks in exact well defined manners. Some machine components are purely physical in nature, because their composition and behavior are strictly by chemical, thermodynamic, and physical properties. For example, an engine is designed to transform the energy released by the combustion of gasoline and oxygen into rotating a crankshaft. Other machines components are algorithmic in nature, because their designs primarily follow constraints necessary to implement a set of logical functions as defined by human beings rather than the law of physics. A traffic light's behavior is predominantly defined by human beings rather than by natural physical laws. Digital logic and arithmetic are critical building blocks in constructing such system named digital system which is made up of digital circuit.

All digital systems are founded on logic design. Boolean algebra is the mathematical basis for logic design and establishes the means by which a task's defining rules are represented digitally. Boolean logic (digital logic) is a branch of mathematics that was discovered in the nineteenth century by an English mathematician named george boole. The basic theory is that logic relationships can be modeled by algebraic equations. Rather than using arithmetic operation such as addition and subtraction, boolean algebra employs logical operations including AND, OR, and NOT. And all of them are achieved by logic gates which is the basic building blocks of digital circuits.

A gate is an electronic component with a number of inputs and, generally, a single output. Corresponding to logical operation, there are three kinds of main gates: AND gate, OR gate, and NOT gate. The inputs and the outputs are normally in one of two states: logic 0 or logic 1, which have two enumerated values: true and false. These logic values are represented by voltages (for instance, 0V for logic 0 and 3.3V for logic 1) or currents. The gate itself performs a logical operation using all of its inputs to generate the output. Ultimately, of course, digital gates are really analogue components, but for simplicity we tend to ignore their analogue nature.

Digital system has many advantages compared with analogue system. For example, it has strong anti-interference and its confidential performance is good. In addition, high transmission rate, high channel utilization and small network delay are also benefit that analogue circuit can't contain.

New Words and Expressions

analogue	[ˈænəlɔg]	n.	模拟，模拟电路
digital	[ˈdidʒitl]	n.	数字，数字电路
disciplines	[ˈdisiplins]	n.	学术，学科
extensive	[ikˈstensiv]	adj.	广泛的，广阔的，大量的
consumer	[kənˈsjuːmə]	n.	消费者，顾客
intelligent	[inˈtelidʒənt]	adj.	智能的，聪明的
volume	[ˈvɔljuːm]	n.	体积，容积
entirely	[inˈtaiəli]	adv.	完全地，完整地
record	[ˈrekɔːd]	v.	记录
communication	[kəˌmjuːniˈkeiʃən]	n.	通信
conference	[ˈkɔnfərəns]	n.	会议，年会
machine	[məˈʃiːn]	n.	机器，机械装置
design	[diˈzain]	v.	设计，计划
perform	[pəˈfɔːm]	v.	执行，履行，运行
task	[tɑːsk, tæsk]	n.	工作，任务
defined	[diˈfaind]	adj.	明确的，定义的
manner	[ˈmænə]	n.	方法，方式
component	[kəmˈpəunənt]	n.	零件，部件
physical	[ˈfizikəl]	adj.	物理的
composition	[ˈkɔmpəˈziʃən]	n.	构成，成分
behavior	[biˈheivjə]	n.	性能，运转状态
chemical	[ˈkemikəl]	n. & adj.	化学，化学的
thermodynamic	[ˌθəːməudaiˈnæmik, -di-]	adj.	热力学的

property	['prɔpəti]	*n.*	性能，特点
combustion	[kəm'bʌstʃən]	*n.*	燃烧，燃烧过程
gasoline	['gæsəli:n]	*n.*	汽油，燃油
oxygen	['ɔksidʒən]	*n.*	氧气
rotate	[rəu'teit, 'rəut-, 'rəuteit]	*v.*	旋转，转动
crankshaft	['kræŋkˌʃa:ft]	*n.*	机轴，转轴
primarily	['praimərəli, prai'me-]	*adv.*	主要的，首先
constraint	[kən'streint]	*n.*	系统参数
implement	['implimənt]	*v.*	实现，完成，履行
predominantly	[ˌpri'dɔminəntli]	*adv.*	显然地，显著地
arithmetic	[ə'riθmətik, ˌæriθ'metik]	*n.*	算法，运算
critical	['kritikəl]	*adj.*	关键的，主要的
construct	[kən'strʌkt]	*v.*	建筑，建设，构造
algebra	['ældʒibrə]	*n.*	代数，代数学
mathematical	[ˌmæθi'mætikəl]	*n. & adj.*	数学，数学上的
basis	['beisis]	*n.*	基础，要素
establish	[i'stæbliʃ]	*v.*	建立，成立
relationship	[ri'leiʃənʃip]	*n.*	关系
model	['mɔdl]	*n.*	模仿，模拟
equation	[i'kweiʒən]	*n.*	方程，方程式
addition	[ə'diʃən]	*n.*	加，加法
subtraction	[səb'trækʃən]	*n.*	减，减法
achieve	[ə'tʃi:v]	*v.*	实现，达到
confidential	[ˌkɔnfi'denʃəl]	*adj.*	秘密的，机密的
transmission	[trænz'miʃən]	*n.*	传输，传送
utilization	[ˌju:tilai'zeiʃən]	*n.*	利用，使用

Notes

1. And the extensive use of digital circuit has led to the development of integrated circuits.

lead to …: 导致

2. 3G is applied in communication to make a video conference and so on.

be applied in …: 被应用于……

3. For example, an engine is designed to transform the energy released by the combustion of gasoline and oxygen into rotating a crankshaft.

transform … into …: 把……转化为……

4. A traffic light's behavior is predominantly defined by human beings rather than by natural physical laws.

rather than: 与其……倒不如……，而不是……

5. The basic theory is that logic relationships can be modeled by algebraic equations.

be modeled by … : 被……模拟，以……为模型

6. Digital system has many advantages compared with analogue system.

compare with ...: 与……比较

7. In addition, high transmission rate, high channel utilization and a small network delay are also benefit that analogue circuit cannot contain.

in addition: 另外，除此之外

Exercises

Ⅰ. Try to match the following columns.

1. anti-interference	信道
2. network delay	集成的
3. channel	交通灯
4. equations	抗干扰能力
5. AND gate	液晶电视机
6. traffic light	网络延时
7. 3G	阴极射线管
8. LCD-TV	方程式
9. CRT	与门
10. integrated	第三代移动通信技术

Ⅱ. Translate the following sentences into Chinese.

1. Some machine components are purely physical in nature, because their composition and behavior are strictly by chemical, thermodynamic, and physical properties.

2. Digital logic and arithmetic are critical building blocks in constructing such system named digital system which is made up of digital circuit.

3. Rather than using arithmetic operation such as addition and subtraction, boolean algebra employs logical operations including AND, OR, and NOT.

4. In addition, high transmission rate, high channel utilization and a small network delay are also benefit that analogue circuit can't contain.

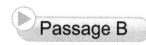

Logical Gate

Questions for passage discussion

In digital electronic systems, which form could the information be represented by?

What can show us the function of a logic gate?

What is the operation of AND gate?

What is the operation of NAND gate?

Text

In digital electronic systems, information is represented by binary digits, bits. A bit may assume either one of two values: 0 or 1. Boolean functions may be practically implemented by using electronic gates.

Gate inputs are driven by voltages having two nominal values, e.g. 0V and 5V representing logic 0 and logic 1 respectively. The output of a gate provides two nominal values of voltage only, e.g. 0V and 5V representing logic 0 and logic 1 respectively. In general, there is only one output to a logic gate except in some special cases. Note that electronic gates require a power supply. There is always a time delay between an input being applied and the output responding. Truth tables are used to help show the function of a logic gate. Digital systems are said to be constructed by using logic gates. These gates are the AND, OR, NOT, NAND, NOR, EOR and ENOR gates. The basic operations are described below with the aid of truth tables. These logical gates are listed as follows.

AND gate (Fig. 3.1): The AND gate is an electronic circuit that gives a high output (1) only if all its inputs are high. A dot (•) is used to show the AND operation i.e. A • B. Bear in mind that this dot is sometimes omitted i.e. AB.

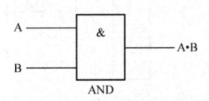

2 Input AND gate		
A	B	A•B
0	0	0
0	1	0
1	0	0
1	1	1

Fig. 3.1   AND gate and its truth table

OR gate (Fig. 3.2): The OR gate is an electronic circuit that gives a high output (1) if one or more of its inputs are high. A plus (+) is used to show the OR operation.

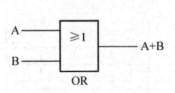

2 Input OR gate		
A	B	A+B
0	0	0
0	1	1
1	0	1
1	1	1

Fig. 3.2   OR gate and its truth table

NOT gate (Fig. 3.3): The NOT gate is an electronic circuit that produces an inverted version of the input at its output. It is also known as an inverter. If the input variable is A, the inverted output is known as NOT A. This is also shown as A', or A with a bar over the top, as shown at the outputs.

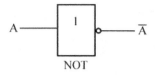

Fig. 3.3   NOT gate and its truth table

NAND gate (Fig. 3.4): This is a NOT-AND gate which is equal to an AND gate followed by a NOT gate. The outputs of all NAND gates are high if any of the inputs are low. The symbol is an AND gate with a small circle on the output. The small circle represents inversion.

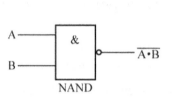

2 Input NAND gate		
A	B	$\overline{A \cdot B}$
0	0	1
0	1	1
1	0	1
1	1	0

Fig. 3.4   NAND gate and its truth table

NOR gate (Fig. 3.5): This is a NOT-OR gate which is equal to an OR gate followed by a NOT gate.   The outputs of all NOR gates are low if any of the inputs are high. The symbol is an OR gate with a small circle on the output. The small circle represents inversion.

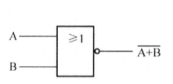

2 Input NOD gate		
A	B	$\overline{A+B}$
0	0	1
0	1	0
1	0	0
1	1	0

Fig. 3.5   NOR gate and its truth table

EOR gate (Fig.3. 6): The Exclusive-OR gate is a circuit which will give a high output if either, but not both, of its two inputs are high. An encircled plus sign ($\oplus$) is used to show the EOR operation.

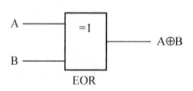

2 Input EOR gate		
A	B	$A \oplus B$
0	0	0
0	1	1
1	0	1
1	1	0

Fig. 3.6   EOR gate and its truth table

ENOR gate (Fig. 3.7): The Exclusive-NOR gate circuit does the opposite to the EOR gate. It will give a low output if either, but not both, of its two inputs are high.

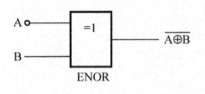

2 Input ENOR gate		
A	B	$\overline{A \oplus B}$
0	0	1
0	1	0
1	0	0
1	1	1

Fig. 3.7   ENOR gate and its truth table

New Words and Expressions

logic gate			逻辑门
binary	['bainəri]	n.	二进制
boolean	[bulən]	n.	布尔
drive	[draiv]	v.	驱动
represent	[,repri'zent]	v.	代表，描述
respectively	[ri'spektivli]	adv.	分别地
responding	[ri'spɔndiŋ]	n.	响应
truth tables			真值表
function	['fʌŋkʃən]	n.	函数
construct	[kən'strʌkt]	v.	构建
operation	[,ɔpə'reiʃən]	n.	运算
inverter	[in'və:tə]	n.	反相器
inversion	[in'və:ʃən]	n.	相反，反相
AND gate			与门
OR gate			或门
NOT gate			非门
NAND gate			与非门
NOR gate			或非门
EOR gate			异或门
ENOR gate			同或门

Notes

1. Boolean functions may be practically implemented by using electronic gates.

布尔函数实际上由电子门来实现。

2. There is always a time delay between an input being applied and the output responding.

在输入和输出响应之间总有时间延迟。

3. A dot (•) is used to show the AND operation i.e. A • B.

一个点(•)用于表示与运算，如 A • B。

4. This is a NOT-AND gate which is equal to an AND gate followed by a NOT gate.

be equal to 等于。

Exercises

Ⅰ. Try to match the following columns.

1. logic gate	反相器
2. power supply	真值表
3. time delay	与运算
4. truth table	电源
5. AND operation	时间延迟
6. inverter	逻辑门

Ⅱ. Translate the following sentences into Chinese.

1. In digital electronic systems, information is represented by binary digits, bits.

2. Truth tables are used to help show the function of a logic gate.

3. The AND gate is an electronic circuit that gives a high output (1) only if all its inputs are high.

4. The Exclusive-OR gate is a circuit which will give a high output if either, but not both, of its two inputs are high.

 Reading

Memory

Questions for passage discussion

What is the memory?
Which kinds of memory are discussed in this passage?
What is the role of memory?

Text

Memory being made of digital device is as fundamental to computer architecture as any other element, as it is used to temporarily store data and programs that are being utilised by the microprocessor. With the development of large scale integrated circuits, the capacity of memory is becoming larger and larger and the storage speed is becoming more and more quickly. And two types of memory are primarily used, ROM and RAM. The following passage will discuss the difference between them.

Random-access memory, or RAM, also known as main memory, internal memory, primary storage, is the kind of memory we usually refer to when we speak of computer memory,whose modules can be purchased in 256MB, 512MB, 1GB, 2GB, and 4GB sizes. And it is typically referred to simply as "memory" even though other types of memory may exist inside a computer. It is the most widely used type, and consists of rows of chips with locations established in tables maintained by the control unit.

As the name suggests, items stored in RAM can be gotten(accessed)both easily and in any order(randomly)rather than in some sequence. RAM relies on electric current for all its operations; moreover, if the power is turned off or interrupted, RAM quickly empties itself of all your hard work. Thus, we say RAM is volatile, or nonpermanent.

A standard "module" or "stick" of memory is long, thin and resembles a short ruler. The bottom of the memory module has one or more notches to guide for proper installation and is lined with numerous, usually gold-plated connectors. Memory is installed in memory module slots located on the motherboard. These slots are easily locatable by looking for the small hinges on either side that lock the memory in place. Certain sizes of modules may need to be installed in certain slots so always check with your motherboard manufacturer before purchase or installation.

Another memory is Read Only Memory (ROM) which is computer memory that can permanently store data and programs within it. These data and programs are manufactured, or "hard-wired" in place on the ROM chips. For example, a microcomputer has a built-in ROM chip(sometimes called ROM BIOS, for ROM basic input/output system)that stores critical programs such as the one that starts up, or boots the computer. Once data has been written onto a ROM chip, it cannot be removed or changed by normal input methods. And the only way to change items in most forms of ROM is to change the actual circuits. ROM is "slower" than RAM memory, and as a result, items in ROM are transferred to RAM when needed for fast processing.

Unlike main memory (RAM), ROM retains its contents even when the computer is turned off. And it is referred to as being nonvolatile, whereas RAM is volatile. There are various types of ROM with names like EPROM (Eraseable ROM) and EEPROM (Electrically Eraseable ROM). EPROM and EEPROM can have their contents rewritten by a special operation. This is called "Flashing the EPROM", a term that came about because ultra violet light is used to clear the contents of the EPROM.

Exercises

I. **Answer the following questions.**

1. What is the difference between RAM and ROM?

2. Which kind of memory is volatile?

3. Where can memory be installed? And how to install?

II. Translate the following sentences into Chinese.

1. Memory being made of digital device is as fundamental to computer architecture as any other element, as it is used to temporarily store data and programs that are being utilised by the microprocessor.

2. Random-access memory, or RAM, also known as main memory, internal memory, primary storage, is the kind of memory we usually refer to when we speak of computer memory, whose modules can be purchased in 256MB, 512MB, 1GB, 2GB, and 4GB sizes.

3. RAM relies on electric current for all its operations; moreover, if the power is turned off or interrupted, RAM quickly empties itself of all your hard work. Thus, we say RAM is volatile, or nonpermanent.

4. Unlike main memory (RAM), ROM retains its contents even when the computer is turned off. And it is referred to as being nonvolatile, whereas RAM is volatile.

Translating Skills

专业英语的构词法

专业英语与普通英语在词汇方面表现出很大的差异，许多单词在普通英语中的意义与在专业英语中的意义大相径庭，同一个词在不同专业中的意义也不尽相同。一般来讲，专业英语词汇由 3 部分组成：专业词汇、半专业词汇和非专业词汇(或普通词)。专业词汇(Technical Words)主要指某一学科、某一专业独有的专用术语，只有一种专业含义，非常单纯，如 histogram(直方图)、probability(概率)、oscillator(振荡器)等。半专业词汇(Semi-technical Words)是指跨学科的出现频率很高的词，在不同的专业领域具有不同的精确含义，如 carrier 在电学中表示"载波，载流子"，在机械领域表示"载重架"，在化学领域表示"载体，吸收剂"，在医学领域表示"带菌者"等。非专业词汇(Non-technical Words)指在非专业英语中很少使用，却严格属于非专业英语性质的词汇，如 application、implementation、to yield 等，这些词也包括出现频率高、在语法上起重要作用的结构功能词，如限定词、介词、连词等。

专业英语词汇中有很大一部分符合构词法。常用构词法主要包括：派生、复合、转换、拼缀和缩略等，下面分别予以介绍。

1. 派生法

派生法(Derivation)通过在原有词或词根的基础上加前缀或后缀而构成新词，前缀通常用以修饰或改变词义，后缀显示词性。

2. 复合法

复合法(Composition)是将两个或两个以上的词按照一定的次序排列而构成新词。多数复合词可通过组成部分猜测词义。例如：trial and error(反复试验)，Q-factor(品质因子)，allowable error(允许误差)等。此外，常用以下两种形式构成复合词。

(1) 直接结合，如 breakthrough(突破)、overestimate(高估)、bandwidth(贷款)等。

(2) 用连字符结合，如 general-purpose(多种用途的)、state-of-the art(达到最新技术水平的)等。

3. 转换法

转换法(Conversion)即单词词性转换，词性转换后其意义与原意有着密切联系，如 function、sound、ground 等词。有些词还会发生音变，如 use、record 等；或音移，如 increase、research、super 等。

4. 拼缀法

拼缀法(Blending)以原有的两个或两个以上的词为基础，经过首尾剪裁(或保留其中一个原词)，重新组合而成，是复合词的缩略形式，如 transistor(晶体管)=transfer + resistor，modem(调制解调器)由 modulator 和 demodulator 拼缀而成。

5. 缩略法

缩略法(Shorting)是将几个单词的首字母以大写形式缩合到一起成为一个新词。该法多用于专有名词，利于记忆，如 radar(Radio Detection And Ranging，雷达)、GPS(Global Positioning System，全球定位系统)等。

随着电子信息及通信类专业技术日新月异的发展，不断有新的专业词汇出现。大多数新词都采用以上 5 种传统的构词法构成，掌握了基本词汇，运用构词知识，一方面可以提高记忆效率，扩大词汇量，另一方面还可以逆向利用构词知识分解单词，了解单词的来历及新添含义，消除阅读障碍。

在专业英语中，派生词出现的频率很高，它是专业英语词汇的特点之一。在此仅介绍派生词中常用的前后缀。

1. 前缀(词头)

(1) anti-/counter- 表示"反，抗"。

    anti-interference 抗干扰   counter flow 反向流动   antiradar 反雷达

(2) auto-表示"自动，自"。

    autocontrol 自控   automodulation 自调制   automobile 自动车

(3) de- 表示相反动作。

modulator 调制器 → demodulator 解调器　　　form 形成 → deform 变形

(4) deci- 表示十分之一，常译为"分"。

decibel(dB) 分贝　　　decimeter(dm) 分米　　　decigram(dg) 分克

(5) di- 表示"二"。

dioxide 二氧化物　　diode 二极管　　dipole 偶极子

(6) dis- 相对应单词的反义词。

connect 连接→ disconnect 解开　　　place 放置→ displace 位移

close 关→ disclose 揭露　　　trust 信任→ distrust 怀疑

(7) in- 表示否定。

accurate 精确的→ inaccurate 不精确的　　　variable 可变的→ invariable 不变的

visible 看得见的→ invisible 看不见的　　　justice 公平→ injustice 不公平

(8) inter- 表示"互相，(在)内，(在)中间"。

interconnect 互连　　　intercarrier 互载的　　　interchange 互换

(9) micro- 表示"微，百万分之一"。

microwave 微波　　　micrometer 微米　　　microelectronics 微电子学

(10) mini- 表示"小"。

minicomputer 微型计算机　　　minicrystal 小晶体　　　minibus 微型公共汽车

(11) over- 表示"超过，太"。

overweight 超重　　　overfrequency 超频　　　overcharge 过量充电

(12) photo- 表示"光，光电，光敏"。

photocell 光电池　　　photohead 光电传感头　　　photorectifier 光电检波器

(13) pre- 表示"在前，预先"。

preheat 预热　　　preamplifier 前置放大器　　　pre-breakdown 未击穿前的

(14) re- 表示"再，重新"。

produce 生产→reproduce 再生产　　　combine 结合→recombine 重新结合

(15) sub- 表示"下，低，亚，次，副"。

sublinear 亚线性的　　　subcircuit 支路　　　subcode 子码

(16) tele- 表示"远"。

television 电视　　　telescope 望远镜　　　telecontrol 遥控

(17) tri- 表示"三"。

triangle 三角形　　　tricycle 三轮车　　　tricar 三轮汽车

(18) thermo- 表示"热"。

thermo-emf 热电(动)势　　　thermoelectric 热电的　　　thermo-fuse 热熔丝

(19) ultra- 表示"超"。

ultra-high-frequency 超高频　　　ultraportable 极轻便的　　　ultrasonic 超声的

(20) un- 表示"不，非，未"等。

unloading 卸载　　　unequal 不等的　　　undecided 未决定的

2. 后缀(词尾)

(1) -able (形容词词尾)：

count 计算→countable 可数的　　　compare 比较→comparable 可比较的

(2) -al (形容词词尾)：

digit 数字→digital 数字的　　　function 功能→functional 功能的

(3) -ance/-ence (名词词尾)：

existence 存在　　　capacitance 电容　　　resonance 谐振

(4) -ary(形容词词尾)：

element 元素→elementary 初步的　　　moment 时刻→momentary 瞬息的

(5) -en(动词词尾)，一般由形容词+en 构成，表示"使……"，例如：

soft 柔软→soften 软化　　　short 短的→shorten 缩短　　　wide 宽的→widen 加宽

(6) -fold 接在数词后，构成形容词或副词，表示"……倍"，例如：

three-fold *adj./adv.* 3 倍的(地)　　　a thousand-fold *adj./adv.* 1000 倍的(地)

(7) -free(形容词词尾)表示"无……的，免于……的"，例如：

oil-free 无油的　　　dust-free 无尘的　　　loss-free 无损耗的

(8) -ful(形容词词尾)：

success 成功→ successful 成功的　　　power 动力→ powerful 强大的：

(9) -ics (名词词尾)表示"学科名称"；- ist，-ician (名词词尾)表示"从事某方面工作的人，……家"，例如：

optics 光学→ opticist 光学家　　　mechanics 力学→ mechanician 机械师

(10) -ity (词尾)构成抽象名词：

reliable 可靠的→reliability 可靠性　　　impure 不纯的→impurity 杂质

(11) -ive (形容词词尾)：

conduct 传导→conductive 导电的　　　act 起作用→active 有源的，活泼的

(12) -less(形容词词尾)，表示"无……"，例如：

limit 极限→limitless 无限的　　　wire 导线→wireless 无线的

(13) -ment(名词词尾)：

displace 位移→displacement 位移　　　equip 装备→equipment 设备

(14) -proof(形容词词尾)，表示"防……的"，例如：

waterproof 防水的　　　fire-proof 防火的　　　lightningproof 防雷的

(15) -tion/-sion(名词词尾)；-or/-er(名词词尾)表示"器、物或人"，例如：

induce 感应　　　induction 感应　　　　　　inductor 电感器

operate 工作　　　operation 工作，运算　　　operator 操作员

transmit 发射　　　transmission 传输，发射　　　transmitter 发射机

Unit Four   Common Instruments

↘ 【Learning Target】

In this Unit, our target is to train your reading comprehension. Try to grasp the main idea of these passages and learn the speciality vocabularies.

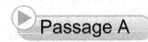

Analog Instruments and Uses

Questions for passage discussion

What is the principle of permanent magnet moving-coil instruments?
What is the principle of moving iron instruments?

Text

1. Permanent Magnet Moving-coil Instruments for Direct Currents and Voltages

The basic principle is that of a moving coil with attached indicator turning in the field of a permanent magnet specially designed so that the angular response of the moving system is uniform and the calibration of the instrument does not change in time due to changes in the value of the field. To measure current values above 20 milliamperes, which would cause overheating in the hairspring used to lead the current into and out of the moving coil, a shunt is used, with a milliammeter connected in parallel. The millimeter scale is marked in terms of the total current in the shunt and the instrument. To measure voltages, the current taken by the instrument must be small. Hence a series resistor or multiplier is used of a value suitable to give full-scale deflection with a current in the range 0.1—10 milliamperes.

2. Moving Iron Instruments of Alternating Currents and Voltages

In these instruments the current or voltage to be measured is used to excite a stationary coil in whose fields placed a moving vane of high permeablility steel together with a spring and pointer. The motion of the vane is such as to increase the flux through it and so the torque produced by the reaction of the magnetic fields of the electromagnet and the vane increases the inductance of the combination. The torque increases with the square of the current in the coil and a suitable scale enables the values to be read off. These moving iron instruments are known as the attraction type. Others are called the repulsion type. Moving iron instruments of the repulsion type are also common.

3. Electrodynamic Instruments for the Measurement of Current and Voltage

These instruments are generally chosen for precision and commercial laboratory measurements. The basic principle is the reaction of the fields of force of two coils, a behavior fixed coil and lighter mobile one. Each of these coils carries a current proportional to the current or voltage being measured and the reaction of the fields supplies the torque which is proportional to the square of the current or the voltage to be measured. For the measurement of relatively and small currents, the fixed and moving coils are connected in series to carry the entire current. For the measurement of higher currents, a parallel-coil arrangement is used. All but a fraction of the current to be measured in the electrodynamic ammeter is carried by the fixed coil which is in series with an appropriate resistor. The moving coil, also with a resistor in series, is connected in parallel with the fixed coil and its resistor.

In the electrodynamic voltmeter, the fixed and moving coils are connected in series to carry the entire current, and a suitable multiplier determines the voltage range.

4. Electrostatic Voltmeters for the Measurement of Low (50V) to Extremely High D.C. and A.C. Voltages

The action of an electric field on charged electrodes produces the deflecting torque in these instruments. This torque is always small. If these instruments are suitably constructed they have a response which is equal for direct or alternating voltages and so they are employed to calibrate the A.C. response of other instruments in terms of D.C. values.

New Words and Expressions

indicator	['indikeitə]	*n.*	指示器
permanent	['pə:mənənt]	*adj.*	永久的
calibration	[,kæli'breiʃən]	*n.*	刻度，标度，校准
milliampere	[,mili'æmpɛə]	*n.*	毫安
hairspring	['hɛəspriŋ]	*n.*	细弹簧，游丝
attraction	[ə'trækʃən]	*v.*	吸引
repulsion	[ri'pʌlʃən]	*v.*	排斥
milliammeter	[,mili'æmitə]	*n.*	毫安表
multiplier	['mʌltiplaiə]	*n.*	乘法器
permeability	[,pə:miə'biliti]	*n.*	渗透性
torque	[tɔ:k]	*n.*	扭矩，转矩
electrodynamic	[i,lektrəudai'næmik]	*adj.*	电力学的，电动
electrostatic	[,lektrə'stætik]	*adj.*	静电学的
electrodynamic ammeter			电表

Notes

1. The basic principle is that of a moving coil with attached indicator turning in the field of a permanent magnet specially designed so that the angular response of the moving system is uniform and the calibration of the instrument does not change in time due to changes in the value of the field.

turning in the field …：动名词短语修饰 coil。

基本原理是带有指示器的可动线圈在特别设计的永久磁场中旋转，从而移动系统的角度响应值恒定，而仪表刻度不随场值的变化而改变。

2. To measure current values above 20 milliamperes, which would cause overheating in the hairspring used to lead the current into and out of the moving coil, a shunt is used, with a

milliammeter connected in parallel.

which 引导的定语从句修饰 current values；used to lead …修饰 hairspring。

为量度高于 20mA 的电流值，即引起用于导入、导出移动线圈的游丝过热的电流，我们使用带有并联毫安计的分流器。

Exercises

Ⅰ. **Try to match the following columns.**

1. permanent magnet   永磁

2. series resistor   校准

3. milliampere   电动仪表

4. milliammeter   毫安

5. in terms of   与……联合起来

6. electrodynamic instruments 毫安计

7. calibrate   以……的方式

8. in combination with   串联电阻

Ⅱ. **Fill in the blank in each of the following sentences.**

1. The millimeter scale is marked_____the total current in the shunt and the instrument.

2. The torque which is _____to the square of the current or the voltage to be measured.

3. The fixed and moving coils are connected _____to carry the entire current.

4. These instruments are generally_____precision and commercial laboratory measurements.

5. The moving coil, also with a resistor in series, is connected _____with the fixed coil and its resistor.

> **Passage B**

Oscilloscope

Questions for passage discussion

What is the function of oscilloscope?

How to use the oscilloscope for voltage measurement?

Text

Oscilloscopes are commonly used when it is desired to observe the exact wave shape of an electrical signal. In addition to the amplitude of the signal, an oscilloscope can show distortion and measure frequency, time between two events (such as pulse width or pulse rise time), and relative timing of two related signals. Some modern digital oscilloscopes can analyze and display the spectrum of a repetitive event. Special-purpose oscilloscopes, called spectrum analyzers, have sensitive inputs and can display spectra well into the GHz range.

An oscilloscope can present an accurate electronic picture of the changing voltages within a circuit. It has both advantage and disadvantage when used to measure voltage (or current). The most obvious advantage is that the oscilloscope shows waveform, frequency and phase simultaneously with the amplitude of the voltage (or current) being measured. The electronic voltmeter shows only amplitude. Likewise, most meters are calibrated in relation to sine waves. When the signals being measured contain significant harmonics, the calibrations are inaccurate. Within the oscilloscope, the voltage is measured from the displayed wave, which includes any harmonic content.

The only major disadvantage of using an oscilloscope for voltage (or current) measurement is the problem of resolution. The scales of simple inexpensive electronic voltmeters are easier to read than an oscilloscope. In most cases, the oscilloscope's vertical scales are used for voltage (or current) measurements, with each scale division representing a given value of voltage (or current). When voltages are large, it is difficult to interpolate between divisions.

The amplitude of a voltage waveform on an oscilloscope screen can be determined by counting the number of centimeters, vertically, from one peak to the other peak of the waveform and multiplying it by the setting of the volts/cm control. As an example, if the amplitude was 4cm and the control was set on 1V/cm, the peak-to-peak voltage would be 4V. Usually the peak-to-peak value is required to be converted to RMS (root-mean-square)(有效值), because most voltages specified in electronic maintenance and troubleshooting manuals are RMS.

To sum up, if the only value of interest is voltage amplitude, use the meter because of its simplicity in readout. Use the oscilloscope when waveform characteristics are of equal importance to amplitude.

New Words and Expressions

oscilloscope	[ɔ'siləuskəup]	*n.*	示波器
obvious	['ɔbviəs]	*adj.*	明显的
simultaneously	[,siməl'teiniəsli]	*adv.*	同时地，同步地
amplitude	['æmplitju:d]	*n.*	振幅，幅度
calibrate	['kælibreit]	*v.*	校准
sine	[sain]	*n.*	正弦
significant	[sig'nifikənt]	*adj.*	重要的，大量的
harmonic	[ha:'mɔnik]	*n.*	谐波
inaccurate	[in'ækjurət]	*adj.*	错误的，不准确的
division	[di'viʒən]	*n.*	分开，分割

vertical	['və:tikəl]	*adj.*	垂直的
scale	[skeil]	*n.*	刻度，进制
interpolate	[in'tə:pəuleit]	*n.*	插入
maintenance	['meintənəns]	*v.*	维护，保持
manual	['mænjuəl]	*n.*	手册
root-mean-square			均方根

Notes

1. The most obvious advantage is that the oscilloscope shows waveform, frequency and phase simultaneously with the amplitude of the voltage (or current) being measured.

最明显的优点是示波器在测量电压(或电流)的波形的幅度时，能同时显示波形、频率和相位。

2. The amplitude of a voltage waveform on an oscilloscope screen can be determined by counting the number of centimeters, vertically, from one peak to the other peak of the waveform and multiplying it by the setting of the volts/cm control.

counting … and multiplying …为并列部分。

示波器屏幕的电压振幅可以通过峰-峰值所占垂直格数乘上所设定的 volts/cm 控制旋钮来确定。

Exercises

I. Answer the following questions.

1. What are the advantages of using an oscilloscope?

2. What are the disadvantages of using an oscilloscope?

II. Translate the following sentences into Chinese.

1. An oscilloscope can present an accurate electronic picture of the changing voltages within a circuit.

2. Within the oscilloscope, the voltage is measured from the displayed wave, which includes any harmonic content.

3. In most cases, the oscilloscope's vertical scales are used for voltage (or current) measurements, with each scale division representing a given value of voltage (or current).

Multimeters

Questions for passage discussion

What is the function of multimeter?
How many kinds can multimeters be divided into?
How to use the multimeter for voltage measurement?

Text

Multimeters are very useful test instruments. By operating a multi-position switch on the meter they can be quickly and easily set to be a voltmeter, an ammeter or an ohmmeter. They have several settings (called "ranges") for each type of meter and the choice of AC or DC. Some multimeters have additional features such as transistor testing and ranges for measuring capacitance and frequency.

There are two basic types of multimeters, digital and analog. Analog multimeters have a needle and the digital has a LED display.

The analog meter usually includes the function and range switches in a single switch. It may also have a polarity switch to facilitate reversing the test leads. The needle will have a screw for mechanical adjust to set it to zero and also a zero adjust control to compensate for weakening batteries when measuring resistance. An analog meter can read positive and negative voltage by simply reversing the test leads or moving the polarity switch. A digital meter usually has an automatic indicator for polarity on its display.

All digital meters contain a battery to power the display so they use virtually no power from the circuit under test. This means that on their DC voltage ranges they have a very high resistance (usually called input impedance) of 1MΩ or more, usually 10MΩ, and they are very unlikely to affect the circuit under test.

Meters must be properly connected to a circuit to ensure a correct reading. A voltmeter is always placed across (in parallel) the circuit or component to be measured. When measuring current, the circuit must be opened and the meter inserted in series with the circuit or component to be measured. When measuring the resistance of a component in a circuit, the voltage to the circuit must be removed and the meter placed in parallel with the component.

1. Measuring Voltage and Current with a Multimeter

(1) Select a range with a maximum greater than you expect the reading to be.

(2) Connect the meter, making sure the leads are the correct way round.

Digital meters can be safely connected in reverse, but an analogue meter may be damaged.

(3) If the reading goes off the scale: immediately disconnect and select a higher range.

Multimeters are easily damaged by careless use so please take these precautions.

(1) Always disconnect the multimeter before adjusting the range switch.

(2) Always check the setting of the range switch before you connect to a circuit.

(3) Never leave a multimeter set to a current range (except when actually taking a reading).

The greatest risk of damage is on the current ranges because the meter has a low resistance.

2. Measuring Resistance with a Multimeter

Another useful function of the digital multimeter is the ohmmeter. An ohmmeter measures the electrical resistance of a circuit. If you have no resistance in a circuit, the ohmmeter will read 0. If you have an open in a circuit, it will read infinite.

Exercises

Translate the following sentences into Chinese.

1. By operating a multi-position switch on the meter they can be quickly and easily set to be a voltmeter, an ammeter or an ohmmeter.

2. All digital meters contain a battery to power the display so they use virtually no power from the circuit under test.

3. This means that on their DC voltage ranges they have a very high resistance (usually called input impedance) of $1M\Omega$ or more, usually $10M\Omega$, and they are very unlikely to affect the circuit under test.

4. The greatest risk of damage is on the current ranges because the meter has a low resistance.

5. Another useful function of the digital multimeter is the ohmmeter.

Translating Skills

数量的表示与翻译

在科技文献中经常有大量数词出现。数词表示事物的数量或数目，其含义十分严格，理解或翻译时的疏忽和差错可能会引起严重后果。由于英语与汉语在数量表达上差别较大，对待数词或数量的表达要特别仔细。

1. 数字的表示

在科技文章中，数字频繁出现，用阿拉伯数字比用单词陈述更有利。但出现下述情形时必须遵循约定俗成的规则：用单词表示不定数量或近似值；句首不用阿拉伯数字，一般用英语的单词，句末要尽量避免用阿拉伯数字；两数连用时，分别用单词和阿拉伯数字表示，习惯上将短的用单词写出；遇到分数，可用带连字符号的单词表示，等等。如：

【例1】 Phase shift is 180°。

(输出电压与输入电压的)相移为 180°。

【例2】 The gain of the voltage follower with the feedback loop closed(closed loop gain)is unity.

电压跟随器的闭环增益为 1。

2. 不确定数字的表示

(1) 大约、左右，常用 about、some、approximately、of the order of、more or less、or so 等词。

(2) 多于，常用 over、above、more than、in excess of 等词。

(3) 少于，常用 less than、under、below、close to 等词。

(4) 以复数形式表示，如 tens/dozens/scores/hundreds/thousands of、thousands upon thousands of 等。

【例3】 The result indicated that actual error probabilities were of the order of 1 percent.
结果表明实际误差概率约为 1%。

【例4】 The microwave communication channel has a very large bandwidth and will accommodate thousands of telephone conversations or dozens of television channels at once.

微波通信信道带宽很宽，可同时容纳几千个电话通话或几十个电视信道。

3. 习惯短语

【例5】 Economies associated with computer-on-a-chip have resulted in the availability of micro-computer systems with the functionality and performance of minicomputer systems costing two orders of magnitude more only a decade ago.

随着单片机的发展，目前微机系统所拥有的功能及性能可以媲美 10 年前的小型机，而价格却下降了两个数量级以上。

【例6】 The resistance of a given section of an electric circuit is equal to the ratio of its voltage to the current through this section of the circuit.

电路中某部分的电阻等于它两端的电压与流过该部分电路的电流的比值。

【例7】 It is found that the heat energy developed in any conductor is proportional to(is in proportion to)the square of the current, the resistance of the conductor and the time.

人们发现，导体中所产生的热能与电流的平方、导体的电阻值和时间成正比。

4. 倍数增减与翻译

倍数的增减在汉语与英语中的表述有较大的差异，在汉语中增加可以是倍数、分数、百分数，而减少只能是分数或百分数，而倍数的增减又常常涉及到是否将基数计入其中，所以要仔细领会。下面是常见的几个句型及其译法。

1) 倍数增加

(1) 表示倍数的增加及百分数的增加，英语常用含有 increase by 的句型，译成汉语时把英语句中的倍数直接译出来，常译成"增加了……倍"、"增加了百分之……"。例如：

New boosters can increase the payload by 150%.

新型推进器可使有效负载增加 150%。

With the new technology, the output of refrigerators has increased by three times.

随着新技术的开发，冰箱的产量增加了 3 倍。

This year the value of our grain output will increase by twice.

今年我国农业产量将比去年增加 2 倍。

(2) …times more than 句型常用于两者比较增加了多少倍，常译为"比……大/高/长/多……倍"，译文的英汉倍数相同。例如：

Some of these stars are one hundred million times brighter than the sun.

这些星体中有些比太阳亮 1 亿倍。

A kilogram of nuclear fuel yields 2.5 million times energy than a kilogram of coal.

1kg 核燃抖的能量比 1kg 煤多 250 万倍。

The speed of red light in glass is approximately 1%greater than the speed of blue light.

在玻璃中红光的速度比蓝光的速度约高 1%。

(3) …as…as 句型常用于表示某物是某物的多少倍或百分之多少，译为汉语时，英汉的倍数相同。例如：

The sun is 330,000 times as large as file earth. 太阳的体积是地球的 33 万倍。

This substance reacts tw0. tenth as fast as the other one.

这种物质的反应速度是另一种物质的 2/10。

We are producing eighty times as many TV sets as we did twenty years ago.

我们现在生产的电视机是 20 年前的 80 倍。

(4) 含有 …the size/amount/figure/that of 的句型常用于表示"……是……的多少倍"，或"……是……的百分之多少"，翻译时英汉倍数相同。例如：

The mass of an electron is 1/1850 that of a hydrogen atom.

电子的质量是氢原子质量的 1/1850。

The earth is 49 times the size of the moon.

地球体积是月亮体积的 49 倍。

Radium was found to radiate with an intensity one million times that of uranium.

人们发现镭的辐射强度是铀的 100 万倍。

(5) 动词 double/treble(triple)常用来说明某物增加了多少倍，译为汉语是"增加……倍时"，把英语的倍数减 1；译为"是……倍"时英汉倍数不变。例如：

As the high voltage was abruptly trebled, all the valves burnt.

由于高压突然增加了两倍，电子管都烧坏了。

The plane has doubled the capacity of that one.

这架飞机的载重量是那架飞机的两倍。

The sales of digital cameras doubled in the first two months this year.

今年头两个月数码相机的销售量翻了一番。

2) 倍数减少

倍数减少的表达中英文有所不同。中文常说"减少了 n 分之……"，而英文常说"减少……倍"，翻译时要注意中英文的表达差异。例如：

(1) 英文说"减少多少倍"，而中文说"减少 n 分之……"，例如：

The length of the laser tube was reduced ten-times.

这种激光管的长度缩短了 9/10。(为原来的 1/10)

Rolling friction is tens of times little than sliding friction.

滚动摩擦是滑动摩擦的几十分之一。

This kind of plastics is three times as light as glass.

这种塑料是玻璃重量的三分之一。

(2) 表示"减少一半"时，英文有多种不同的句型和表达方法，翻译时要多加注意。例如：

The new-type electronic device shortened the circuit two times.

新型电子装置使线路缩短了一半。

This kind of film is twice thinner than ordinary paper，but its quality is good.

这种薄膜的厚度只是普通纸张的一半，可是质量很好。

The laptop is only half as heavy as the old one.

这台手提电脑比旧型号的要轻一半。

(3) 表示一般意义上的减少，英文表达非常灵活。例如：

The price of cars in China last year fell about one-third.

去年中国的车价下降了 1/3。

The loss of metal has been reduced to less than 30%.

金属损耗已经减少到 30%以下。

The ordinary smelting time has been cut by one-forth.

普通溶解时间缩短了 1/4。

Part II

Automatic Control Technology

Unit Five   Computer-Based Control Systems

↘ 【Learning Target】

In this Unit, our target is to train your reading comprehension. Try to grasp the main idea of these passages and learn the speciality vocabularies.

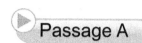
Passage A

Introduction of a Single Chip Microcomputer

Questions for passage discussion

What is a single chip microcomputer?

What are the basic elements of a single chip microcomputer? What's the function of each element?

Text

A single chip microcomputer, also called microcontroller, is a computer with most of the necessary resources on a single integrated circuit. The predominant family of microcontrollers are 8-bit types, such as AT80C51 and TMS370, since this word size has been popular for the vast majority of tasks the devices have been required to perform.

There are a wide range of devices available in the 8051 family, differing in terms of memory type and capacity, number of counter/timers, types of serial interface, number of input/output ports, etc. The 80C51 is available in three different package types and is basically a 40-pin device with the architecture shown in the block diagram of Fig. 5.1.

1. CPU

The CPU is the brain of the microcontrollers reading user's programs and executing the expected task as per instructions stored there. Its primary elements are an 8-bit arithmetic logic unit (ALU), accumulator, few more registers, B register, stack pointer (SP), program status word (PSW) and 16-bit registers, program counter (PC) and data pointer register (DPTR).

2. Internal RAM

The 80C51 has 128 bytes of on-chip RAM plus a number of SFRs. Including the SFR space it gives 256 addressable locations but the addressing modes for internal RAM can accommodate 384 bytes by splitting the memory space into three blocks viz. the lower 128, the upper 128 and the SFR space. The lower 128 bytes can be accessed using direct and indirect addressing. The upper 128 bytes may be accessed using direct addressing only; locations in this space with addresses ending with 0H or 8H are also bit addressable.

3. Internal ROM

The ROM in a microcontroller is provided so that the control program can be resident on-chip. If the control program can be accommodated within the 4 KB, then no external program memory is required; if however, the control program needs greater memory capacity external memory can be added up to 64 KB.

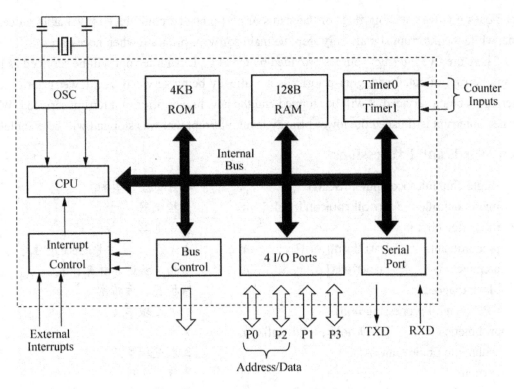

Fig. 5.1   80C51 block diagram

4. Input/Output Ports

The 80C51's I/O port structure is extremely flexible and versatile. The device has 32 I/O pins configured as four 8 bit parallel ports (P0, P1, P2, and P3). Each pin can be used as an input or as an output under the software control. Even within a single port, different pins can be configured as input or output independent of each other or the same pin can be used as an input or an output at different time. All the pins of P0, P2 and P3 can also be made to do many different tasks apart from their regular I/O function executions.

5. Timer/Counters

The 80C51 has two 16-bit timer/counter registers known as Timer 0 and Timer 1. Timers 0 and 1 are up-counters and may be programmed to count internal clock pulses (timer) or count external pulses(counter). Each counter is divided into two 8-bit registers to give timer low and timer high bytes i.e.TL0, TH0 and TL1, TH1.

6. Serial interface

The 80C51 possesses an on-chip serial port to enable serial data transmission between the device and external circuits.The serial port is full duplex so that it can receive and transmit data simultaneously.The port is also buffered in receive mode so that it can receive a second data byte before the first data byte has been read from the register.

7. Interrupts

Whenever a computer program is running it can be forced to respond to external conditions either by software techniques or the use of hardware signals called interrupts. Software techniques involve checking flags or the status of port pins and could take up valuable processor time, while the interrupt signals only stop the main software program when necessary.

There are five interrupt sources provided by the 80C51. An interrupt will be serviced as long as an interrupt of equal or higher priority is not already being serviced. If a lower priority level interrupt is being serviced, it will be stopped and the new higher priority interrupt serviced. When the new interrupt is finished the lower priority level interrupt that was stopped will be completed.

New Words and Expressions

single chip microcomputer (SCM)			单片微型计算机
microcontroller	[ˌmaikrəukənˈtrəulə]	n.	微控制器
integrated circuit			集成电路
predominant	[ˌpriˈdɔminənt]	adj.	占优势的；占主导地位的；主导的
architecture	[ˈɑːkitektʃə]	n.	结构，构造，体系结构
block diagram			结构图，方框图
CPU (central processing unit)			中央处理单元
arithmetic	[əˈriθmətik, ˌæriθˈmetik]	n.	算术
arithmetic Logic Unit (ALU)			算术逻辑单元
execute	[ˈeksikjuːt]	vt.	执行，实行
accumulator	[əˈkjuːmjuleitə]	n.	累加器
program status word (PSW)			程序状态字
program counter (PC)			程序计数器
register	[ˈredʒistə]	n.	寄存器
stack pointer (SP)			堆栈指针
data pointer register (DPTR)			数据指针寄存器
addressable location			可寻址单元
addressing mode			寻址方式
accommodate	[əˈkɔmədeit]	v.	容纳，提供空间
viz.	[viz]	adv.	即，就是
indirect addressing			间接寻址
direct addressing			直接寻址
bit addressable			位寻址
external memory			外部存储器
versatile	[ˈvəːsətail]	adj.	通用的，万能的
flexible	[ˈfleksəbl]	adj.	柔韧性，灵活的
pin		n.	管脚，引脚
configured as			配置为
apart from			除……以外，除了
up-counter			加法计数器
internal clock pulses			内部时钟脉冲

serial data transmission			串行数据传输
full duplex			全双工，全双向的
simultaneously	[siməl'teiniəsli]	*adv.*	同时，同时发生地
buffer	['bʌfə]	*v. & n.*	缓冲，缓冲器
interrupt	[ˌintəˌrʌpt]	*n.*	中断
take up			占据，占用
as long as			只要，既然，如果
priority	[prai'ɔrəti]	*n.*	优先，优先级，优先权

Notes

1. The predominant family of microcontrollers are 8-bit types, … , since this word size has been popular for the vast majority of tasks the devices have been required to perform.

句中 the devices have been required to perform 作 the vast majority of tasks 的定语从句，其前省略了引导词 that。

2. Including the SFR space it gives 256 addressable locations but the addressing modes for internal RAM can accommodate 384 bytes by splitting the memory space into three blocks viz. the lower 128, the upper 128 and the SFR space.

译为：包括特殊功能寄存器空间在内，它有 256 个可寻址单元，但是通过将存储空间分成 3 个区，即低 128 字节、高 128 字节和特殊功能寄存器空间，内部 RAM 的寻址方式能容纳 384 字节。

3. Whenever a computer program is running it can be forced to respond to external conditions either by software techniques or the use of hardware signals called interrupts.

called interrupts 作 hardware signals 的后置定语。

4. Software techniques involve checking flags or the status of port pins and could take up valuable processor time, while the interrupt signals only stop the main software program when necessary.

while 是连词，表示前后对比，译为 "而……"。

Exercises

Ⅰ. Try to match the following columns.

single chip microcomputer	程序状态字
microcontroller	优先，优先级，优先权
arithmetic logic unit (ALU)	累加器
accumulator	寄存器
register	加法计数器
stack pointer (SP)	缓冲，缓冲器
pin	堆栈指针
up-counter	算术逻辑单元
serial data transmission	微控制器
buffer	管脚，引脚

priority   串行数据传输

program status word (PSW)   单片机

II. Place a "T" after the sentence which is true and an "F" after the sentence which is false.

1. The predominant family of microcontrollers are 16-bit types.   ( )

2. The CPU is the brain of the microcontrollers which reads user's programs and executing the expected task.   ( )

3. The lower 128 bytes of the internal RAM can be accessed only by direct addressing. ( )

4. The ROM in a microcontroller is provided to store the control program.   ( )

5. The 80C51 has three 8-bit timer/counter registers known as timer0, timer1 and timer2. ( )

6. The serial port of the 80(5) is half-duplex so that it can only receive or transmit data at a time.   ( )

7. The 80C51 provides six interrupt sources.   ( )

8. When a computer program is running it cannot respond to external conditions.   ( )

III. Translate the following paragraph into Chinese.

A microcontroller (also called microcomputer, MCU or μC) is a small computer on a single integrated circuit consisting internally of a relatively simple CPU, clock, timers, I/O ports, and memory. Microcontrollers are designed for small or dedicated applications. Thus, in contrast to the microprocessors used in personal computers and other high-performance or general purpose applications, simplicity is emphasized. Some microcontrollers may use four-bit words and operate at clock rate frequencies as low as 4 kHz, as this is adequate for many typical applications, enabling low power consumption (milliwatts or microwatts). They will generally have the ability to retain functionality while waiting for an event such as a button press or other interrupt; power consumption while sleeping (CPU clock and most peripherals off) may be just nanowatts, making many of them well suited for long lasting battery applications. Other microcontrollers may serve performance-critical roles, where they may need to act more like a digital signal processor (DSP), with higher clock speeds and power consumption.

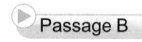

Microcomputer Controlled Systems

Questions for passage discussion

What can be used to control the industrial processes?

What are the limitations of pure analog systems?

What is a microcomputer controlled system composed of? What's the function of each part?

Text

Industrial processes can be controlled by microcomputers or by anolog controllers. In such systems, a variety of different types of transducers are used, e.g., potentiometers, strain gauges, LVDTs, or synchros. The parameter being measured, e.g., position, temperature, pressure, flow velocity, or density, is usually defined by an electrical voltage.

The limitations of pure analog systems lie in the limited processing of data that can be accomplished, and in the difficulties of changing the type of data manipulation if this is found to be necessary. Additional costs are incurred if it is necessary to provide digital readouts of any analog signals, since it is necessary to provide an A/D converter for each such readout.

The introduction of a digital microcomputer to such a system permits the range of signal manipulation to be considerably extended giving, in some cases, a quick analysis to determine characteristics that cannot be measured directly. It also provides an easy method of processing a control signal. A further advantage is that the microcomputer can condition the electrical voltages representing the measurements to identify any rogue readings and filter any unwanted "noise" present.

A typical control system using a digital microcomputer can illustrate conventional on-line digital control, in which analog transducers produce electrical voltages proportional to the parameters to be measured. As the microcomputer can only accept one measurement signal at a time, the transducer signals are taken in order before being converted in the A/D converter. The input data to the microcomputer is processed by the microcomputer under the control of the programs held in store. The digital outputs to various control devices which control the process are first fed from the microcomputer in a prescribed sequence. Each is converted to an analog signal by the digital-to-analog (D/A) converter, and then switched as analog signals to the appropriate control unit by an output multiplexer. In most control systems there will also be a number of direct digital lines between the microcomputer and the process for information which requires switching actions only.

An instrumentation system follows the same pattern as the control system except that there are no outputs from the microcomputer to the process and no control devices. Generally speaking a microcomputer would be incorporated into an instrumentation system only where the amount of data to be collected is very large, where processing of this data is complex or time-consuming and where it would probably be necessary to use an off-line microcomputer. There is obviously considerable advantage in such a system which collects the necessary measurements and processes them and presents the data in the form required, and especially, the process can be readily changed by inputting a new program to the microcomputer.

One of the most commonly controlled quantities is temperature, for heating and cooling rooms or for controlling the reaction rates of chemical or biological processes. When fuel combustion or electrical resistance heating is used, the control engineer can actively control heating but must rely on heat losses for cooling. On the other hand, heat pumps or peltier thermoelectric devices can both heat and actively cool.

Fig. 5.2 shows the schematic of a typical microcomputer-based temperature-control system. The thermistor and bridge provide a voltage that is converted with an A/D converter and read by the microcomputer program. A control program writes a number to the D/A converter, whose output is amplified to drive an oven resistor. A thermistor is used for temperature sensing and a cylindrical ceramic resistor is used for heating.

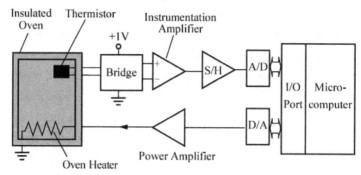

Fig. 5.2   A temperature-control system

Microcomputers are also widely used in automatically controlled products and devices, such as automobile engine control systems, implantable medical devices, remote controls, power tools and toys.

New Words and Expressions

transducer	[trænz'dju:sə]	*n.*	传感器，换能器，变换器
potentiometer	[pə,tenʃi'ɔmitə]	*n.*	电位计，分压器，电位差计，电位器
strain	[strein]	*v. & n.*	拉紧张力，应变
gauge	[geidʒ]	*n.*	规格，计量器，测量仪表
strain gauge			应变仪，变形测量器
LVDT =linear variable differential transformer			线性可调差接变压器
synchros = synchronous devices		*n.*	同步设备
velocity	[vi'lɔsəti]	*n.*	速度
incur	[in'kə:]	*vt.*	遭受，招致，引起
readout	['ri:daut]	*n.*	示值，读数
rogue	[rəug]	*adj.*	行为失常的，异常的
filter	[filtə]	*vt. & n.*	过滤，滤波器
proportional to			与……成(正)比例
digital-to-analog (D/A) converter			数-模拟转换器
multiplexer	['mʌltipleksə]	*n.*	多路复用器，多路转换器
incorporate	[in'kɔ:pəreit, in'kɔ:pərət]	*vt.*	包含，合并，使……并入
reaction rate			反应率，反应速率
combustion	[kəm'bʌstʃən]	*n.*	燃烧，燃烧过程

rely on	依靠，依赖，信赖
heat pump	热(力)泵；蒸汽泵
thermoelectric [ˌθəːməuiˈlektrik] *adj.*	热电的
thermistor [θəːˈmistə]	热敏电阻，热元件
cylindrical ceramic resistor	圆柱形陶瓷电阻
implantable medical device	植入式医疗设备
remote control	远程控制，遥控，遥控器，遥控装置

Notes

1. The limitations of pure analog systems lie in the limited processing of data that can be accomplished, and in the difficulties of changing the type of data manipulation if this is found to be necessary.

lie in … and in …: 两个介词短语指出了纯模拟系统所受的两个限制。

that can be accomplished 是 limited processing of data 的定语从句。

of changing the type of data manipulation … 作 difficulties 的定语。

2. The introduction of a digital microcomputer to such a system permits the range of signal manipulation to be considerably extended giving, in some cases, a quick analysis to determine characteristics that cannot be measured directly.

The introduction of a digital microcomputer to system 作本句主语，permits 作谓语。

giving … 对前面内容进行补充说明。

3. A further advantage is that the microcomputer can condition the electrical voltages representing the measurements to identify any rogue readings and filter any unwanted "noise" present.

representing the measurements 作 electrical voltages 的定语。

to identify … and filter … 作目的状语。

4. A typical control system using a digital microcomputer can illustrate conventional on-line digital control, in which analog transducers produce electrical voltages proportional to the parameters to be measured.

句中 using a digital microcomputer 作 a typical control system 的定语。

in which analog transducers produce … 作 conventional on-line digital control 的非限制性定语从句。

5. The digital outputs to various control devices which control the process are first fed from the microcomputer in a prescribed sequence.

to various control devices 作 digital outputs 的定语，which control the process 作 control devices 的定语从句。

6. In most control systems there will also be a number of direct digital lines between the microcomputer and the process for information which requires switching actions only.

between the microcomputer and the process 作 direct digital lines 的定语。

for information 作目的状语。

which requires switching actions only 是 information 的定语从句。

7. Generally speaking a microcomputer would be incorporated into an instrumentation system only where the amount of data to be collected is very large, where processing of this data is complex or time consuming and where it would probably be necessary to use an off-line microcomputer.

where …, where … and where … 都是 instrumentation system 的定语从句。

8. There is obviously considerable advantage in such a system which collects the necessary measurements and processes them and presents the data in the form required, and especially, the process can be readily changed by inputting a new program to the microcomputer.

which 引导 system 的定语从句，从句的谓语有 collects、processes、presents。

9. The thermistor and bridge provide a voltage that is converted with an A/D converter and read by the microcomputer program. A control program writes a number to the D/A converter, whose output is amplified to drive an oven resistor.

that is converted … and read …是 a voltage 的定语从句。

whose output … 是 D/A converter 的非限制性定语从句。

Exercises

I. Try to match the following columns.

transducer	电位计，分压器，电位差计
potentiometer	与……成(正)比例
strain gauge	模/数转换器
digital-to-analog (D/A) converter	多路复用器，多路转换器
multiplexer	应变仪，变形测量器
thermistor	数-模转换器
remote control	热敏电阻，热元件
power tool	远程控制，遥控
A/D converter	电动工具
proportional to	传感器，换能器

II. Place a "T" after the sentence which is true and an "F" after the sentence which is false.

1. Industrial processes can only be controlled by anolog controllers. ( )

2. The parameter being measured, such as position, temperature, pressure, and density, is usually defined by an electrical current. ( )

3. In some cases, the anolog control system can give a quick analysis to determine characteristics that cannot be measured directly. ( )

4. The digital output from the microcomputer is converted to an analog signal by a D/A converter. ( )

5. The microcomputer can only accept one measurement signal at a time. ( )

6. In the instrumentation system where a microcomputer is incorporated, the process can be

readily changed by inputting a new program to the microcomputer.   (   )

7. In a typical microcomputer-based temperature-control system, a thermistor is used for temperature sensing and a cylindrical ceramic resistor is used for heating.   (   )

8. The anolog controller can condition the electrical voltages representing the measurements to identify any rogue readings and filter any unwanted "noise" present.   (   )

III. Translate the following paragraph into Chinese.

Feedback in most cases is analogous. To turn analogue feedback into digital signals that a digital microprocessor can handle, an analogue-to-digital converter (ADC) is used. With an ADC, an analogue signal is digitized into a digital signal which is represented in a form of a series of on/off pulse, a form that stands for a binary figure. In a similar way, the output of the microprocessor, which is used as a control signal exerted on the mechanism to manipulate the controlled object, can be converted into an analogue signal that can drive those mechanisms, using a digital-to-analogue converter (DAC). Today, both ADC and DAC can work with high efficiency and at high frequency. Their functions can be implemented by means of either hardware or software or their combination.

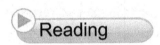

Reading

Use of Microcontrollers in Numerical Control Systems

Questions for passage discussion

How does a Numerical Control System work?

What are the advantages to be gained from the use of microcontrollers in numerical control systems?

Text

Microcontrollers are widely used in numerical control systems. Briefly, the variable to be controlled, such as temperature, position, is monitored and the output from the sensor monitoring this variable is subtracted from a reference signal. The difference signal resulting from the comparator is measure of error, called the actuating signal, which is used as an input to the process. A typical system is shown schematically in Fig.5.3.

A microcontroller can be used in such a system, which is referred to as direct digital control (DDC). The motor speed is the variable to be controlled. The tachometer acts as a speed transducer, generating a voltage proportional to speed. The comparator is an electronic device. If the speed is low for any reason, the actuating signal is positive, causing the amplifier to feed more current to the motor which increases the torque and therefore the speed. If the speed is too high, the actuating signal is negative and the motor reduces torque and slows down. Clearly a stable operating speed will reached when the tacho-voltage is roughly equal to the reference voltage and hence the speed is proportional to the potentiometer position. Externally applied loads try to slow the motor down, but this causes the actuating signal to increase, the motor developing more torque to counteract the external load. The speed of the output shaft, which may be delivering thousands of watts, can be controlled simply by turning the reference potentiometer.

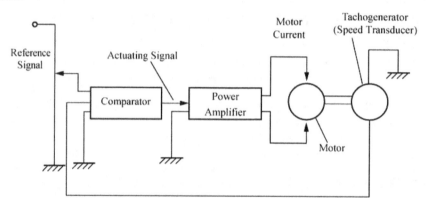

Fig. 5.3　A velocity control system using negative feedback

The advantages to be gained from the use of microcontrollers are (1) regulation against unwanted disturbances; (2) indirect control of what may be a high power by the low power reference signal; (3) a reduction in the undesirable effects of nonlinearities.

There is a wide variety in the performance of such systems and in many cases the comparator is much more complex. It is normally called a controller, in which a microcontroller can be used. This is referred to as direct digital controller (DDC), although far more complex digital control schemes are being configured.

The output from the transducer is sampled at regular intervals of time close enough together so that the output cannot change appreciably between samples. This information is converted to the binary form by an analog-to-digit controller (ADC) and stored by the microcontroller. And the reading entered into the microcontroller is used by a program which subtracts it from a reference number to create a digital equivalent to the signal to be fed back to the process. This number is thus output from the microcontroller to a digital analog converter (DAC) which produces a proportional voltage which stays constant until reset (a hold circuit). The transducer is then re-sampled, the sample processed and the hold circuit reset by the DAC, and so on.

The reference signal used by the control program may be a fixed number (a set point), but it may be varied by resetting from a teletype. Alternatively it may be a digital reference signal transmitted from another microcontroller. The hierarchy in large scale systems is becoming common, with a number of microcontrollers' control functions supervised by a central computer.

The reference signal may itself be continually varying and the ease with which this can be handled in the microcontroller is one advantage of digital control.

While it may prove practical by using specially tailored controllers, with the program stored in read only memory (ROM), to control a single system as just explained, the economic use is for one microcontroller to control, say fifty closed loops. One transducer output is sampled, processed and used to set the hold circuit feeding the appropriate process input. This, since the microcontroller is so fast, may only take one hundredth of the time before another sample is required. Thus a number of process outputs are multiplexed into the microcontroller with an appropriately "ganged" demultiplexor feeding the hold circuits. In this way, the microcontroller is "time-multiplexed" to control fifty or so individual loops before repeating first loop.

Common examples of microcontroller control exist in the process industries: e.g. chemical plants, oil refineries, and steel works, and sophisticated mechanical systems: e.g. radar systems, tracking telescopes, aircraft control systems, etc.

New Words and Expressions

microcontroller	[ˌmaikrəukən'trəulə]	n.	微控制器
subtract	[səb'trækt]	v.	减去，减
comparator	[kəm'pærətə]	n.	比较发生器
schematically	[ski'mætikəli]	adv.	示意地，原理性地
tachogenerator	['tækə'dʒenəreitə]	n.	测速发电机，测速传感器
tachometer	[tæ'kɔmitə]	n.	转速表，转数计
transducer	[trænz'djuːsə]	n.	传感器，变换器，换能器
tacho-voltage		n.	转速电压
counteract	[ˌkauntə'rækt]	v.	抵消，反作用于
disturbance	[di'stəːbəns]	n.	干扰，骚乱，扰动
nonlinearity	[ˌnɔnlini'ærəti]	n.	非线性
interval	['intəvəl]	n.	间隔，距离，时间间隔
appreciably	[ə'priːʃiəbli]	adv.	明显地
equivalent	[i'kwivələnt]	adj.	相等的，相当的
		n.	当量
inaccessible	[ˌinæk'sesəbl]	adj.	不能接近的，达不到的
configure	[kən'figə]	vt.	使……成形，安装
teletype	['telitaip]	n.	电传打字机，打字电报通信
hierarchy	['haiəˌrɑːki]	n.	分级系统，分级结构，数据层次
supervise	['sjuːpəvaiz]	v.	监控，检测，操纵
tailor	['teilə]	v.	制作，改装，使合适
incorporate	[in'kɔːpəreit, in'kɔːpərət]	v.	(使)合并，并入，合编
refinery	[ri'fainəri]	n.	精炼厂

65

| sophisticated | [sə'fistikeitid] | adj. | 非常复杂的，非常精密的 |

sophisticated   [sə'fistikeitid]   *adj.*   非常复杂的，非常精密的

direct digital controller (DDC)   直接数字控制器

analog-to digit controller (ADC)   模数转换器

digit-to analog controller (DAC)   数模转换器

hold circuit   自保持电路

routine maintenance   例行保养

read only memory (ROM)   只读存储器

Notes

1. The difference signal resulting from the comparator is measure of error, called the actuating signal, which is used as an input to the process.

called the actuating signal 作 measure of error 的后置定语。

which is used as an input to the process 是 actuating signal 的非限制性定语从句。

2. If the speed is low for any reason, the actuating signal is positive, causing the amplifier to feed more current to the motor which increases the torque and therefore the speed.

causing the amplifier to feed more current to the motor 作 the actuating signal is positive 的定语。

which increases the torque and therefore the speed 作 more current to the motor 的定语从句。

3. Externally applied loads try to slow the motor down, but this causes the actuating signal to increase, the motor developing more torque to counteract the external load.

the motor developing more torque to counteract the external load 是独立结构作状语。

4. And the reading entered into the computer is used by a program which subtracts it from a reference number to create a digital equivalent to the signal to be fed back to the process.

which 引导 a program 的定语从句。

equivalent to the signal 作 a digital 的后置定语。

to be fed back to the process 作 the signal 的后置定语。

5. This number is thus output from the computer to a digital analog converter (DAC) which produces a proportional voltage which stays constant until reset (a hold circuit).

第一个 which 引导 digital analog converter (DAC)的定语从句，第二个 which 引导 proportional voltage 的定语从句。

6. The reference signal may itself be continually varying and the ease with which this can be handled in the computer is one advantage of digital control.

and 前后是两个并列的句子。

and 后的句子: the ease 为主语，is one advantage of digital control 为谓语，with which this can be handled in the computer 作 the ease 的定语从句。

7. While it may prove practical by using specially tailored microcontrollers, with the program stored in read only memory (ROM), to control a single system as just explained, the economic use is for one computer to control, say fifty closed loops.

主句为 the economic use is for one computer to control, say fifty closed loops。

之前是 while 引导的让步状语从句。

Exercises

Ⅰ. **Try to match the following columns.**

monitor	直接数字控制器
comparator	转速电压
tachometer	转速表，转数计
tacho-voltage	电位计，电势计
potentiometer	抵消，反作用于
counteract	非线性
nonlinearity	常量，恒量，恒定的
constant	只读存储器
direct digital controller (DDC)	保持电路
hold circuit	监控，监视
read only memory (ROM)	比较发生器

Ⅱ. **Fill in the blanks according to the words given in Chinese.**

With the development of science and technology, a new term, _____ (数字控制) appeared. Controlling a machine tool using a punched tape or stored_____ (程序) is known as numerical control. When numerical control is performed under computer supervision, it is called _____ (计算机数字控制). Computers are the control units of CNC machines, they are built in or linked to the machines via communications channels. CNC means the operation of machine tools and other processing machines by a series of _____ (命令) of the tool to the work-piece. An organized list of commands constitutes a CNC program. The program may be used repeatedly to obtain identical results. When the job changes, we can only change the program of _____ (指令). The capability to change the program for each new job gives CNC its flexibility.

Ⅲ. **Translate the following paragraph into Chinese.**

Numerical control (NC) refers to the automation of machine tools that are operated by abstractly programmed commands encoded on a storage medium, as opposed to manually controlled via handwheels or levers, or mechanically automated via cams alone. The first NC machines were built in the 1940s and 1950s, based on existing tools that were modified with motors that moved the controls to follow points fed into the system on paper tape. These early servomechanisms were rapidly augmented with analog and digital computers, creating the modern computed numerically controlled (CNC) machine tools that have revolutionized the design process.

Translating Skills

词的增译与省译

英语和汉语是两种不同的语言，其表达方式各不相同，语言特点各有其异。把英文译为汉语，首先要忠实于原著的内容，保持原著的风格，把原著用汉语通畅易懂地表达出来，并让读者能够领略到原著的意境，这就是翻译的原则，即翻译史上著名翻译家严复提出的"信、达、雅"翻译标准。

为了使译文更符合汉语的表达习惯，让其读起来更像汉语，通常在译文能够保持原意的情况下，将词类、词量加以处理，或转换，或增加或减少，以达到翻译的更高层次。

1. 词的增译

增译法就是在翻译时，为了能更忠实地表达原文的思想内容，根据意义上、修辞上的需要，增加一些无其词而有其义的词汇。最常见的增译方法有以下几种。

1) 增译名词复数

英语名词复数表现在词形的变化上，而汉语名词复数需要通过数量词、重叠词等来表现，因此通常可增加诸如"一些"、"许多"、"各类"、"种种"、"们"等词汇，以提高修辞效果。例如：

The first electronic computers went into operation in 1945.

第一批电子计算机在 1945 年开始使用。

The data are stored in the memory—another category of computer hardware，which is used to store data, and also hold the program.

各种数据都存储在存储器中——另一种计算机硬件，用来存储各种数据，也存放程序。

Iraq has gone through years of turmoil. 伊拉克经历了多年的动乱。

2) 增译动词

进行英译汉时，根据上下文需要，在一些名词或名词词组前增加动词，能使其意思更加明白，更符合汉语的表达习惯。例如：

Einstein received Iris Nobel Prize for the theory of photoemission.

爱因斯坦由于创立了光电发射理论而荣获诺贝尔奖。

We see airplane in the sky and ships in the sea.

我们看见飞机在空中飞行，船舶在海上行驶。

An electric switch is often on a wall near the door of a room.

电开关通常安装在靠房门的墙上。

3) 增译语气助词

为了更好地表达原著的意思，增加修辞色彩，可以增译一些汉语中常用的语气助词，如"呢"、"嘛"、"啦"、"的"、"了"等，使译文更富有生活气息。例如：

Great! Any other tips on the design?　好极了! 对设计还有什么建议吗?

As for me，I shall not go back there，either.　至于我呢，也不会再回那儿了。

Go easy on the water——it's the last bottle! We still have a long way to go.
水要省着点喝——这是最后一瓶了!我们还要走远路呢。

4) 增译量词

在英语中很少使用量词，数词一般可直接与可数名词连用，译为汉语时，常需要加上量词。例如:

The successful landing of two robots on Mars is another landmark of man's exploring outer-space.

两个机器人的成功着陆火星，是人类探测外太空的又一个里程碑。

Each material has its own specific resistance.　每种材料都有自己的电阻率。

The heavenly, body "Sedna" may not be the tenth planet in the solar system.
天体"塞德娜"不一定就是太阳系的第 10 颗行星。

2. 词的省译

由于英汉语言的差异，一些词译为汉语是无法译出的，例如冠词、物主代词、形式主语、形式宾语等，按照英文逐字译出，反而使译文累赘，不符合汉语习惯。这时，在不违背原文的原则下，常可省译一些词语。

1) 省译物主代词

英语物主代词的运用具有其鲜明的特色，有些已成为固定用法，缺之不可。为了使表达更加汉语化，在进行汉译时，这些物主代词常可省去。例如:

Different metals differ in their electrical conductivity.
不同金属具有不同的导电性能。

The keyboard has lost one of its keys.　键盘少了一个键。

Falling water has kinetic energy due to its motion.　落水由于运动具有动能。

No two electrons may have all their quantum numbers alike.
没有两个电子其所有量子数都相同。

2) 省译形式主语 it

英语中 it 引导的句型很常见，译为汉语时，形式主语 it 常可省去而译成无主句。例如:

It is quite impossible for a body speeds faster than that of light.
要让一个物体获得比光速还快的速度是完全不可能的。

It was not until the 19th century that heat was considered a form of energy.
直到 19 世纪，热才被认为是能的一种形式。

It is damp and cold. I think it's going to rain.　又潮又冷，我想要下雨了。

It is thought that in the universe there is as much positive as negative charge.
人们都认为宇宙间的正电荷和负电荷一样多。

3) 省译形式宾语 it

it 作为形式宾语是英语的一个特别用法，汉语并无对应的成分，翻译时常可省译。例如:

By using electric computers, meteorologists are able to perform mathematical computations speed which makes it possible to use the results to make more accurate weather forecasts.

通过使用计算机，气象学家就能够高速进行数学运算，这种高速可将运算结果用来更准确地预报天气。

We have made it clear that binary arithmetic is crucial to understanding computer operation.
我们已经讲清楚了，二进制运算对了解计算机的操作是至关重要的。

I heard it said that he has great concern for our biological experiments.
我听说他很关心我们的生物实验。

4) 省译介词

介词在英语中使用频率很高，译成汉语时，一些表示时间、地点的介词可以省译。例如：

The difference between the two machines consists in power.
这两台机器的差别在于功率不同。

On October 16, 2003, China's first manned spaceship safely returned to the earth.
2003 年 10 月 16 日，中国第一艘载人太空飞船安全地回到地球。

Everything in our physical world is continually changing.
我们的物质世界的一切都在不断变化。

Unit Six　Foundation of PLC

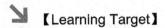 【Learning Target】

In this Unit, our target is to train your reading comprehension. Try to grasp the main idea of these passages and learn the speciality vocabularies.

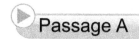

PLC Overview

Questions for passage discussion

What is the PLC? What are the main units of the PLC? And what are their functions?
What are the main differences of the PLC from other computers?

Text

Programmable logic controllers, or programmable controllers, or PLCs for short, are specialized industrial devices for interfacing to and controlling analog and digital devices. They are also special computer devices used for automation of real-world processes, such as control of machinery on factory assembly lines. The PLC usually uses a microprocessor. The program can often be used to control complex sequencing and is often written by engineers. The program is stored in battery-backed memory or EEPROMs.

PLCs come in many shapes and sizes. They can be so small as to fit in your shirt pocket, while more involved control systems require large PLC racks. Smaller PLCs are typically designed with fixed I/O points.

All PLCs have the basic structure, shown in Fig. 6.1.

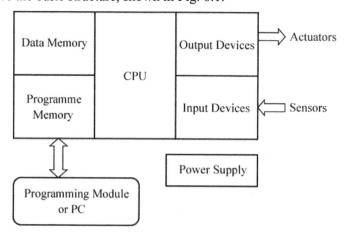

Fig. 6.1   Schematic of a PLC

From Fig. 6.1, the PLC has five main units: the central processing unit (CPU), the programme memory, the data memory, the output devices and the input devices.

The CPU is dedicated to run one program that monitors a series of different inputs and logically manipulates the outputs for the desired control. They are meant to be very flexible in how they can be programmed while also providing the advantages of high reliability (no program crashes or mechanical failures), compact and economical over traditional control systems. The programme memory is used for storing the instructions for the logical control sequence. The status of switches, interlocks, past values of data and other working data is stored in the data memory.

The main differences from other computers are the special input/output arrangements. These connect the PLC to sensors and actuators. PLCs can read limit switches, temperature indicators and the positions of complex positioning systems. Some even use machine vision. On the actuator side, PLCs drive any kind of electronic motors, pneumatic or hydraulic cylinders, diaphragms, magnetic relays or solenoids. The input/output arrangements may be built into a simple PLC, or the PLC may have external I/O modules attached to a proprietary computer network that plugs into the PLC. PLCs were invented as less expensive replacements for older automated systems that would use hundreds or thousands of relays and cam timers. Often, a single PLC can be programmed to replace thousands of relays. Programmable controllers were initially adopted by the automotive manufacturing industry, where software revision replaced the rewiring of hard-wired control panels.

The functionality of the PLC has evolved over the years to include typical relay control, sophisticated motion control, process control, distributed control systems and complex networking.

The earliest PLCs expressed all decisions making logic in simple ladder logic inspired from the electrical connection diagrams. The electricians were quite able to trace out circuit problems with schematic diagrams using ladder logic. This was chosen mainly to reduce the apprehension of the existing technicians.

Today, the PLCs have been proven very reliable, but the programmable computer still has a long way to go. With the IEC61131-3 standard, it is now possible to program these devices using structured programming languages, and logic elementary operations.

A graphical programming notation called sequential function charts is available on certain programmable controllers.

However, it should be noted that PLCs no longer have a very high cost (often thousands of dollars), typical of a "generic" solution. Modern PLCs with full capabilities are available for a few hundred USD. There are other ways for automating machines, such as a custom microcontroller-based design, but there are differences among both: PLCs contain everything needed to handle high power loads right out of the box, while a microcontroller would need an electronics engineer to design power supplies, I/O modules, etc. Also a microcontroller based design would not have the flexibility of in-field programmability of a PLC. That is why PLCs are used in production lines.

New Words and Expressions

programmable logic controller (PLC)		可编程逻辑控制器
interface ['intəfeis]	vt.	(使通过界面或接口)接合，连接

machinery	[məˈʃiːnəri]	n.	机械，机器
assembly line			装配线，生产流水线
fit …in			装得下，放得进去
involved	[inˈvɔlvd]	adj.	有关的，复杂的
dedicated	[ˈdedikeitid]	adj.	专用的，专门用途的
manipulate	[məˈnipjuleit]	vt.	操作，控制
crash	[kræʃ]	v. & n.	崩溃，失效，停机
interlock	[ˌintəˈlɔk, ˈintəlɔk]	v. & n.	联锁，互锁
actuator	[ˈæktjueitə]	n.	执行机构
pneumatic	[njuːˈmætik]	adj.	气动的，气压的
hydraulic	[haiˈdrɔːlik]	adj.	液压的
hydraulic cylinder			液压缸
relay	[ˈriːlei, riˈlei]	n.	[电工]继电器
solenoid	[ˈsəulənɔid]	n.	[电]螺线管
proprietary	[prəuˈpraiətəri]	adj.	专用的，专有的
cam	[kæm]	n.	凸轮
automate	[ˈɔːtəmeit]	v.	使自动化，自动操作
initially	[iˈniʃəli]	adv.	最初，开头
ladder	[ˈlædə]	n.	梯形，阶梯，途径
ladder logic			梯形图，梯形逻辑
inspire	[inˈspaiə]	vt.	作为……的原因或根源，引起，激励
diaphragm	[ˈdaiəfræm]	n.	隔板，膜片
electrician	[ˌilekˈtriʃən]	n.	电工，电气专家
revision	[riˈviʒən]	n.	修改，校正
evolve	[iˈvɔlv]	vt.	演变，进化，发展
sophisticated	[səˈfistikeitid]	adj.	复杂的，高级的，尖端的，精密的
trace out			描绘出，提出，追查
apprehension	[ˌæpriˈhenʃən]	n.	担心，忧虑
power supply			电源
module	[ˈmɔdjuːl]	n.	模数，模块
flexibility	[fleksiˈbiliti]	n.	弹性，适应性，柔韧性

Notes

1. Programmable logic controllers, … are specialized industrial devices for interfacing to and controlling …. They are also special computer devices used for …

for interfacing to and controlling…作 programmable logic controllers 的后置定语。

used for …为分词结构，作 special computer devices 的定语。

2. They can be so small as to fit in your shirt pocket, while more involved control systems

require large PLC racks.

so small as to: so … as to 结构，意为 "如此…… 以致于……"。

3. They are meant to be very flexible in how they can be programmed while also providing the advantages of … over traditional control systems.

be meant to: 打算，有意要。

how 引导 be very flexible in 中介词 in 的宾语，while 引导时间状语。

advantages … over …: 与……相比的优点或长处

4. The input/output arrangements may be built into a simple PLC, or the PLC may have external I/O modules attached to a proprietary computer network that plugs into the PLC.

attached to … 作 external I/O modules 的后置定语。

that plugs into the PLC 是 external I/O modules 的定语从句。

5. PLCs were invented as less expensive replacements for older automated systems that would use hundreds or thousands of relays and cam timers.

that would …作 older automated systems 的定语从句。

6. Programmable controllers were initially adopted by the automotive manufacturing industry, where software revision replaced the rewiring of hard-wired control panels.

where 引导 automotive manufacturing industry 的非限制性定语从句。

7. The earliest PLCs expressed all decisions making logic in simple ladder logic inspired from the electrical connection diagrams.

making logic 作 all decision 的定语，inspired … 作 ladder logic 的后置定语。

Exercises

I. Try to match the following columns.

interface	模块
assembly line	监测，检测
monitor	装配线，生产流水线
actuator	接口，连接
relay	继电器
ladder logic	负载
load	传感器
power supply	电源
module	执行机构
sensor	梯形图

II. Fill in the blanks according to the words given in Chinese.

The development of low cost _____ (计算机) has brought the most recent revolution, the _____ (可编程逻辑控制器). The advent of the PLCs began in the 1970s, and has become the most common choice for _____ (生产) controls. _____ (梯形图) is the main _____ (编程) method used for PLCs and has been developed to mimic _____ (继电器) logic. The relays allow _____ (电源) to be switched on and off without a mechanical switch.

III. Place a "T" after the sentence which is true and an "F" after the sentence which is false.

1. The instructions for the logical control sequence are stored in the data memory.　　(　　)

2. The I/O modules only can be built into PLCs.　　(　　)

3. Now, we can use structured programming languages, and logic elementary operations to program PLCs.　　(　　)

4. The simple ladder logic used to program PLCs are inspired from the electrical connection diagrams.　　(　　)

5. It is very flexible in how to program PLCs.　　(　　)

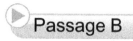

PLCs versus Other Types of Controls

Questions for passage discussion

Which means can be used to control the industrial processes?

What are the differences between PLC control and other types of controls?

Text

Though PLC is widely used in industrial control, it is not the only choice for controlling a process. Sticking with only basic relays may be of a benefit depending upon your application. Yet, on the other hand, a computer might also be the way to go. The PLC vs. microcontroller debate has been going on for a long time. More often though it doesn't come down to an "either or" situation but involves a mix of technologies.

1. PLC vs. Relay

When we first started programming PLCs it was still questionable if a PLC was necessary over just relay control. With PLC prices going down, size shrinking, and performance of PLCs improving over the years this has become less of a battle. Yet the designer has to ask themselves if a PLC is really overkill for their application. Some questions should be asked.

(1) Is there a need for future growth?

A PLC can easily accept a new module in a slot or get an expansion base.

(2) Is there a need for high reliability?

PLCs are seen as more robust over individual components.

(3) Is downtime a concern?

Any change or troubleshooting on a relay system means the system might have to go offline. Changes in a PLC can often be made online with no downtime.

(4) Are increased capability and output required?

PLCs can be faster than their mechanical counterparts.

(5) Are there data collection and communications required?

Only possible with a PLC or computer.

2. PLC vs. Dedicated Controller

A dedicated controller is a single instrument that is dedicated to controlling one parameter such as a PID controller measuring a temperature for heating control. They have the advantages of an all in one package, typically with display and buttons. This can be a very good thing to use in simple applications. A PLC these days can compete price wise and functionally with these controllers especially if more than one controller is needed. PLCs offer a greater degree of flexibility too because they can be programmed to handle all sorts of different scenarios.

3. PLC vs. Microcontroller

PLCs are well-adapted to a range of automation tasks. These are typically industrial processes in manufacturing where the cost of developing and maintaining the automation system is high relative to the total cost of the automation, and where changes to the system would be expected during its operational life. PLCs contain input and output devices compatible with industrial pilot devices and controls; little electrical design is required, and the design problem centers on expressing the desired sequence of operations. PLC applications are typically highly customized systems so the cost of a packaged PLC is low compared to the cost of a specific custom-built controller design. On the other hand, in the case of mass-produced goods, customized control systems are economic due to the lower cost of the components, which can be optimally chosen instead of a "generic" solution, and where the non-recurring engineering charges are spread over thousands or millions of units.

For high volume or very simple fixed automation tasks, different techniques are used. For example, a consumer dishwasher would be controlled by an electromechanical cam timer costing only a few dollars in production quantities.

A microcontroller-based design would be appropriate where hundreds or thousands of units will be produced and so the development cost (design of power supplies, input/output hardware and necessary testing and certification) can be spread over many sales, and where the end-user would not need to alter the control. Automotive applications are an example; millions of units are built each year, and very few end-users alter the programming of these controllers. However, some specialty vehicles such as transit buses economically use PLCs instead of custom-designed controls, because the volumes are low and the development cost would be uneconomic.

Very complex process control, such as used in the chemical industry, may require algorithms and performance beyond the capability of even high-performance PLCs. Very high-speed or precision controls may also require customized solutions; for example, aircraft flight controls.

PLCs may include logic for single-variable feedback analog control loop, a "proportional, integral, derivative" or "PID controller". A PID loop could be used to control the temperature of a manufacturing process, for example. Historically PLCs were usually configured with only a few analog control loops; where processes required hundreds or thousands of loops, a distributed control system (DCS) would instead be used. As PLCs have become more powerful, the boundary between DCS and PLC applications has become less distinct.

New Words and Expressions

versus	['və:səs]	*prep.*	对，对抗，比较
stick with			坚持，继续，坚持做
depend upon			依赖，依靠，取决于
debate	[di'beit]	*v. & n.*	辩论，争论
come down to			到达，归结为
shrink	[ʃriŋk]	*v. & n.*	收缩，缩小
overkill	['əuvəkil, ,əuvə'kil]	*n.*	过度的杀伤力
robust	[rəu'bʌst, 'rəubʌst]	*adj.*	强壮的，结实的，耐用的，坚固的
downtime	['dauntaim]	*n.*	停机时间，停工期
troubleshoot	['trʌblʃu:t]	*v.*	故障检测
offline	['ɔflain]	*adj.*	脱机的，离线的
capability	[,keipə'biləti]	*n.*	能力，性能，功能，容量
counterpart	['kauntə,pa:t]	*n.*	对手，对方
dedicated	['dedikeitid]	*adj.*	专用的，专门用途的
instrument	['instrumənt]	*n.*	仪器，器具，装置
have the advantages of			有……的优点
scenario	[si'na:riəu]	*n.*	情况
operational life			使用年限，使用寿命，使用限期
compatible	[kəm'pætəbl]	*adj.*	兼容的，相容的
pilot	['pailət]	*n.*	指示器，调节器
customized	['kʌstəmaizd]	*adj.*	定制的，用户化的
spread over			分散，传开
in the case of			在……的情况下
generic	[dʒi'nerik]	*adj.*	通用的，一般的
non-recurring		*adj.*	非定期的，临时性的，一次性的
electromechanical	[i,lektrəumi'kænikəl]	*adj.*	机电的
certification	[,sə:tifi'keiʃən]	*n.*	认证，确认，鉴定
specialty vehicles			特种车辆，专用车
transit	['trænsit]	*v. & n.*	运输，过境，中转
boundary	['baundəri]	*n.*	边界，界限，分界线
distinct	[dis'tiŋkt]	*adj.*	清晰的，明显的，清楚的，有区别的

Notes

1. With PLC prices going down, size shrinking, and performance of PLCs improving over the years this has become less of a battle.

with …years 是独立结构作状语，主句为 this has become less of a battle。

2. These are typically industrial processes in manufacturing where the cost of developing and maintaining the automation system is high relative to the total cost of the automation, and where changes to the system would be expected during its operational life.

where … and where …: 两个 where 都引导 manufacturing 的定语从句。

3. PLCs contain input and output devices compatible with industrial pilot devices and controls; little electrical design is required, and the design problem centers on expressing the desired sequence of operations.

compatible with … 作 input and output devices 的后置定语。

centers on: 集中于……，以……为中心，重点在于……

4. On the other hand, in the case of mass-produced goods, customized control systems…, which can be …, and where ….

which 和 where 均引导 customized control systems 的非限制性定语从句。

5. A microcontroller-based design would be appropriate where …, and where …

句中两个 where 均引导状语从句。

6. Historically PLCs were usually configured with only a few analog control loops; where processes required hundreds or thousands of loops, a distributed control system (DCS) would instead be used.

where … loops 是状语从句。

Exercises

Ⅰ. **Try to match the following columns.**

relay	模块
module	故障检测
downtime	继电器
troubleshoot	停机
counterpart	对手，对方
compatible	机电的
electromechanical	能力，性能，功能，容量
boundary	仪器，器具，装置
instrument	边界，界限，分界线
capability	兼容的，相容的

Ⅱ. **Fill in the blanks according to the words given in Chinese.**

The PLC was specifically designed for harsh conditions with _____ (电噪声), magnetic fields, vibration, extreme temperatures or humidity. By design PLCs are friendly to

_____ (电工) since they are in ladder logic and have easy connections.PLCs execute a single _____ (程序) in sequential order. The have better ability to handle events in real time.A PLC never _____ (崩溃) over long periods of time ("never" may not be the right word but it's close enough to be true) . _____ (数据存储器) is limited in its ability to store a lot of data.

Ⅲ. Place a "T" after the sentence which is true and an "F" after the sentence which is false.

1. PLC is the only choice for controlling a industrial production process.　　　(　　)

2. The dedicated controllers have the advantages of an all in one package, typically with display and buttons.　　　(　　)

3. PLCs offer a greater degree of flexibility because they can not be programmed to handle all sorts of different scenarios.　　　(　　)

4. PLCs do not contain input and output devices compatible with industrial pilot devices and controls.　　　(　　)

5. Very complex process control, such as used in the chemical industry, may require algorithms and performance beyond the capability of even high-performance PLCs.　　　(　　)

6. When processes required hundreds or thousands of loops, a distributed control system (DCS) would prefer to be used.　　　(　　)

Reading

Applications of PLC

Questions for passage discussion

What are the general characteristics of the PLC?
Where can a programmable logic controller be applied?

Text

A programmable logic controller is a digitally operating apparatus that uses a programmable memory for the internal storage of instructions that implement specific functions such as logic, sequence, timing, counting, and arithmetic, to control machines and processes. As electronic components become smaller and more reliable, PLC becomes faster, more powerful, and capable of controlling more inputs and outputs. In the late 1970s high-speed local communication networks were developed that allow a large process or a machine to be controlled by several smaller controllers.

The 1980s brought ever faster and more powerful PLC; with expandable instruction set and the 16 bits capabilities instead of 8 bits, and even floating point calculation instead of integer ones. The size of the PLC shrank to the point that a single card can do what it took an entire rack to do in the past. Small and very small PLCs also appeared for application that would normally have required as little as half a dozen relays.

Recent developments have been in the area of communication between different brands of PLC's and personal and mainframe computer. There has also been an ever-increasing selection of devices for operator interfacing that can be added to PLC without having to be controlled directly by the PLC. Some PLC's now have computer module available for analog and special input/output modules.

PLC are used everywhere. They are found in doc levelers and stretch wrappers, packing machines and assembly lines, power distribution systems and process plants. With the advent of small self contained PLCs, it is now very easy for average electrician to design, install and program small application that previously would have been done with relay logic.

Some of the actual PLC applications in industry are listed, with a brief description of each control system.

Boiler control: A separate PLC is used for each of four boilers in a chemical plant to control the process of purging, pilot light-off, flame safety checks, all interlock and safety shut down checks, main burner light-off, temperature control, and valve switching from natural gas to fuel oil. The PLC is programmed to be an energy management system for maximum efficiency and safety.

Compressor station control: A compressor station with multiple compressors is controlled by a PLC, which handles start-up and shutdown sequence and all safety interlocks.

Ethylene drying facility: In an ethylene drying facility, where moist gas is first removed from salt domes and then dried and pumped into the main pipeline, two PLCs are used for controlling the entire operation. One PLC is used to control heater combustion controls and shutdown system. The second PLC is used to control the drying and regeneration cycles in the dryer units. Both PLCs act as slaves and are tied into a master PLC located in a central operation control room. The master PLC has control over shutdown sequences, and also monitors some of the critical process variables.

Automatic welding: PLCs have been successfully applied to the control of automatic welding machines in the automotive industry. The use of aluminum in automobile bodies for weight reduction created a load distribution problem because welding aluminum consumes more current per weld than welding steel. To eliminate this, time-share automatic welding machines on a priority scheme utilizes the data handling and arithmetic capability of the PLCs.

Coal fluidizing process: A PLC is installed on a fluidized bed to determine the amount of energy generated from a given amount of coal. A mixture of crushed coal and limestone is blown through jets over a heated bed. Burning rates and temperature are monitored. The PLC controls the sequencing of the valve, and takes the place of a relay control system. The analog capabilities of the PLC enable jet valves to be controlled by the control system that is doing the sequencing. Control devices are also monitored on a CRT.

Material handling: In a storage/retrieval system controlled by a PLC, parts are loaded and carried through the system in totes bins. The controller keeps track of the totes. An operator's console allows parts to be rapidly loaded or unloaded. A printer provides inventory printout, such as storage lane number, parts assigned to each lane, and a quantity of parts in a lane.

New Words and Expressions

apparatus	[ˌæpəˈreitəs]	*n.*	仪器，设备，仪表，装置
as little as			与……一样少，少则，少到
leveler	[ˈlevələ]	*n.*	轧平机，校平器
stretch wrapper			包装设备
purge	[pəːdʒ]	*v.*	清洗，净化
compressor	[kəmˈpresə]	*n.*	压缩机
ethylene drying facility			乙烯干燥装置
dome	[dəum]	*n.*	拱形结构，圆屋顶
combustion	[kəmˈbʌstʃən]	*n.*	燃烧
slave	[sleiv]	*adj.*	从属的
weld	[weld]	*v.*	焊接
aluminum	[əˈljuːminəm]	*n.*	铝
eliminate	[iˈlimineit]	*vt.*	消除，排除，除去
priority	[praiˈɔrəti]	*n.*	优先权，优先级，优先
fluidize	[ˈfluːidaiz]	*vt.*	使液化，流(态)化
limestone	[ˈlaimstəun]	*n.*	石灰岩，石灰石
take the place of			代替
tote	[təut]	*v.*	手提，拖拉，携带
keep track of			记住，留意

Notes

1. A programmable logic controller is a digitally operating apparatus that uses a programmable memory for the internal storage of instructions that implement …

that uses …作 operating apparatus 的定语从句。

that implement …作 instructions 的定语从句。

2. There has also been an ever-increasing selection of devices for operator interfacing that can be added to PLC without having to be controlled directly by the PLC.

that 引导 operator interfacing 的定语从句。

3. With the advent of small self contained PLCs, it is now very easy for average electrician to design, install and program small application that previously would have been done with relay logic.

that 引导 small application 的定语从句。

4. A compressor station with multiple compressors is controlled by a PLC, which handles start-up and shutdown sequence and all safety interlocks.

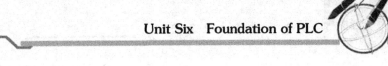

which 引导 PLC 的非限制性定语从句。

5. In an ethylene drying facility, where …, two PLCs are used for controlling the entire operation.

where 引导 ethylene drying facility 的非限制性定语从句。

6. The use of aluminum in automobile bodies for weight reduction created a load distribution problem because welding aluminum consumes more current per weld than welding steel.

句中主语为 the use of aluminum in automobile bodies，谓语为 created。

Exercises

Ⅰ. Try to match the following columns.

apparatus	包装机械
compressor	焊接
weld	优先权，优先级
priority	压缩机
eliminate	记住，留意
take the place of	可编程存储器
keep track of	消除，排除
programmable memory	代替
packing machine	装配线
assembly line	仪器，设备，仪表，装置

Ⅱ. Translate the following paragraph into Chinese.

The link with the industrial equipment is accomplished by means of the input/output interface. The input interface is designed to receive signals from the process and machine operation and to convert them into an acceptable form for the PLCs. The output interface converts PLC control signals into a form that can be used by the process equipment. The input interfaces and the output interfaces are kept separate, and both types are designed to be modular in structure. The processor is the central component of the PLC, and it executes the various logic functions, performs operations on inputs, and determines the appropriate outputs. The memory in the programmable controller is used to store the program that specifies the logic of the input/output processing.

Translating Skills

动词非谓语形式

如前所述，科技文章要求行文简练，结构紧凑，为此，往往使用分词短语代替定语从句或状语从句；使用分词独立结构代替状语从句或并列分句；使用不定式短语代替各种从句，使用介词加动名词构成的短语代替定语从句或状语从句。这样可缩短句子，又比较醒目。非谓语动词有 4 种形式：动名词、现在分词、过去分词和不定式。

1. 动名词

动名词由动词原形后+ing 构成，它以名词为主，可充当主语、宾语(动词宾语或介词宾语)、宾补、表语及定语，同时保留了动词性，可带宾语和状语。动名词名词性较强，表示经常性动作。

【例 1】 Selecting a desired signal is one of three important functions performed by the tuning circuit. (作主语)

选择所需的信号只是调谐电路所执行的 3 个重要功能之一。

【例 2】 This reliability can further be improved by using error-detecting and error-correcting codes. (作介词 by 的宾语)

利用检错码和纠错码可以进一步提高可靠性。

【例 3】 One of the greatest advantages of the transistor is its being able to be made very small. (作表语，its 是逻辑主体)

晶体管的最大优点之一，就是能够把它做得很小。

2. 现在分词

现在分词与动名词一样，由动词原形后+ing 构成，它以形容词性、副词性为主，也保留了动词性，可作定语、状语用。现在分词含有主动和进行的意义。

【例 4】 In the process of transmission，the signals bearing the information are contaminated by noise. (作定语)

在传输的过程中，载信息信号会混入噪声。

注：动名词作定语时，动名词和它所修饰的词没有逻辑上的主谓关系，而分词作定语时，分词和它所修饰的词有逻辑上的主谓关系。

【例 5】 The left-most bit, excluding the sign bit, is the most significant bit(MSB)and the right-most bit is the least significant bit(LSB). (作主语补足语)

除符号位最左边的位是最高有效位，而最右边的位是最低有效位。

【例 6】 Using time multiplexing, a digital system can be used to process a number of digital signals. (作方式状语)

利用时间多路传输，数字系统可用于处理许多数字信号。

【例 7】 Physically, the transistor consists of three parts, emitter, base and collector, the base region being very thin. (分词独立结构，作状语，逻辑主体与句中主语不一致)

晶体管由发射极、基极和集电极 3 部分构成，基区很薄。

【例 8】 This article deals with microwaves, with particular attention being paid to radio location. (分词复合结构，with/without+名词+分词)

这篇文章是研究微波的，其中特别注意无线电定位问题。

3. 过去分词

过去分词由动词原形后+ed 构成，同现在分词一样，以形容词性、副词性为主，也保留了动词性，只作定语、状语。过去分词含有被动和完成的意义。

【例9】 Messages sent by telegraph are digital signals. (作定语)

由电报传送的信息是数字信号。

【例10】 Given a pattern, its recognition/classification may consist of one of the following two tasks: supervised classification or unsupervised classification. (作条件状语)

已知某个模式，其分类方式可以是有监督分类与无监督分类中的一种。

4. 不定式

不定式由动词原形前+to 构成，兼有名词、形容词、副词性，也保留了动词性，可用做定语、状语、表语、主语及宾语。不定式常表示具体的(特别是未来的)一次性动作。

【例11】 If you want to specialize in DSP, these are the allied areas you will also need to study. (作宾语)

要想精通数字信号处理，还需学习这些相关领域(的知识)。

【例12】 The only convenient way to store analog signals is to tape or film them.

(to store 作定语，to tape/film 与助动词 be 构成复合谓语)

存储模拟信号的唯一便捷的办法是将它存放在磁带或胶卷上。

注：除 way 外，要求不定式作定语的名词还有 ability, power, tendency, capacity, chance, time, method, attempt, opportunity, thing, work, property 等。

【例13】 In analog systems, it is difficult or very expensive to have a number of components with identical value. (作主语，it 为形式主语)

在模拟系统中，实现元器件参数相同很难，或者说代价不菲。

【例14】 To simplify the discussion, we use decimal numbers to illustrate this point. (to simplify 作状语，表目的，to illustrate 作宾语补足语)

为简化讨论，我们用十进制数来说明这一点。

【例15】 In some filter design problems, a primary objective may be to control some aspect of the time response such as the impulse response or the step response. (作表语)

在某些滤波器设计问题中，主要的目的可能是控制时间响应，如冲击响应或阶跃响应的某些方面。

注：常用的主语有下列名词：aim，task，duty，goal，work，job，role，problem，mistake 等。

Unit Seven   Electrical Machines

【Learning Target】

In this Unit, our target is to train your reading comprehension. Try to grasp the main idea of these passages and learn the speciality vocabularies.

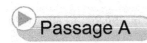

Introduction to Electrical Machines

Questions for passage discussion

What is an electrical machine? Where can electrical machines be applied?
How does the electrical machine be classified?

Text

Electrical machine is an electromagnetic device which can be used to achieve energy conversion or transfer according to Faraday's Law of Electromagnetic Induction. By the classic definition, electric machine is synonymous with electric motor or electric generator, all of which are electro-mechanical energy converters: converting electricity to mechanical power (i.e., electric motor) or mechanical power to electricity (i.e., electric generator). The movement involved in the mechanical power can be rotating or linear. Although transformers do not contain any moving parts they are also included in the family of electric machines because they utilize electromagnetic phenomena.

1. Brief History of Electrical Machines

Electrical machinery has been in existence for many years. The applications of electrical machines have expanded rapidly since their first use many years ago. At the present time, applications continue to increase at a rapid rate.

Most early discoveries related to electrical machinery operation dealt with direct-current systems. Alternating-current (AC) power generation and distribution became widespread a short time later. Presently, almost all electrical power systems produce and distribute three-phase alternating current. Thansformers allow the voltage produced by an AC generator to be increased while decreasing the current level by a corresponding amount. This allows long-distance distribution at a reduced current level, reduces power losses, and increases system efficiency.

The use of electrical motors has increased for home appliances and industrial and commercial applications for driving machines and sophisticated equipment. Many machines and automated industrial equipment now require precise control. Thus motor design and complexity has changed since early DC motors which were used primarily with railroad trains.

Our complex system of transportation has also had an impact on the use of electrical machines. Automobiles and other means of ground transportation use electrical motors for starting and generators for their battery-charging systems. There has recently been emphasis in the development of electric motor-driven automobiles.

2. Classification of Electric Machines

When classifying of electric machines (motors and generators) it is reasonable to start with physical principle for converting electric energy to mechanical energy.

Electric machines can be synchronous meaning that the magnetic field set up by the stator coils rotates with the same speed as rotor; or asynchronous, meaning that there is a speed difference. PM machines and reluctance machines are always synchronous. Brushed machines with rotor windings can be synchronous when rotor is supplied with DC or AC with same frequency as stator or asynchronous when stator and rotor are supplied with AC with different frequencies. Induction machines are usually asynchronous, but can be synchronous, if there are superconductors in the rotor windings.

With that in mind, it is correct to classify common electric machines as follows.

1) Electromagnetic-rotor machines

Electromagnetic-rotor machines are machines having some kind of electric current in rotor which creates a magnetic field which interacts with the stator windings. The rotor current can be the internal current in a permanent magnet (PM machine), a current supplied to rotor through brushes (brushed machine) or a current set up in closed rotor windings by a varying magnetic field (induction machine).

2) Reluctance machines (step machines).

Reluctance machines (reluctance motor) has no windings in rotor, only a ferromagnetic material shaped so that "electromagnets" in stator can "grab" the teeth in rotor and move it a little. The electromagnets are then turned off, while another set of electromagnets is turned on to move stator further. Another name is step motor, and it is suited for low speed and accurate position control. Reluctance machines can be supplied with PMs in stator to improve performance.

3) Electrostatic machines

In Electrostatic machines (electrostatic motor) torque is created by attraction or repulsion of electric charge in rotor and stator.

4) Homopolar machines

Homopolar machines (homopolar motor) are true DC machines where current is supplied to a spinning wheel through brushes. The wheel is inserted in a magnetic field, and torque is created as the current travels from the edge to the centre of the wheel through the magnetic field.

New Words and Expressions

electrical machine			电机
electromagnetic	[ilektrəumæg'netik]	*adj.*	电磁的
transfer	[træns'fə:]	*n. & v.*	转移
synonymous	[si'nɔniməs]	*adj.*	同义的，类义的
electric motor			电动机
electric generator			发电机
transformer	[træns'fɔ:mə]	*n.*	变压器

utilize	['juːtilaiz]	*vt.*	利用，应用
alternating-current (AC)			交流电流
direct-current			直流电流
three-phase alternating current			三相交流电流
principle	['prinsəpl]	*n.*	原理
mechanical energy 机械能			
stator	['steitə]	*n.*	定子，固定片
synchronous	['siŋkrənəs]	*adj.*	同步的
asynchronous	[ei'siŋkrənəs]	*adj.*	异步的
rotor	['rəutə]	*n.*	转子
PM machine			永磁电机
reluctance machine			磁阻电机
brushed machine			有刷电机
induction machine			感应电机
superconductor	[ˌsjuːpəkən'dʌktə]	*n.*	超导体
magnetic field			磁场
winding	['waindiŋ]	*n.*	线圈，绕组
ferromagnetic	['ferəumæg'netik]	*adj.*	铁磁的，铁磁体的
grab	[græb]	*vt.*	抓，抓住
performance	[pə'fɔːməns]	*n.*	性能，表现
electrostatic machine			静电机
torque	[tɔːk]	*n.*	转矩
repulsion	[ri'pʌlʃən]	*n.*	排斥
homopolar	[ˌhɔmə'pəulə]	*adj.*	单极的，同极的
spin	[spin]	*v.*	旋转

Notes

1. By the classic definition, electric machine is synonymous with electric motor or electric generator, all of which are electro-mechanical energy converters: converting electricity to mechanical power (i.e., electric motor) or mechanical power to electricity (i.e., electric generator).

句中 which 引导 electric motor or electric generator 的非限制性定语从句。

2. Transformers allow the voltage produced by an AC generator to be increased while decreasing the current level by a corresponding amount.

while 引导伴随状语，译为：而使电流值相应减小。

3. The use of electrical motors has increased for home appliances and industrial and commercial applications for driving machines and sophisticated equipment.

home appliances 与 industrial and commercial applications 作介词 for 的宾语。

for driving machines and sophisticated equipment: for 引导介词短语作状语，表示目的。

4. Brushed machines with rotor windings can be synchronous when rotor is supplied with DC or AC with same frequency as stator or asynchronous when stator and rotor are supplied with AC with different frequencies.

can be synchronous …or asynchronous … 作 brushed machines 的表语。

5. Electromagnetic-rotor machines are machines having some kind of electric current in rotor which creates a magnetic field which interacts with the stator windings.

having …：动名词结构作 machines 的定语。

which creates a magnetic field 作 electric current 的定语从句。

which interacts with the stator windings 作 magnetic field 的定语从句。

Exercises

Ⅰ. Try to match the following columns:

electrical machine	同步的
electric motor	变压器
electric generator	电动机
transformer	发电机
alternating-current (AC)	异步的
direct-current	转矩
stator	交流电流
synchronous	转子
asynchronous	定子，固定片
rotor	感应电机
induction machine	电机
magnetic field	直流电流
winding	线圈，绕组
torque	磁场

Ⅱ. Fill in the blank in each of the following sentences.

1. Electrical machine is an _____ device which can be used to achieve energy conversion or transfer.

2. Although _____ do not contain any moving parts they are also included in the family of electric machines.

3. _____ can used to increased the voltage produced by an AC generator while decreasing the current level by a corresponding amount.

4. Electric machines can be _____ meaning that the magnetic field set up by the stator coils rotates with the same speed as rotor.

5. Induction machines can be _____, if there are superconductors in the rotor windings.

6. PM machines and reluctance machines are always _____.

7. _____ machines can be supplied with PMs in stator to improve performance.

8. Electromagnetic-rotor machines have some kind of electric current in _____ which creates a magnetic field which interacts with the stator windings.

III. Translate the following paragraphs into Chinese.

We know that electricity and magnetism are related. When an electric current flows through a wire, a magnetic field is created.

Magnets are used in electric motors. In one kind of motor, a coil of wire is wound around an iron rod. The coil is placed between the poles of a permanent magnet, so that the coil can rotate.

When the motor is turned on, an electric current runs through the wire, the brush and the commutator and then into the electro-magnet coil.

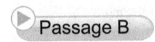

Passage B

Basic Construction of Electrical Machines

Questions for passage discussion

What's the function of an electric machine?
What is an electric machine composed of? What are the functions of each part?

Text

All electric machines comprise coupled electric and magnetic circuits that convert electrical energy to/or from mechanical energy. The term electric machine tends to be used to describe the machine used in an industrial drive, regardless of whether it is converting electrical energy to mechanical motion as a motor or if it is producing electrical energy from mechanical energy as a generator.

Rotating electrical machines accomplish electromechanical energy conversion. The energy-conversion process usually involves the presence of two important features in a given electromechanical device. These are the field winding, which produces the flux density, and the armature winding, in which the "working" emf is induced.

In rotating machines, voltages are generated in windings or groups of coils by rotating these windings mechanically through a magnetic field, by mechanically rotating a magnetic field past the winding, or by designing the magnetic circuit so that the reluctance varies with rotation of the rotor. By any of these methods, the flux linking a specific coil is changed cyclically, and a time-varying voltage is generated.

Generators convert mechanical energy into electrical energy, while motors convert an electrical energy input into a mechanical energy output. Generators and motors have basic construction characteristics which are common among many types of machines. The functions of various machines differ even though their construction is similar. Generators have rotary motion supplies by prime movers which provide mechanical energy input. Relative motion between the conductors and a magnetic field of generators produces an electrical energy output. Motors have electrical energy supplied to their windings and a magnetic field that develops an electromagnetic interaction to produce mechanical energy or torque.

The construction of most rotating electrical machines is somewhat similar. Most machines have a stationary part called the stator and a rotating set of conductors called the rotor. The stator consists of a yoke or frame which serves as a support and a metallic path for magnetic flux developed in a machine.

Fig. 7.1 illustrates the construction and components of a typical electric motor.

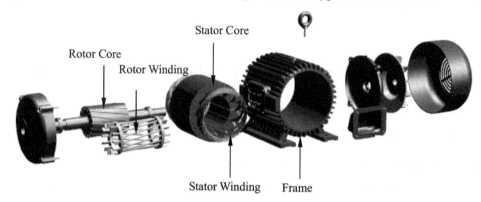

Fig. 7.1　The construction and components of a typical electric motor

1. Field poles and Windings

Rotating machines have field poles which are part of the stator assembly. Field poles are constructed of laminated sheets of steel and secured to machine frame. They are usually curved on the portion near the rotor to provide a low-reluctance path for magnetic flux. The field windings or field coils are placed around the poles. The field coils are electromagnets that develop an electromagnetic field interaction with the rotor to generate a voltage or to produce torque in a machine.

2. Rotor Construction

In the study of electrical machines, there is a need to understand the electromagnetic fields produced by the rotating section of a motor or a generator. This section is called armature or rotor. Some types of machines use solid metal rotors called squirrel-cage rotors.

3. Slip Rings, Split Rings, and Brushes

In order for electrical energy to be supplied to a rotating device such as the armature, some sort of sliding brush contact must be established. Sliding brush contacts are either slip rings or split rings. Slip rings are constructed of a cylinder of insulating material with two separate solid metal rings glued to it. Sliding brushes made of carbon and graphite ride on the metal rings and permit application or extraction of electrical energy from the rings during rotation. The split ring commutator is similar to the slip ring except a solid metal ring is cut into two or more separate sections. As a general rule, slip rings are used in AC motors and generators, while DC machines employ the split-ring commutating device. The gap or split in the commutator is kept at a minimum to reduce sparking of the brushes.

4. Other Machine Parts

There are several other parts used in the construction of rotating machines. Among these is rotor shaft, while rotates between a set of bearings. Bearings may be either the ball, roller, or sleeve type. Bearing seals, often made of felt material, are used to keep lubricant around the bearing and keep dirt out. A rotor core is usually constructed of laminated steel to provide a low-reluctance magnetic path between the field poles of a machine and to reduce eddy currents. Internal and external electrical connections provide a means of delivering or extracting electrical energy.

New Words and Expressions

comprise	[kəm'praiz]	v.	包含，包括，由……组成
generator	['dʒenəreitə]	n.	发电机
flux	[flʌks]	n.	磁通，(电，磁，光)通量
armature	['a:mətjuə]	n.	电枢
emf =electromotive force			电动势
induce	[in'dju:s]	v.	感应
magnetic field			磁场
reluctance	[ri'lʌktəns]	n.	磁阻
cyclically	['saiklikəli]	adv.	周期性地，循环地
interaction	[,intər'ækʃən]	n.	相互作用，相互影响，配合
stationary	['steiʃənəri]	adj.	不动的，静止的，固定的
metallic	[mi'tælik]	adj.	金属的；金属制的；含金属的
stator assembly			定子总成
laminated	['læmineitid]	adj.	分层的，迭片的
secure	[si'kjuə]	v.	拴牢；扣紧，固定
squirrel-cage rotor			鼠笼式转子
slip ring			滑动环；集电环
split ring			开口环，扣环
insulating	['insjuleitiŋ]	adj.	绝缘的
glue	[glu:]	v.	用胶水将物体粘合，粘牢，粘贴
carbon	['ka:bən]	n.	碳
graphite	['græfait]	n.	石墨，石墨电极
commutator	['kɔmjuteitə]	n.	整流子，换向器
shaft	[ʃa:ft]	n.	轴，转轴
bearing	['bɛəriŋ]	n.	轴承，支座

roller	['rəulə]	n.	滚轮(轴，筒)，滚动
sleeve	[sli:v]	n.	套筒，套管
felt material			毛毡；毛布；毡制品；油毛毡材料
lubricant	['lu:brikənt]	n.	润滑剂〔油〕 adj. 润滑的
deliver	[di'livə]	vt.	排放，供给，发出，提出
extract	[ik'strækt, 'ekstrækt]	vt.	抽取，提取

Notes

1. The term electric machine tends to be used to describe the machine used in an industrial drive, regardless of whether it is converting electrical energy to mechanical motion as a motor or if it is producing electrical energy from mechanical energy as a generator.

used in an industrial drive 作 the machine 的定语。

regardless 引导让步状语从句。

2. These are the field winding, which produces the flux density, and the armature winding, in which the "working" emf is induced.

which 引导 field winding 的非限制性定语从句。

in which 引导 armature winding 的非限制性定语从句。

3. In rotating machines, voltages are generated in windings or groups of coils by rotating these windings mechanically through a magnetic field, by mechanically rotating a magnetic field past the winding, or by designing the magnetic circuit so that the reluctance varies with rotation of the rotor.

句中 3 个 by 引导的是方式状语。本句可译为：在旋转电机中，通过使绕组在磁场中机械旋转，使磁场经过绕组，或者设计磁路使其磁阻随转子的旋转而改变，就会在绕组或一组线圈中产生电压。

4. Motors have electrical energy supplied to their windings and a magnetic field that develops an electromagnetic interaction to produce mechanical energy or torque.

supplied to their windings 作 electrical energy 的定语。

that develops an electromagnetic interaction to produce mechanical energy or torque 作 magnetic field 的定语。

5. The stator consists of a yoke or frame which serves as a support and a metallic path for magnetic flux developed in a machine.

which 引导 yoke or frame 的定语从句。

6. The field coils are electromagnets that develop an electromagnetic field interaction with the rotor to generate a voltage or to produce torque in a machine.

that 引导 electromagnet 的定语从句。

7. Sliding brushes made of carbon and graphite ride on the metal rings and permit application or extraction of electrical energy from the rings during rotation.

本句的主语是 sliding brushes，谓语是 ride 和 permit。

made of carbon and graphite 作 sliding brushes 的定语。

Exercises

Ⅰ. Try to match the following columns.

generator	磁场
winding	绕组，线圈
armature	扭矩，转矩
emf (electromotive force)	定子
magnetic field	电枢
torque	转子
stator	电刷
rotor	整流子，换向器
brush	发电机
commutator	电动势

Ⅱ. Place a "T" after the sentence which is true and an "F" after the sentence which is false.

1. The important features involved by the energy-conversion process in an electrical machine are the field winding and the armature winding.   (   )

2. In rotating machines, voltages are generated in windings or groups of coils when the flux linking them is changed.   (   )

3. Electrical motors convert an electrical energy input into a mechanical energy output. (   )

4. Electrical motors have rotary motion supplies by prime movers which provide mechanical energy input.   (   )

5. Most machines have a stationary part called the rotor and a rotating set of conductors called the stator.   (   )

6. Field poles, which are part of the stator assembly in rotating machines, are constructed of laminated sheets of steel and secured to machine frame.   (   )

7. In electrical machines, the rotating section of a motor or a generator, called armature or rotor, produces the electromagnetic fields.   (   )

8. The split-ring commutator which is employed in DC machines is similar to the slip ring used in AC motors and generators except a solid metal ring is cut into two or more separate sections.   (   )

Ⅲ. Translate the following paragraphs into Chinese.

The current enters and leaves the armature only when the brushes touch the commentators. But as the armature rotates, the commentators rotate past the brushes. Without current from the brushes, the armature loses its magnetic field. However, momentum keeps the armature rotating until it comes in contact with the brushes again. Once more, current flows through the armature, but now the commentators are in the opposite positions from what they were when the motor was started. Again poles that are the same are together. They repel each other, and the armature keeps turning. The poles change with once each half turn the armature makes, and so the motor keeps running.

Special Purpose Electric Motors

Questions for passage discussion

Where can special purpose electric motors be used? What are their characteristics?
Where can be stepper motors be used? And where can be servomotors be used?

Text

In a large number of special applications, some special electric motors are widely used, which are usually called special purpose motors. Some common examples are included here.

1. Integrated Starter Generator

The electronically controlled integrated starter generator (ISG) used in mild hybrid electric vehicles (HEVs) combines the automotive starter and alternator into a single machine. The conventional starter is a low speed, high current DC machine, while the alternator is a variable speed 3 phase AC machine.

2. Maglev Traction Motors

The principle of the linear induction motor is used to propel high speed Maglev (magnetic levitation) trains which float on a magnetic field created by electromagnets in the track bed under the train. A separate set of trackside guidance magnets is used to control the lateral position of the train relative to the track. Thus the maglev train uses electromagnetic forces for three different tasks, to suspend, to guide and to propel the train.

3. Geared motors

Standard industrial motors are often unsuitable as direct drives for low-speed applications. Moreover, the use of motors with low and medium ratings is uneconomical at low speeds. Geared motors are available for such applications. These units consist of a high-speed motor and a gear reducer assembled to form an integral unit. The hardened teeth of the gear wheel resist high stressing and ensure long life of the assembly.

Geared motors are widely used on single machines such as tower cranes, lifts/elevators, construction machinery, in agriculture, and so on, as well as in industrial plants.

4. Brake motors

Mechanical brakes are often used in conjunction with motors instead of, or as well as, electrical braking circuits. These units consist of a motor and a brake, assembled to form an integral unit. It is important to note that the brake may be rated to brake the motor and its load, or may be rated to provide a holding duty only. A holding only brake will be quickly destroyed if it is used to brake a load from speed. It is common practice, particularly on brushless servo motors, that the brake be rated for holding duty only.

Brake motors can be designed to be fail-safe. If the power is lost then the brake will automatically be applied.

5. Torque motors

Torque motors have been developed from the basic designs of three-phase squirrel-cage induction motors. They are not designed for a definite output, but for a maximum torque, which they are capable of delivering at standstill and/or at low speed(when supplied from a fixed-frequency supply).

6. Stepper Motors

A special type of DC motor, known as a stepper motor, is a permanent magnet or variable reluctance DC motor that has the following performance characteristics: it can rotate in both directions, move in precise angular increment, sustain a holding torque at zero speed, and be controlled with digital circuits. It moves in accurate angular increments, known as steps, in response to the application of digital pulses to an electric drive circuit. The number and rate of the pulses control the position and speed of the motor shaft. Generally, stepper motors are manufactured with steps per revolution of 12, 24, 72, 144, 180, and 200, resulting in shaft increments of $30°$, $15°$, $5°$, $2.5°$, $2°$, and $1.8°$ per step.

Stepper motors are either bipolar, requiring two power sources or a switchable polarity power source, or unipolar, requiring only one power source. They are powered by DC sources and require digital circuitry to produce coil energizing sequences for rotation of motor. Generally, stepper motors produce less than 735W and are therefore used only in low-power position control applications.

7. Servomotors

Servomotors are available as AC or DC motors. Early servomotors were generally DC motors because the only type of control for large currents was through SCRs for many years. As transistors became capable of controlling larger currents and switching the large currents at higher frequencies, the AC servomotor became used more often. Early servomotors were specifically designed for servo amplifiers. Today a class of motors is designed for applications that may use a servo amplifier or a variable-frequency controller, which means that a motor may be used in a servo system in one application, and used in a variable-frequency drive in another application. Some companies also call any closed-loop system that does not use a stepper motor a servo system, so it is possible for a simple AC induction motor that is connected to a velocity controller to be called a servomotor.

New Words and Expressions

integrated starter generator		集成启动发电机
hybrid	['haibrid]　*n.*	混合物，合成物

maglev traction motor			磁悬浮列车牵引电机
propel	[prə'pel]	vt.	推进；推动 驱动
magnetic	[mæg'netik]	adj.	磁性的，有磁性的
levitation	[ˌlevi'teiʃən]	n.	轻轻浮起，悬浮
electromagnet	[iˌlektrəu'mægnit]	n.	电磁体，电磁铁
trackside	['træksaid]	adj.	轨道旁的，轨道附近的
lateral	['lætərəl]	adj.	外侧的，侧面的，横向的
suspend	[sə'spend]	v.	悬浮，悬，挂，吊
assemble	[ə'sembl]	v.	装配，组合，组装
assembly	[ə'sembli]	n.	零件，部件，配件，总成
stress	[stres]	n.	压力，应力
conjunction	[kən'dʒʌŋkʃən]	n.	联合，结合
in conjunction with			共同，与……一起，与……共同
common practice			司空见惯的事，惯例，习惯做法，常见的惯例
fail-safe	['feilseif]	adj.	自动防故障装置的
squirrel-cage induction motor			鼠笼式感应电机
standstill	['stændstil]	n.	停止，停顿，停止状态
reluctance	[ri'lʌktəns]	n.	磁阻
revolution	[ˌrevə'ljuːʃən]	n.	旋转，旋转周
angular	['æŋɡjulə]	n.	角度，用角度测量的
sustain	[sə'stein]	vt.	维持，保持，承受，支持
in response to			对……的响应，对……的反应
bipolar	[bai'pəulə]	adj.	有两极的，双极的
unipolar	[ˌjuːni'pəulə]	adj.	单极的
coil energizing sequence			线圈激励序列
SCR abbr. = semiconductor control rectifier			晶闸管，可控硅
servo amplifier			伺服放大器
variable-frequency controller			变频控制器

Notes

1. The electronically controlled integrated starter generator used in light hybrid electric vehicles (HEVs) combines the automotive starter and alternator into a single machine.

句子的主语为 integrated starter generator，谓语为 combines，used in light hybrid electric vehicles (HEVs)作 integrated starter generator 的后置定语。

2. Geared motors are widely used on single machines such as tower cranes, lifts/elevators, construction machinery, in agriculture, and so on, as well as in industrial plants.

in agriculture 和 in industrial plants 作 tower cranes, lifts/elevators, construction machinery, and so on 的定语。

译为：齿轮电机在农业、工厂等领域中被广泛地用于塔吊、升降机、建筑机械这样的独立机械中。

3. Mechanical brakes are often used in conjunction with motors instead of, or as well as, electrical braking circuits.

in conjunction with: 与……一起，与……共同

instead of: 而不是……

4. They are not designed for a definite output, but for a maximum torque, which they are capable of delivering at standstill and/or at low speed (when supplied from a fixed-frequency supply).

not ... but ...: 不是……而是……

which 引导 a maximum torque 的非限制性定语从句。

5. Generally, stepper motors are manufactured with steps per revolution of 12, 24, 72, 144, 180, and 200, resulting in shaft increments of 30°, 15°, 5°, 2.5°, 2°, and 1.8° per step.

with steps per revolution of 12, 24, 72, 144, 180, and 200 译为 "每转一圈需要 12、24、72、144、180 和 200 步。"

resulting in ...: 介词短语作状语，进行补充说明。

6. Today a class of motors is designed for applications that may use a servo amplifier or a variable-frequency controller, which means that a motor may be used in a servo system in one application, and used in a variable-frequency drive in another application.

that 引导 applications 的定语从句。

which 引导非限制性定语从句。

7. Some companies also call any closed-loop system that does not use a stepper motor a servo system, so it is possible for a simple AC induction motor that is connected to a velocity controller to be called a servomotor.

call ... sth.: 将……称为……

that does not use a stepper motor 是 any closed-loop system 的定语从句。

that is connected to a velocity controller 是 AC induction motor 的定语从句。

Exercises

I. Try to match the following columns.

maglev traction motor	磁阻
magnetic	磁性的，有磁性的
electromagnet	有两极的，双极的
gear	角度，用角度测量的
assembly	伺服放大器
reluctance	晶闸管，可控硅
angular	电磁体，电磁铁
shaft	轴，杆状物
unipolar	磁悬浮列车牵引电机
bipolar	单极的

SCR	变频控制器
servo amplifier	零件，配件，总成
variable-frequency controller	齿轮，传动装置

Ⅱ. Place a "T" after the sentence which is true and an "F" after the sentence which is false.

1. The conventional starter in a vehicle is a high speed, high current DC machine.　(　　)

2. Standard industrial motors are often suitable as direct drives for low-speed applications.　(　　)

3. Torque motors are not designed for a definite output, but for a maximum torque.　(　　)

4. A stepper motor is characterized by rotating in both directions, moving in precise angular increment, sustaining a holding torque at zero speed, and being controlled with digital circuits.　(　　)

5. Stepper motors are bipolar, requiring two power sources or a switchable polarity power source.　(　　)

6. As transistors became capable of controlling larger currents and switching the large currents at higher frequencies, the DC servomotor became used more often.　(　　)

7. Today servomotors were specifically designed for servo amplifiers.　(　　)

8. A simple AC induction motor that is connected to a velocity controller can be called a servo system.　(　　)

Ⅲ. Fill in the blanks according to the words given in Chinese.

A _____ (步进电机) is an _____ (机电装置) which converts electrical _____ (脉冲) into discrete mechanical movements. The shaft or spindle of a stepper motor rotates in discrete step increments when electrical command pulses are applied to it in the proper sequence.The motors rotation has several direct relationships to these applied input pulses.The sequence of the applied pulses is directly related to the _____ (方向) of motor shafts rotation.The speed of the motor shafts rotation is directly related to the _____ (频率) of the input pulses and the length of rotation is directly related to the number of input pulses applied.

Translating Skills

句子成分的强调、倒装、分隔和省略

在专业英语中经常使用各种类型的强调、倒装、分隔和省略。对句子的某些成分或整个句子进行强调，主要是为了产生鲜明的概念，具有更充分的说服力；倒装的使用或是强调句子的表达意义，或是强调一种表达语气；将语法关系密切的两个句子成分用其他语法成分分隔是为了平衡句子结构，避免头重脚轻；而省略则主要是为了避免重复，突出关键词并使上下文紧密连接，下面分别予以介绍。

1. 强调

强调是指通过添加强调词，采用强调句型或改变成分的结构位置等手段来突出某一部分。

(1) 添加强调词。

【例 1】 Beta is approximately constant for an individual transistor, although it does vary with temperature and slightly with the collector current. (强调动词 do)

对某个晶体管而言，β 近似为常数，尽管它确实会随温度及集电极电流的变化而变化。

(2) 采用强调句型 It is (was)+被强调的成分+that(which, who, whom)，可强调主语、宾语和状语，不能强调定语和谓语。

【例 2】 We conclude that it is the ratio of the average signal power to the average noise power that is important, and not the magnitudes of S and N themselves.

我们断定，重要的是平均信号功率与平均噪声功率之比，而不是信号与噪声本身幅度的大小。(强调主语)

【例 3】 Ironically, it was Bell himself who invented one of the earliest light-wave communication devices in 1880.

具有讽刺意味的是，正是比尔本人于 1880 年发明了最早的光波通信设备之一。

(3) 改变句子成分的结构位置。

【例 4】 Very obvious is the ever-growing influence on mankind by the adoption of radio-broadcasting both sound and television. (倒装强调)

很明显，无线电及电视广播的应用对人类产生了深远的影响。

2. 倒装

由于表达的需要，将主谓语序颠倒，表语(系动词)、宾语或定语提前，称为倒装。

(1) 强调倒装成分或避免头重脚轻，符合句子结构本身要求。

【例 5】 Surrounding the cladding is a buffer material, used to help shield the core and cladding from damage during the manufacturing or installation process. (使主语紧靠其修饰语)

包在纤包外面的是缓冲材料，用于防护纤芯和纤包，使其在制造或安装过程中不受损害。

(2) 否定词位于句首、例如 by no means、hardly、in no way、little、neither、never、no、no more、nor、no sooner than、not、not only、not until、scarcely、seldom、trivial 等，强调句子中的某一成分。

【例 6】 Not since Alexander Graham Bell's invention of the telephone has communications experienced such revolutionary development. (强调状语)

人们并非从亚历山大·格雷厄姆·贝尔的电话发明中体验到通信创新性的发展。

(3) 副词位于句首，例如，hence、here、now、often、only、so、then、thus 等，需要倒装。

【例 7】 Hence (comes) the name magnet. 故有磁铁之称。

(4) 其他。

【例 8】 The better conductor a substance is, the less its resistance, and vise versa.

导体材料越好，电阻就越小，反之亦然。

【例9】 And of course, there is always some electricity needed, be it day or night. (there be 句型，be it day or night 是省略 if 的虚拟条件句)

当然，不论白天还是夜里，人们都需要用电。

【例10】 Digital circuits are less subject to distortion and interference than are analog circuits.

与模拟电路相比，数字电路不易失真和受到干扰。(比较状语从句)

3. 分隔

分隔修饰可使结构变化，以免头重脚轻，使得句子平稳，造句生动而不呆滞。

(1) 定语与其先行词分隔(两个以上后置定语时先短后长)。

【例11】 An insulator offers a very high resistance to the passage through it of an electric current.

绝缘体对通过它本身的电流会呈现很高的阻抗。

【例12】 Some new methods of making electronic circuits have been found by which many of the electronic devices have become quite small. (定语从句)

人们找到了几种制作电子电路的新方法，因此许多电子器件变得十分小巧。

(2) 动宾分隔。

【例13】 A fusion splice, by contrast, involves actually melting (fusing) together the ends of two pieces of fiber. (by contrast 将主语和谓语分离)

相比之下，熔接头实际上是将光纤的两头熔接(熔化)在一起。

(3) 系表分隔。

【例14】 The phenomena of electricity at rest are both historically and practically of great significance in the development of science.

在科学发展过程中，静电现象在历史上和实践中都具有很重要的意义。

(4) 其他分隔。

【例15】 In solids, very few, if any, of the molecules are free to move from one point to another.

在固体中能自由地从一处运动到另一处的分子，即使有也很少见。

4. 省略

省略能在不影响句子意义完整的前提下使句子变得简洁。

(1) 并列复合句的省略(如果后面的分句和前面的分句有相同的部分，常把这些相同的部分省略，以免重复)。

【例16】 For each type of modulation used(i. e., AM, FM, SSB, PM), a number of different circuits exist. Some will have gain, others(will have)a loss.

对所用的每种调制方式(如调幅、调频、单边带和脉冲调制)，都存在不同的电路，有些会产生增益，另一些则会造成损耗。

(2) 不完全从句。

【例17】 Although(it is)still in its infancy, fly-by-light flight control system may someday replace fly-by-wire system with cabling which is both lighter, smaller and safer. (让步状语从句)

尽管光线仍处于发展初期，但总有一天光控飞行控制系统会用重量轻、直径小又使用安全的光缆取代线控飞行系统。

【例18】　Electromagnetic waves travel as fast as light(waves travel fast). (比较状语从句)

电磁波和光波传播得一样快。(比较状语从句)

注：常见省略句型(在状语从句中省略主语和谓语)

As already/previously discussed/mentioned	前已讨论，前已述及
As described/explained/indicated above/before/in the figure	如前所述，前已解释，如图所示
If necessary/possible	如果必要的话，如果可能的话
If so	尚若，如此
When necessary/needed	必要时，需要时
Where feasible/possible	在实际可行的场合，在可能的情况下

(3) 关系代词、关系副词在从句中作宾语，可以省略。

【例19】　An electron is millions of times smaller than. the smallest thing(that)you have ever seen.

电子比人们见到过的最小物质还要小数百万倍。

Unit Eight   Automatic Control

In this Unit, our target is to train your reading comprehension. Try to grasp the main idea of these passages and learn the speciality vocabularies.

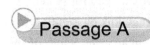

Passage A

Introduction to Automatic Control Systems

Questions for passage discussion

What is an automatic control system? What are the basic functions of automatic control?

What are the functional elements in an automatic control system? And what's the function of each element?

What is a feedback control system? How does it work?

Text

Automatic control has played a vital role in the advancement of engineering and science. In addition to its extreme importance in space-vehicle, missile-guidance, and aircraft-piloting systems, etc., automatic control has become an important and integral part of modern manufacturing and industrial processes. For example, automatic control is essential in such industrial operations as controlling pressure, temperature, humidity, viscosity, and flow in the process industries; tooling, handling, and assembling mechanical parts in the manufacturing industries, among many others.

An automatic control system is a preset closed-loop control system, which has two process variables associated with it: a controlled variable and a manipulated variable. A controlled variable is the process variable that is maintained at a specified value or within a specified range. For example, in the water tank level control system, the storage tank level is the controlled variable. A manipulated variable is the process variable that is acted on by the control system to maintain the controlled variable at the specified value or within the specified range. For the previous example, the flow rate of the water supplied to the tank is the manipulated variable.

1. Functions of automatic Control

In any automatic control system, the four basic functions that occur are: measurement, comparison, computation, correction. In the water tank level control system in the example above, the level transmitter measures the level within the tank. The level transmitter sends a signal representing the tank level to the level control device, where it is compared to a desired tank level. The level control device then computes how far to open the supply valve to correct any difference between actual and desired tank levels.

2. Elements of Automatic Control

The three functional elements needed to perform the functions of an automatic control system are: a measurement element, an error detection element and a final control element.

Relations between these elements and functions they perform in an automatic control system are shown in Fig. 8.1. The measuring element performs the measuring function by sending and evaluating the controlled variable. The error detection element first compares the value of the controlled variable to the desired value, and then signals an error if a deviation exists between the actual and desired values. The final control element responds to the error signal by correcting the manipulated variable of the system.

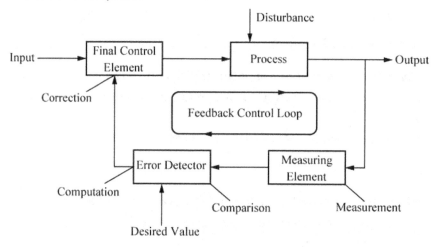

Fig. 8.1   Automatic Control System

3. Feedback Control

Feedback control is an operation which, in the presence of disturbances, tends to reduce the difference between the output of a system and the reference input (or an arbitrarily varied, desired state) and which does so on the basis of this difference.

Fig. 8.2 shows basic elements of a feedback control system as represented by a block diagram.

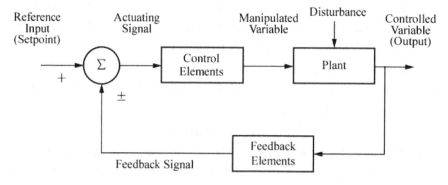

Fig. 8.2   Feedback Control System Block Diagram

The feedback elements are components needed to identify the functional relationship between the feedback signal and the controlled output. The reference input is an external signal applied to the summing point of the control system to cause the plant to produce a specified action. This signal represents the desired value of a controlled variable and is also called the "setpoint". The controlled output is the quantity or condition of the plant which is controlled.

This signal represents the controlled variable. The feedback signal is sent to the summing point and algebraically added to the reference input signal to obtain the actuating signal. The actuating signal represents the control action of the control loop and is equal to the algebraic sum of the reference input signal and feedback signal. This is also called the "error signal". The manipulated variable is the variable of the process acted upon to maintain the plant output (controlled variable) at the desired value. The disturbance is an undesirable input signal that upsets the value of the controlled output of the plant.

4. Feedback Control Systems

A feedback control system is one which tends to maintain a prescribed relationship between the output and the reference input by comparing these and using the difference as a means of control.

New Words and Expressions

in addition to			除……之外，另外，加之
space-vehicle			宇宙飞船
missile-guidance			导弹制导
aircraft-piloting			飞机驾驶
humidity	[hjuː'midəti]	n.	湿气，潮湿，湿度
viscosity	[vi'skɔsəti]	n.	黏质，黏性
flow	[fləu]	n.	流程，流量，流动 vi. 流动，涌流
tooling	['tuːliŋ]	v.	用刀具加工
manipulate	[mə'nipjuleit]	vt.	(熟练地)操作，使用(机器等)
preset	[priː'set]	vt.	事先调整，预先安置，预先调试
tank	[tæŋk]	n.	(盛液体、气体的大容器)桶、箱、池、槽
closed-loop control system			闭环控制系统
variable	['vɛəriəbl]	n.	变量
controlled variable			被控变量
manipulated variable			控制变量
act on/upon			对……起作用，按照……而行动，施加于，作用于
transmitter	[trænz'mitə]	n.	变送器，转送者，传导物
final control element			末级控制元件
evaluate	[i'væljueit]	vt.	评估，评价，计算
deviation	[ˌdiːvi'eiʃən]	n.	背离，偏离
feedback	['fiːdbæk]	n.	反馈，反应
tend to			易于，倾向于，有助于
disturbance	[di'stəːbəns]	n.	扰动
on the basis of			以……为基础，根据……，基于……
identify	[ai'dentifai]	vt.	确定，打出，识别
actuating signal			执行信号

error signal			误差信号
upset	[ʌpˈset, ˈʌpset]	vt.	打乱，扰乱，搅动
prescribed	[prisˈkraibd]	adj.	规定的，法定的

Notes

1. For example, automatic control is essential in such industrial operations as controlling …; tooling, handling, and assembling mechanical parts in the manufacturing industries, among many others.

controlling, tooling, handling 和 assembling 均属名词，作 such … as …结构中介词 as 的宾语。

2. An automatic control system is a preset closed-loop control system, which …

which 引导 an automatic control system 的非限制性定语从句。

3. A manipulated variable is the process variable that is acted on by the control system to maintain the controlled variable at the specified value or within the specified range.

句中 that 引导的是 process variable 的限制性定语从句。

该句可译为：控制量是控制系统对其施加作用，以使被控量保持在给定值或给定范围内的过程变量。

4. The level transmitter sends a signal representing the tank level to the level control device, where it is compared to a desired tank level.

where 引导的是 the level control device 的非限制性定语从句。

该句可译为：变送器将表示水池水位的信号送到水位控制装置，在那里将信号与期望水池水位相比较。

5. Relations between these elements and functions they perform in an automatic control system are shown in Fig. 8.1.

该句主语为 relations and functions，between …作 relations 的定语，they perform 作 functions 的定语。

6. Feedback control is an operation which, in the presence of disturbances, tends to reduce … and which does so on the basis of this difference.

which … and which …，两个 which 引导 an operation 的两个定语从句。

7. The manipulated variable is the variable of the process acted upon to maintain the plant output (controlled variable) at the desired value.

句中 acted upon to …之前省略了 that is，属于过去分词作 the variable of the process 的定语。

Exercises

I. **Try to match the following columns.**

closed-loop control system	被控变量
controlled variable	变送器
manipulated variable	末端控制元件

transmitter	自动控制
disturbance	执行信号
actuating signal	反馈信号
automatic control	测量元件
measurement element	误差检测元件
error detection element	控制变量
final control element	偏差
deviation	闭环控制系统
feedback signal	干扰，扰动

II. **Place a "T" after the sentence that is true and an "F" after the sentence that is false.**

1. In open-loop control systems, the output values can be fed back to the summing point of the control system.   (   )

2. An automatic control system has two process varibles; they are the controlled variable and the manipulated variable.   (   )

3. The disturbance is a desirable input signal for the control system.   (   )

4. The variable that is fed back to the summing point is the error signal in a feedback control system.   (   )

5. In the water tank level control system, the storage tank level is the manipulated variable, and the flow rate of the water supplied to the tank is the controlled variable.   (   )

6. In a feedback control system, the "setpoint" represents the desired value of a controlled variable.   (   )

7. A measurement element, an error detection element and a final control element are the functional elements in an automatic control system.   (   )

8. A feedback control system uses the difference between the output and the reference input to maintain the output at a specified value or within a specified range.   (   )

▶ **Passage B**

Applications of Automatic Control

Questions for passage discussion

Where can the automatic control be applied?

What is a servomechanism?

What is the process control? And what is DDC?

How does the automatic control be used in the electric power generation and distribution?

What is the numeric control?

Text

Although the scope of automatic control is virtually unlimited, we will limit this discussion to examples which are commonplace in modern industry.

1) Servomechanisms

A servomechanism is commonplace in automatic control. A servomechanism, or "servo" for short, is a close-loop control system in which the controlled variable is mechanical position or motion. It is designed so that the output will quickly and precisely respond to a change in the output command. Thus we may think of a servomechanism as a flowing device.

Another form of servomechanism in which the rate of change or velocity of the output is controlled is known as a rate or velocity servomechanism.

2) Process control

Process control is a term applied to the control of variables in a manufacturing process. Chemical plants, oil refineries, food processing plants, blast furnaces and steel mill are examples of production processes to which automatic control is applied. Process control is concerned with maintaining at a desired value such variables as temperature, pressure, flow rate, liquid level, viscosity, density, and composition.

Much current work in process control involves extending the use of the digital computer to provide direct digital control (DDC) of the process variables. In direct digital control the computer calculates the values of the manipulated variables directly from the values of the set points and the measurements of the process variables. The decisions of the computer are applied to digital actuators in the process. Since the computer duplicates the analog controller action, these conventional controllers are no longer needed.

3) Power generation

The electric power industry is primarily concerned with energy conversion and distribution. Large modern power plants which may be exceeded several hundred megawatts of generation require complex control systems to account for the interrelationship of the many variables and provide optimum power production. Control of power generation has many as 100 manipulated variables under computer control.

Automatic control has also been extensively applied to the distribution of electric power. Power systems are commonly made up of a number of generation plants. As load requirements fluctuate, the generation and transmission of power is controlled to achieve minimum cost of system operation. In addition, most large power systems are interconnected with each other, and the flow of power between systems is controlled.

4) Numeric control

There are many manufacturing operations such as boring, drilling, milling and welding which must be performed with high precision on a repetitive basis. Numerical control is a system that uses redetermined instructions called a program to control a sequence of such operations. The instructions to accomplish a desired operation are coded and stored on some medium such as punched paper tape, magnetic tape, or punched cards. These instructions are usually stored in the form of numbers, hence the name numeric control. The instructions identify what tool is to be used, in what way (e.g., cutting speed), and the path of the tool movement (position, direction, velocity, etc.).

5) Transportation

To provide mass transportation systems for modern urban areas, large, complex control systems are needed. Several automatic transportation systems now have high-speed trains running at several-minute intervals. Automatic control is necessary to maintain a constant flow of trains and to provide comfortable acceleration and braking at station stops.

Aircraft flight control is another important application in the transportation field. This has been proven to be one of the most complex control applications due to the wide range of system parameters and the interaction between controls. Aircraft control systems are frequently adaptive in nature, that is, the operation adapts itself to the surrounding conditions. For examples, since the behavior of an aircraft may differ radically at low and high altitudes the control system must be modified as a function of altitude.

Ship-steering and roll-stabilization controls are similar to flight control but generally require far higher powers and involve lower speed of response.

New Words and Expressions

virtually	['vəːtʃuəli]	adv.	实际上，差不多，几乎
commonplace	['kɔmənpleis]	adj.	平凡的，普通的，平常的
velocity	[vi'lɔsəti]	n.	速度
servomechanism	[ˌsəːvəu'mekənizəm]	n.	伺服机构(系统)，自动控制装置
mechanical	[mi'kænikəl]	adj.	机械的，机器的
chemical plant			化工厂
refinery	[ri'fainəri]	n.	提炼，精炼厂
blast furnace			鼓风炉
concerned with			与……有关，关于，涉及
desired value			期望值，预定值，期待值
viscosity	[vi'skɔsəti]	n.	黏性，黏度
liquid level			液位
direct digital control (DDC)			直接数字控制
actuator	['æktjueitə]	n.	执行机构，执行器，驱动器，调节器
duplicate	['djuːplikət, 'djuːplikeit]	v.	复制，重复，重做
megawatt	['megəwɔt]	n.	兆瓦
account for			说明……的原因，解释，对……负责
optimum	['ɔptiməm]	adj.	最适宜的；最有利的，最佳的
fluctuate	['flʌktjueit]	v.	波动，起伏
numeric control			数字控制

boring	['bɔːriŋ]	n.	镗削，镗孔
drill	[dril]	v.	钻孔，打眼 n. 钻头，钻床
mill	[mil]	v.	磨，研磨
weld	[weld]	v.	焊接
precision	[pri'siʒən]	n.	精确度，准确(性)
repetitive	[ri'petətiv]	adj.	重复的
redetermine	[,riːdi'təːmin]	v.	重新决定，重新确定
a sequence of			一系列，一连串
punched card			穿孔卡片
medium	['miːdiəm]	n.	介质，(存储)媒体
cutting speed			切削速度
mass	[mæs]	adj.	大规模的，大量的，许多的
in operation			运转中；实施中；操作中
brake	[breik]	n.	制动器 v. 刹(车)
adapt to			变得习惯于……，使适应于，能应付……
adaptive	[ə'dæptiv]	adj.	适合的，适应的，自动适配；自适应
radically	['rædikəli]	adv.	根本地；彻底地，完全地；激进地，极端地
behavior	[bi'heivjə]	n.	(机器等的)运转状态，性能，行为
altitude	['æltitjuːd]	n.	高度，海拔
steer	[stiə]	v.	驾驶，掌舵；操纵；控制；引导
stabilization	[,steibilai'zeiʃən]	n.	稳定性

Notes

1. Another form of servomechanism in which the rate of change or velocity of the output is controlled is known as a rate or velocity servomechanism.

in which the rate of change or velocity of the output is controlled 作主语 another form of servomechanism 的定语从句。

2. Process control is concerned with maintaining at a desired value such variables as temperature, pressure, flow rate, liquid level, viscosity, density, and composition.

such variables as temperature…，此处将 maintaining 的宾语后置了。

3. Large modern power plants which may be exceeded several hundred megawatts of generation require complex control systems to account for the interrelationship of the many variables and provide optimum power production.

which may be exceeded several hundred megawatts of generation 为主语 large modern power plants 的定语从句。

4. There are many manufacturing operations such as boring, drilling, milling and welding which must be performed with high precision on a repetitive basis.

which must be performed with high precision on a repetitive basis 作 many manufacturing operations 的定语从句。

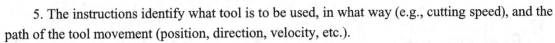

5. The instructions identify what tool is to be used, in what way (e.g., cutting speed), and the path of the tool movement (position, direction, velocity, etc.).

what tool…, in what way…, and the path of…作动词 identify 的宾语。

6. This has been proven to be one of the most complex control applications due to the wide range of system parameters and the interaction between controls.

due to…，介词短语作状语。

Exercises

Ⅰ. Try to match the following columns.

velocity	切削速度
servomechanism	伺服机构(系统)
chemical plant	期望值，预定值
desired value	速度
liquid level	化工厂
direct digital control (DDC)	执行机构，执行器
actuator	波动，起伏
fluctuate	直接数字控制
numeric control	一系列，一连串
a sequence of	数字控制
cutting speed	相互作用
interaction	(机器等的)运转状态，性能
behavior	稳定性
stabilization	液位

Ⅱ. Place a "T" after the sentence that is true and an "F" after the sentence that is false.

1. The scope of automatic control is virtually limited. (   )

2. A servomechanism is a open-loop control system in which the controlled variable is mechanical position or motion. (   )

3. Process control can be used to maintain some process variables at a desired value. (   )

4. In DDC, the computer calculates the values of the manipulated variables, then make decisions which are applied to digital actuators in the process. Since the computer duplicates the analog controller action, these conventional controllers are no longer needed. (   )

5. In DDC, although the computer performs the analog controller action, those conventional controllers are needed. (   )

6. The electric power industry is only concerned with energy conversion. (   )

7. To achieve minimum cost of system operation when load requirements fluctuate, the generation and transmission of power is controlled. (   )

8. Boring, drilling, milling and welding are all manufacturing operations. (   )

9. All automatic transportation systems now have high-speed trains running at several-hour intervals. (   )

10. Ship-steering controls generally require far higher powers and involve higher speed of response. (   )

▶ Reading

Introduction to PID Controllers

Questions for passage discussion

What does PID mean?
What is the basic principle of the PID control algorithm?
How does the PID controller be used in process control?

Text

The proportional–integral–derivative (PID) control algorithm has been successfully used for over 50 years. It is a robust easily understood algorithm that can provide excellent control performance despite the varied dynamic characteristics of process plant.

The PID control algorithm involves three separate parameters, and is accordingly sometimes called three-term control: the proportional, the integral and derivative values, denoted P, I, and D. The proportional value determines the reaction to the current error, the integral value determines the reaction based on the sum of recent errors, and the derivative value determines the reaction based on the rate at which the error has been changing. The weighted sum of these three actions is used to adjust the process via a control element such as the position of a control valve or the power supply of a heating element. Heuristically, these values can be interpreted in terms of time: P depends on the present error, I on the accumulation of past errors, and D is a prediction of future errors, based on current rate of change.

Fig.8.3 shows a block diagram of a PID controller.

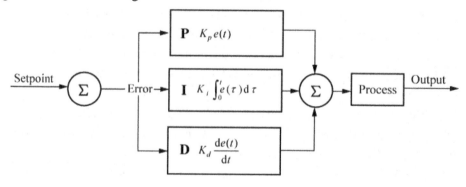

Fig.8.3　A block diagram of a PID controller

A PID controller is a generic control loop feedback mechanism (controller) widely used in industrial control systems—a PID is the most commonly used feedback controller. In the absence of knowledge of the underlying process, PID controllers are the best controllers.

Some applications may require using only one or two modes to provide the appropriate system control. Thus the PID controller will be called a PI, PD, P or I controller. PI controllers are particularly common, since derivative action is very sensitive to measurement noise, and the absence of an integral value may prevent the system from reaching its target value due to the control action.

A familiar example of a control loop is the action taken when adjusting hot and cold faucet valves to maintain the faucet water at the desired temperature. This typically involves the mixing of two process streams, the hot and cold water. The person touches the water to sense or measure its temperature. Based on this feedback he performs a control action to adjust the hot and cold water valves until the process temperature stabilizes at the desired value.

Sensing water temperature is analogous to taking a measurement of the process value or process variable (PV). The desired temperature is called the setpoint (SP). The input to the process (the water valve position) is called the manipulated variable (MV). The difference between the temperature measurement and the setpoint is the error (e), which quantifies whether the water is too hot or too cold and by how much.

After measuring the temperature (PV), and then calculating the error, the controller decides when to change the tap position (MV) and by how much. When the controller first turns the valve on, they may turn the hot valve only slightly if warm water is desired, or they may open the valve all the way if very hot water is desired. This is an example of a simple proportional control. In the event that hot water does not arrive quickly, the controller may try to speed-up the process by opening up the hot water valve more-and-more as time goes by. This is an example of an integral control. By using only the proportional and integral control methods, it is possible that in some systems the water temperature may oscillate between hot and cold.

In the interest of achieving a gradual convergence at the desired temperature (SP), the controller may wish to damp the anticipated future oscillations. So in order to compensate for this effect, the controller may elect to temper their adjustments. This can be thought of as a derivative control method.

PID controllers have survived many changes in technology, from mechanics and pneumatics to microprocessors via electronic tubes,transistors,integrated circuits.The microprocessor has had a dramatic influence on the PID controller.Practically all PID controllers made today are based on microprocessor. This has given opportunities to provide additional features like automatic tuning, gain scheduling, and continuous adaptation.

New Words and Expressions

mechanism	['mekənizəm]	*n.*	机构，机制，机械装置
proportional	[prəu'pɔːʃənəl]	*adj.*	比例的，成比例的
integral	['intigrəl]	*adj.*	作为组成部分的　*n.* 积分
derivative	[di'rivətiv]	*n.*	导数，微商

underlying	[ˌʌndə'laiiŋ]	adj.	基础的，根本的
denote	[di'nəut]	vt.	代表，表示
responsiveness	[ri'spɔnsivnis]	n.	响应性，反应性，应答性
heuristically	[hjuə'ristikəli]	adv.	启发式地，几乎都是
interpret	[in'tə:prit]	vt.	解释，说明
overshoot	[ˌəuvə'ʃu:t, 'əuvəʃu:t]	vt.	过冲，超调，超越，超过
oscillation	[ˌɔsi'leiʃən]	n.	振荡，波动
guarantee	[ˌgærən'ti:]	vt.	保证，确保，使必然发生
optimal	['ɔptiməl]	adj.	最佳的，最优的，最理想的
stability	[stə'biliti]	n.	稳定(性)
in the absence of			在缺乏……的情况下，缺乏……时；当……不在时，缺乏，不存在
sensitive	['sensitiv]	adj.	敏感的
familiar	[fə'miljə]	adj.	熟悉的，惯用的
faucet	['fɔ:sit]	n.	水龙头，旋塞
typically	['tipikəli]	adv.	代表性地，典型地；通常，一般
process stream			工艺流程，过程流
base on			以……为根据，以……为基础
analogous	[ə'næləgəs]	adj.	相似的，可比拟的，类似的
quantify	['kwɔntifai]	v.	确定数量，用数量表示
in the event that			如果，在……的情况下
in the interest of			为了……的利益，为了
convergence	[kən'və:dʒəns]		收敛，会聚，集中
damp	[dæmp]	v.	减弱，抑制，使沮丧，使败兴
temper	['tempə]	v.	使缓和，使温和，减轻
thought of as			将看做，视为
governor	['gʌvənə]	n.	调节器，控制器
essential	[i'senʃəl]	adj.	必不可少的，绝对必要的；本质的，实质的，基本的
sequential	[si'kwenʃəl]	adj.	顺序的，相继的，连续的
strategy	['strætidʒi]	n.	策略，战略，行动计划
sophisticated	[sə'fistikeitid]	adj.	精密的，尖端的，复杂巧妙的，先进的
hierarchically	[ˌhaiə'ra:kikəli]	adv.	分等级地，分级体系地
mechanics	[mi'kæniks]	n.	力学，机械学
pneumatics	[nju:'mætiks]	n.	气动，气动装置，气动元件

Notes

1. The weighted sum of these three actions is used to adjust the process via a control

element such as the position of a control valve or the power supply of a heating element.

该句的主语为 the weighted sum of these three actions，译为 "这 3 种作用的加权和"。

via: 通过，借助。其后为方式状语。

2. PI controllers are particularly common, since derivative action is very sensitive to measurement noise, and the absence of an integral value may prevent the system from reaching its target value due to the control action.

since 引导原因状语从句。

prevent … from …: 防止……，使……不能……。

3. A familiar example of a control loop is the action taken when adjusting hot and cold faucet valves to maintain the faucet water at the desired temperature.

taken when …: 过去分词结构作 action 的定语。

4. In the event that hot water does not arrive quickly, the controller may try to speed-up the process by opening up the hot water valve more-and-more as time goes by.

in the event that …: 如果，在……的情况下，后面引导状语从句。

Exercises

Ⅰ. Try to match the following columns.

PID control	导数，微商
parameter	控制变量
PI controller	比例-积分控制器
measurement noise	集成电路
be based on…	参数
process variable	以……为基础，根据
manipulated variable	收敛
oscillate	过程变量
convergence	减弱，抑制
damp	振荡，摆动
compensate	测量噪声
temper	弥补，补偿
derivative	缓和
integrated circuit	比例-积分-微分控制

Ⅱ. Translate the following paragraphs into Chinese.

Examples of "continuous process control" are temperature, pressure, flow, and level control. For example, controlling the heating of a tank. For simple control, you have two temperature limit sensors(one low and one high)and then switch the heater on when the low temperature limit sensor turns on and thrn tum the heater off when the temperature rises to the high temperature limit sensor. This is similar to most home air conditioning & heating thermostats.

In contrast, the PID controller would receive input as the actual temperature and control a valve that regulates the flow of gas to the heater. The PID controller automatically finds the correct (constant) flow of gas to the heater that keeps the temperature steady at the setpoint.

Instead of the temperature bouncing back and forth between two points, the temperature is held steady. If the setpoint is lowered, then the PID controller automatically reduces the amount of gas flowing to the heater. If the setpoint is raised, then the PID controller automatically increases the amount of gas flowing to the heater. Likewise the PID controller would automatically for hot, sunny days(when it is hotter outside the heater)and for cold, cloudy days.

Translating Skills

否定的表示

在专业英语中为了描述事物所具有的客观规律，常使用各种形式的否定句。有些否定句型不能完全采用直译法进行翻译，否则，就会造成误译，甚至与原意背道而驰。下面介绍科技英语中常见的否定类型及其译法。

1. 全部否定

常用 never、no、nobody、nothing、nowhere、neither、neither...nor 等词。

【例1】 In many emerging applications，it is clear that no single approach for classification is optimal and that multiple methods and approaches have to be used.

显然，在许多新兴的应用中，没有一种单一的分类方法是最佳的，而需要采用多种方法。

【例2】 Nothing in the world travels faster than the electromagnetic waves.

世界上不存在比电磁波传播得更快的东西。

【例3】 The new medium also offered a number of possibilities for special effects，not possible in conventional film production.

这种新方法也提供了传统的电影制作不可能实现的许多特殊效果。

【例4】 Energy can be changed from one form to another, but can neither be created nor destroyed.

能量可以从一种形式转换成另一种形式，但它既不能被创造出来，也不能消失。

2. 部分否定

all、every、both 及某些副词 always、often、entirely、altogether 等与否定词连用时表示部分否定。

【例5】 Both of the instruments are not precision ones.

这两台仪器并非都精密。

【例6】 The electrons within a conductor are not entirely free to move.

导体中的电子运动并不是完全自由的。

【例7】 Not every communication system makes use of all indicated operations.

并非每个通信系统都使用指定的所有操作。

3. 双重否定

not、no、never、neither、nobody、nothing 与其他有否定意义的词搭配使用，双层否定形式上是否定，实质上是肯定。

【例 8】　Without a series of rely towers, it is impossible for microwaves to send messages over long distances to remote places.

要是没有一系列的转播塔，微波就不能越过漫长的距离，将消息传递到远方。

【例 9】　In the absence of radar, the pilot in an airplane could not fly for a long distance at night.

没有雷达，飞行员在夜间不能进行长途飞行。

4. 内容否定

英语中有些词本身不是否定词，但也有否定的意义，如 few、little、seldom、too…to、but for、instead of、rather than、hardly、scarcely、barely、fail to、free from、keep …from、prevent from、suffer from 等。

【例 10】　There is little doubt that human beings and computers are getting more friendly.

计算机正日益便于人们使用，这是毫无疑问的。

【例 11】　There are many substances through which currents will scarcely flow at all.

【例 12】　As rubber prevents electricity from passing through it, it is used as insulating material.

橡胶不导电，所以用做绝缘材料。

【例 13】　Small distant objects cannot easily be seen with the eye because the image on the retina is too small for details to be apparent.

肉眼不易看到小而远的物体，因为在视网膜上所成的像太小，因而细节不那么清楚。

【例 14】　In 1990，the FCC announced that HDTV would be simultaneously broadcast rather than augmented.

1990 年，美国通信委员会宣布将会同时播放高清晰度电视，而不是在原有的基础上扩增。

5. 形式否定

有的句子在使用上表面是否定的，而在意义上却并不表示否定，可译为肯定句。

【例 15】　Source programs cannot be directly processed by the computer until it has been compiled which means interpreted into machine code.

源程序只有经过编译(即翻译为机器代码)后才能由计算机来直接处理。

【例 16】　Its importance cannot be stressed too much. (决不会……太……)

它的重要性怎样强调也不过分。

6. 其他常见否定短语的翻译

at no time　从来没有

by no means/under no circumstances/in no account　决不

come to nothing　毫无结果

have nothing in common　与……毫无共同之处

make no difference　没有关系，没有印象

more often than not 多半，通常

not a bit 一点也不

not a quarter 远不是，完全不是

not amount too much 没有什么了不起

not to speak of 更不用说，当然

nothing but, nothing else but(than), nothing more/less than 只不过是，不外是

spare no pains 不遗余力

to say nothing of 更不用说……

these is no(1ittle)doubt 毫无疑问

in no way 决不，无论如何不……

no longer 不再，不能再

no more…than (not…any more than) =not…just as…not 与……同样不是……

Part III
Communications

Unit Nine   Communication Systems

↘ 【Learning Target】

In this Unit, our target is to train your reading comprehension. Try to grasp the main idea of these passages and learn the speciality vocabularies.

Communication Systems

Questions for passage discussion

What is a communication system?
What are the components of a communication system?

Text

Today, communication enters our daily lives in so many different ways that it is very easy to overlook the multitude of its facets. The telephones at our hands, the radios and televisions in our living rooms, the computer terminals with access to the Internet in our offices and homes, and our newspapers are all capable of providing rapid communications from every corner of the globe.

In the most fundamental sense, communication involves implicitly the transmission of information from one point to another through a succession of processes, as described here.

(1) The generation of a message signal: voice, music, picture or computer data.

(2) The description of that message signal with a certain measure of precision, by a set of symbols: electrical, aural, or visual.

(3) The encoding of these symbols in a form that is suitable for transmission over a physical medium of interest.

(4) The transmission of the encoded symbols to the desired destination.

(5) The decoding and reproduction of the original symbols.

(6) The re-creation of the original message signal, with a definable degradation in quality: the degradation is caused by imperfections in the system.

A generalized communication system has the following components (as shown in Fig. 9.1).

(1) Information source. This produces a message which may be written or spoken words, or some form of data.

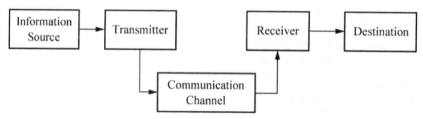

Fig. 9.1 Communication system

(2) Transmitter. The transmitter converts the message into a signal, the form of which is suitable for transmission over the communication channel.

(3) Communication channel. The communication channel is the medium used to transmit the signal from the transmitter to the receiver. The channel may be a radio link or a direct wire connection.

(4) Receiver. The receiver can be thought of as the inverse of the transmitter. It converts the received signal back into a loudspeaker, teleprinter or computer data bank.

An unfortunate characteristic of all communication channels is that noise is added to the signal. This unwanted noise may cause distortions of sound in a telephone, or errors in a telegraph message or data.

The purpose of a communication system is to transmit information bearing signals through a communication channel. Information bearing signals are also referred to as baseband signals. The term baseband is used to designate the band of frequencies representing the original signal as delivered by a source of information. The proper use of the communication channel requires a shift of the range of baseband frequencies into other frequency ranges suitable for transmission, and corresponding shift back to the original frequency range after reception. For example, a radio system must operate with frequencies of 30kHz and upward, whereas the baseband signal usually contains frequencies in the audio frequency range, and so some form of frequency band shifting must be used for the system to operate satisfactorily. A shift of the range of frequencies in a signal is accomplished by using modulation, which is defined as the process by which some characteristics of a carrier is a varied in accordance with a modulation wave. A common form of the carrier is a sinusoidal wave, in which case we speak of a continuous wave modulation process. The baseband signal is referred to as the modulated wave. Modulation is performed at the transmitting end of the communication system. At the receiving end of the system, we usually require the original baseband signal to be restored. This is accomplished by using a process known as demodulation, which is the reverse of the modulation process.

New Words and Expressions

multitude	['mʌltiˌtjuːd]	n.	大量，众多
facet	['fæsit]	n.	方面
implicitly	[im'plisitli]	adv.	含蓄地，暗中地
transmission	[trænz'miʃən]	n.	传输
succession	[sək'seʃən]	n.	连续
generation	[ˌdʒenə'reiʃən]	n.	产生
symbol	['simbəl]	n.	符号
aural	['ɔːrəl]	adj.	听觉的
encoding	[in'kəudiŋ]	n.	编码
medium	['miːdiəm]	n.	媒介，媒质
decoding	[ˌdiː'kəudiŋ]	n.	解码

degradation	[ˌdegrə'deiʃən]	*n.*	衰减，衰弱
transmitter	[trænz'mitə]	*n.*	发射机
receiver	[ri'si:və]	*n.*	接收机
loudspeaker	['laud'spi:kə]	*n.*	扬声器
teleprinter	['teliˌprintə]	*n.*	电传打字机
characteristic	[ˌkærəktə'ristik]	*n.*	特性
noise	[nɔiz]	*n.*	噪声
distortion	[dis'tɔ:ʃən]	*n.*	失真
telegraph	['teligra:f]	*n.*	电报
baseband	['beisbænd]	*n.*	基带
designate	['dezigneit]	*v.*	指明
shift	[ʃift]	*v.*	移动
audio	['ɔ:diəu]	*adj.*	音频的
carrier	['kæriə]	*n.*	载波
modulation	[ˌmɔdju'leiʃən]	*n.*	调制
sinusoidal wave			正弦波
demodulation	[di:ˌmɔdju'leiʃən]	*n.*	解调
imperfection	[ˌimpə'fekʃən]	*n.*	缺陷

Notes

1. In the most fundamental sense, communication involves implicitly the transmission of information from one point to another through a succession of processes, as described here.

从最基本的意义上来讲，通信本身包含了从一点到另一点的一系列过程的传输，如下所述。

in some sense 在某种意义上

implicitly 含蓄地，暗中地

2. The encoding of these symbols in a form that is suitable for transmission over a physical medium of interest.

将这些物理量符号以适合于物理媒介传输的形式进行编码。

3. The proper use of the communication channel requires a shift of the range of baseband frequencies into other frequency ranges suitable for transmission, and corresponding shift back to the original frequency range after reception.

为了恰当地使用通信信道传输，需要把基带频率成分迁移到其他的频率范围内，在传输完成后相应地将基带频率成分再迁移回来。

4. A shift of the range of frequencies in a signal is accomplished by using modulation, which is defined as the process by which some characteristic of a carrier is a varied in accordance with a modulation wave.

一种完成频带迁移的方法是采用调制技术，用调制波来改变载波的某个参数。

Exercises

Ⅰ. **Try to match the following columns.**

1. sinusoidal wave   衰减
2. baseband   发射机
3. modulation   正弦波
4. loudspeaker   调制
5. transmitter   物理媒介
6. degradation   基带
7. encoding   扬声器
8. physical medium   编码

Ⅱ. **Fill in the blank in each of the following sentences.**

1. The description of that message signal with a certain measure of precision, by a set of _____: electrical, aural, or visual.

2. _____ produces a message which may be written or spoken words, or some form of data.

3. The term _____ is used to designate the band of frequencies representing the original signal as delivered by a source of information.

4. A shift of the range of frequencies in a signal is accomplished by using _____.

5. The re-creation of the original message signal, with a definable degradation caused by _____ in the system.

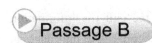

Digital Communication Technology

Questions for passage discussion

Illustrate some examples of the digital communication system.

How many elements does the digital communication system include? And what are the functions?

Text

In some applications, the information to be transmitted is inherently digital; e.g., in the form of English text, computer data, etc. In such cases, the information source that generates the data is called a discrete (digital) source.

In a digital communication system, the functional operations performed at the transmitter and receiver must be expanded to include message signal discretization at the transmitter and message signal synthesis or interpolation at the receiver. Additional functions include redundancy removal, and channel coding and decoding.

Fig. 9.2 illustrates the functional diagram and the basic elements of a digital communication system. The source output may be either an analog signal, such as audio or video signal, or a digital signal, such as the output of a computer which is discrete in time and has a finite number of output characters. In a digital communication system, the message produced by the source are usually converted into a sequence of binary digits. Ideally, we would like to represent the source output (message) by as few binary digits as possible. In other words, we seek an efficient representation of the source output that results in little or no redundancy. The process of efficiently converting the output of either an analog or a digital source into a sequence of binary digits is called source encoding or data compression.

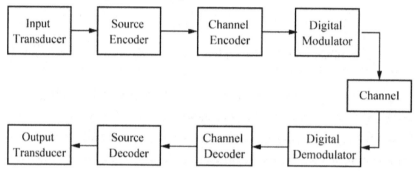

Fig. 9.2   Basic diagrams of a digital communication system

The sequence of binary digits from the source encoder, which we call the information sequence is passed to the channel encoder. The purpose of the channel encoder is to introduce, in a controlled manner, some redundancy in the binary information sequence which can be used at the receiver to overcome the effects of noise and interference encountered in the transmission of the signal through the channel. The binary sequence at the output of the channel encoder is passed to the digital modulator, which serves as the interface to the communications channel. Since nearly all of the communication channels encountered in practice are capable of transmitting electrical signals (waveforms), the primary purpose of the digital modulator is to map the binary information sequence into signal waveforms.

At the receiving end of a digital communication system, the digital demodulator processes the channel-corrupted transmitted waveform and reduces each waveform to a single number that represents an estimate of the transmitted data symbol. Using the redundancy in the transmitted data, the decoder attempts to fill in the position where erasures occurred. When there is no redundancy in the transmitted information, the demodulator must decide which of the waveforms was transmitted in any given time interval. On the other hand, when there is redundancy introduced by a discrete channel encoder at the transmitter, the output from the demodulator is fed to the decoder which attempts to reconstruct the original information sequence.

As a final step, when an analog output is desired, the source decoder accepts the output sequence from the channel decoder and, from knowledge of the source-encoding method used, attempts to reconstruct the original signal from the source. Due to channel-decoding errors and possible distortion, the signal of output of the source decoder is an approximation to the original source output. The difference or some function of the difference between the original and the reconstructed signal is a measure of the distortion introduced by the digital communication system.

New Words and Expressions

inherently	[in'hiərəntli]	*adv.*	固有地
discrete	[dis'kri:t]	*adj.*	离散的
discretization	[dis'kri:tai'zeiʃən]	*n.*	散化
synthesis	['sinθisis]	*n.*	综合，合成
interpolation	[in,tə:pəu'leiʃən]	*n.*	插补，内插
redundancy	[ri'dʌndənsi]	*n.*	冗余
illustrate	['iləstreit]	*n.*	阐明
binary	['bainəri]	*adj.*	二进位的，二元的
data compression			数据压缩
waveform	['weivfɔ:m]	*n.*	波形
modulator	['mɔdjuleitə]	*n.*	调制器
demodulator	[di:'mɔdjuleitə]	*n.*	解调器
interval	['intəvəl]	*n.*	间隔
approximation	[ə,prɔksi'meiʃən]	*n.*	近似值
reconstruct	[,ri:kən'strʌkt]	*v.*	重建，重构

Notes

1. In other words, we seek an efficient representation of the source output that results in little or no redundancy

换句话说，信源的输出或多或少含有冗余，我们要寻求一种有效的表示方法。

that 引导 the source output 的非限制性定语从句。

2. As a final step, when an analog output is desired, the source decoder accepts the output sequence from the channel decoder and, from knowledge of the source-encoding method used, attempts to reconstruct the original signal from the source.

最后一步，如果要求模拟输出，源解码器结合源编码方法，接收信道解码器的输出，来重构原始信号。

Exercises

Ⅰ. **Answer the following questions.**

1. In a digital communication system, what's the function of source encoder?

2. What's the purpose of channel encoder?

II. Translate the following sentences into Chinese.

1. In a digital communication system, the functional operations performed at the transmitter and receiver must be expanded to include message signal discretization at the transmitter and message signal synthesis or interpolation at the receiver.

2. The process of efficiently converting the output of either an analog or a digital source into a sequence of binary digits is called source encoding or data compression.

3. At the receiving end of a digital communication system, the digital demodulator processes the channel-corrupted transmitted waveform and reduces each waveform to a single number that represents an estimate of the transmitted data symbol.

4. Due to channel-decoding errors and possible distortion, the signal of output of the source decoder is an approximation to the original source output.

Analog Communications

Questions for passage discussion

What is the purpose of communication systems?
What are the benefits of modulation schemes?
What is the function of multiplexing technique?

Text

The purpose of any communication system is the transmission of information (speech, video, data) from a source to a receiver through a medium or channel. The channel for transmission can be wires as in wired communications (telephone lines, cable television) or free space (air) as in wireless communications (commercial radio and television, cell phones). The transmitter broadcasts the source information through free space using radiated power from an antenna. This power is picked up at the receiving end by an antenna and is processed by the receiver block. Since the information signals occupy similar frequency bands (the base band), one cannot transmit these signals over a single communication channel without resorting to the signal multiplexing either in the time domain or frequency domain.

Amplitude modulation (AM) and frequency modulation (FM) are two analog techniques for multiplexing signals in the frequency domain and are used extensively in commercial radio broadcast systems, AM and FM radios, respectively. The base band signals are translated to different locations (channels) at higher frequencies in the frequency spectrum using these modulation techniques. A secondary signal called the carrier is used for the frequency translation. Another benefit of the modulation schemes is that the low frequency base band signals are up converted to a higher frequency with the aid of the carrier and this makes their transmission through free space easier.

One of the most common modulation methods is to alter a carrier wave of the form

$$A \cdot \cos(\omega t + \theta)$$

where θ is an arbitrary constant, A is the wave peak amplitude, and ω is the carrier frequency. More or less obvious modulation approaches are to make A a function of the information signal $f(t)$ or to add a phase term to the cosine argument which depends on $f(t)$. These methods may be characterized as continuous wave (cw) modulation. The result of cw modulation is usually a bandpass signal because the carrier frequency is often much higher than the largest significant frequency component in $f(t)$.

Multiplexing is the process of combining several signals for simultaneous transmission on one channel. Frequency-division multiplexing (FDM) uses cw modulation to put each signal on a different carrier frequency, and a bank of filters separates the signals at the destination. Applications of multiplexing include data telemetry, FM stereophonic broadcasting, and long-distance telephone. As many as 1800 voice signals can be multiplexed on a coaxial cable less than one centimeter in diameter. Multiplexing thereby provides another way of increasing communication efficiency.

Exercises

Translate the following sentences into Chinese.

1. The purpose of any communication system is the transmission of information (speech, video, data) from a source to a receiver through a medium or channel.

2. Since the information signals occupy similar frequency bands (the base band), one cannot transmit these signals over a single communication channel without resorting to the signal multiplexing either in the time domain or frequency domain.

3. The base band signals are translated to different locations (channels) at higher frequencies in the frequency spectrum using these modulation techniques.

4. Another benefit of the modulation schemes is that the low frequency base band signals are up converted to a higher frequency with the aid of the carrier and this makes their transmission through free space easier.

5. Multiplexing is the process of combining several signals for simultaneous transmission on one channel.

Translating Skills

状 语 从 句

在专业英语中为表示事物之间复杂的逻辑关系，常使用状语从句。状语从句通常由从属连词引导，按其意义和作用可分为时间、地点、条件、原因、让步、目的、结果、方式、比较共 9 种。学习和掌握英语的状语从句的最佳方法是熟记引导各种状语的从属连词和词组，如表 1 所示。

表 1　常用引导状语从句的连词

类　型	常用连词
时间	when, while, as, as soon as, before, after, since, till, (not) …until, once, immediately, directly, the moment, every time, each time, the minute, the instant, no sooner…than, hardly…when
地点	where, wherever
条件	if, unless, as/so long as, on condition that, provided/supposing that, in the event that, in case that
原因	because, as, since, now (that) , seeing (that) , in that, considering (that)
让步	though, although, even if, even though, as, no matter(what, when…), whatever, whether, granted that
方式	as ,as if ,as though, the way
目的	so that, in order that, lest, for fear that, in case
结果	so that, so…that, such…that
比较	than, (not)as…as, not so …as, the …the …

1. 时间状语从句

【例1】 We take this ability for granted until we face the task of teaching a machine how to do the same.
我们一直对这种能力视为当然，直到我们遇到怎样让机器来做同样的事的问题。

【例2】 Once the analog signal is distorted, the distortion cannot be removed by amplification.
一旦模拟信号产生失真，该失真无法通过放大器消除。

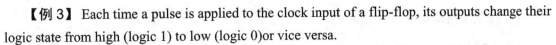

【例 3】 Each time a pulse is applied to the clock input of a flip-flop, its outputs change their logic state from high (logic 1) to low (logic 0)or vice versa.

　　每当对触发器的时钟输入端施加一个脉冲时，输出端的逻辑状态就会从高电平(逻辑 1)跳变到低电平(逻辑 0)，或者相反。

　　2.　地点状语从句

【例 4】 Communication systems are found wherever information is to be transmitted from one point to another.

　　哪里需要把信息从一地传到另一地，哪里就有通信系统。

【例 5】 The detected video signal is fed to the input of the audio string, where tuned circuits isolated the audio carrier, which is now at 4.5MHz.

　　检测出的视频信号再反馈入音频电路系列的输入端，在此处调谐电路将 4.5MHz 的音频载波分离出来。

　　3.　条件状语从句

【例 6】 For instance, it would fail if the patterns are distorted due to the imaging prozcess, viewpoint change, or large intra-class variations among the patterns.

　　例如，该方法(模板匹配法)不适用于由于成像过程、视点变化或同类模式间存在较大差异而产生失真的模式。

【例 7】 The output of a NAND gate, however, stays high unless all its inputs are high.

　　然而一个与非门的输出总是高电平，除非它的所有输入均为高电平。

　　4.　原因状语从句

【例 8】 Structural pattern recognition is intuitively appealing because, in addition to classification, this approach also provides a description of how the given pattern is constructed from the primitives.

　　结构模式识别不仅可用于分类，而且提供了从原词中构造已知模式的描述方法，所以直观地讲，很有吸引力。

【例 9】 This is hopeful news to proponents of artificial intelligence, since computers can surely be taught to recognize patterns.

　　这对人工智能的支持者来说是个好消息，因为肯定能教会计算机识别模式。

　　5.　让步状语从句

【例 10】 Although storage technology has improved significantly over the past decade, the same cannot be said for transmission capacity.

　　尽管过去 10 年间存储技术取得了令人瞩目的进展，但传输容量却并非如此。

【例 11】 While the subject of coding often carries with it an air of secrecy, a more important motive in many modern coding systems is the improved efficiency in conveying information.

　　尽管编码问题常常有保密的性质，但在很多现在的编码系统中，更主要的是提高信息传输的效率。

6. 结果状语从句

【例 12】 Often the function generator is used with an oscilloscope so that a visual display of the waveform can be seen.

函数发生器常常和示波器一起使用，以使波形清晰可见。

【例 13】 Insulators resist the flow of electrons so much that practically no current can flow through them.

绝缘体对电子流的阻力很大，因而实际上电流不能通过绝缘体。

7. 目的状语从句

【例 14】 The learning process involves updating network architecture and connection weights so that a network can efficiently perform a specific classification/clustering task.

学习的过程包含对网络结构和连接权重的更新，以使网络能够更好地完成某一特定的分类或聚类工作。

【例 15】 In order that an electric current can be produced in a conductor, an electric field must be built in it.

为了在导体中产生电流，必须在导体中建立电场。

8. 方式状语从句

【例 16】 The audio signals can be combined with the RF carrier wave in such a way that it varies the amplitude of the carrier.

音频信号通过改变载波的振幅叠加到射频波上。

【例 17】 It acts as if it had a resistance associated with it.

它工作起来就好像有一个电阻与它连在一起似的。

9. 比较状语从句

【例 18】 Unlike ordinary cassettes, digital recording is used with the result that the sound quality is as good as CDs—much better than ordinary audiotape.

与普通的盒式磁带不同，数字录音的音质同 CD 一样好，比普通录音磁带要好得多。

【例 19】 To understand how the radio works, it is more important to understand the function of each unit than to know what components are used.

为了了解收音机是怎样工作的，了解每个单元的功能比知道使用什么元件更为重要。

【例 20】 The higher the frequency of the analogue signal, the more often it must be sampled.

模拟信号的频率越高，取样就必须越频繁。

Unit Ten　Communication Applications

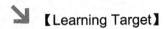【Learning Target】

In this Unit, our target is to train your reading comprehension. Try to grasp the main idea of these passages and learn the speciality vocabularies.

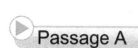
▶ Passage A

Radio Receiver

Questions for passage discussion

What is the usage of radio receiver?
What is the function of amplification stage?
What is the function of detection stage?

Text

A block diagram for a modern radio receiver is shown in Fig. 10.1. The input signals to this radio are amplitude-modulated radio waves. The basic electronic circuits include: antenna, tuner, mixer, local oscillator, IF amplifier, audio detector, AF amplifier, loudspeaker, and power supply.

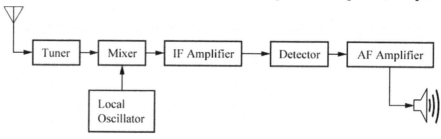

Fig. 10.1   Block diagram of a radio receiver

Any antenna system capable of radiating electrical energy is also able to abstract energy from a passing radio wave. Since every wave passing the receiving antenna induces its own voltage in the antenna conductor, it is necessary that the receiving equipment be capable of separating the desired signal from the unwanted signals that are also inducing voltages in the antenna. This separation is made on the basis of the difference in frequency between transmitting stations and is carried out by the use of resonant circuits, which can be made to discriminate very strongly in favor of a particular frequency. It has already been pointed that, by making antenna circuit resonant to a particular frequency, the energy abstracted from radio waves of that frequencies; this alone gives a certain amount of separation between signals. Still greater selective action can be obtained by the use of additional suitably adjusted resonant circuits located somewhere in the receiver in such a way as to reject all but the desired signal. The ability to discriminate between radio waves of different frequencies is called selectivity and the process of adjusting circuits to resonance with the frequency of a desired signal is spoken of as tuning.

Although intelligible radio signals have been received from the stations thousands of miles distant, using only the energy abstracted from the radio wave by the receiving antenna much more satisfactory reception can be obtained if the received energy is amplified. This amplification may be applied to the radio-frequency currents before detection, in which case it is called radio-frequency amplification or it may be applied to the rectified currents after detection, in which case it is called audio-frequency amplification. The use of amplification makes possible the satisfactory reception of signals from waves that would otherwise be too weak to give an audible response.

The process by which the signal being transmitted is reproduced from the radio-frequency currents present at the receiver is called detection, or sometimes demodulation. Where the intelligence is transmitted by varying the amplitude of the radiated wave, detection is accomplished by rectifying the radio frequency current. The rectified current thus produced varies in accordance with the signal originally modulated on the wave radiated at the transmitter and so reproduces the desired signal. Thus, when the modulated wave is rectified, the resulting current is seen to have an average value that varies in accordance with the amplitude of the original signal.

Receiver circuits are made up of a number of stages. A stage is a single transistor connected to components which provide operating voltages and currents and also signal voltages and currents. Each stage has its input circuit from which the signal comes in and its output from which the signal, usually amplified, goes out. When one stage follows another, the output circuit of the first feeds the signal to the circuit of the second. And so the signal is amplified, stage by stage, until it is strong enough to operate the loudspeaker.

New Words and Expressions

diagram	['daiəgræm]	n.	框图
amplitude	['æmplitjuːd]	n.	幅度，振幅
modulate	['mɔdjuleit]	v.	调制
antenna	[æn'tenə]	n.	天线
tuner	['tjuːnə]	n.	调谐器
mixer	['miksə]	n.	混频器
oscillator	['ɔsileitə]	n.	振荡器
IF amplifier			中频放大器
detector	[di'tektə]	n.	检波器
AF			音频
loudspeaker	['laud'spiːkə]	n.	扬声器
power supply			电源
conductor	[kən'dʌktə]	n.	导体
discriminate	[dis'krimineit]	v.	区别
resonant	['rezənənt]	adj.	共振的，共鸣的
reject	[ri'dʒekt]	v.	拒绝，抵制，丢弃

selectivity	[silek'tiviti]	*n.*	选择性
amplification	[ˌæmplifi'keiʃən]	*n.*	放大，扩大
intelligence	[in'telidʒəns]	*n.*	信息
rectify	['rektifai]	*v.*	调整，矫正
radio-frequency			射频

Notes

1. Since every wave passing the receiving antenna induces its own voltage in the antenna conductor, it is necessary that the receiving equipment be capable of separating the desired signal from the unwanted signals that are also inducing voltages in the antenna.

passing the receiving antenna 现在分词短语修饰 wave; it is necessary that 结构中的 that 引导主语从句的谓语动词要用虚拟语气，即 should + 动词原形，其中的 should 可省略，这里谓语动词为 be; the unwanted signals that …其中 that 引导定语从句来修饰 signals。

2. Still greater selective action can be obtained by the use of additional suitably adjusted resonant circuits located somewhere in the receiver in such a way as to reject all but the desired signal.

still greater selective 更好的选择性，resonant circuits 谐振电路。

3. This amplification may be applied to the radio-frequency currents before detection, in which case it is called radio-frequency amplification or it may be applied to the rectified currents after detection, in which case it is called audio-frequency amplification.

radio-frequency 射频，audio-frequency 音频，in which case 在这种情况下。这里由 or 连接两个并列的语句，具有相同的主语 this amplification。

Exercises

Ⅰ. **Try to match the following columns.**

1. local oscillator　　　　　　　　天线电路
2. IF amplifier　　　　　　　　　　谐振电路
3. block diagram　　　　　　　　　本地振荡器
4. power supply　　　　　　　　　与……一致，依照
5. antenna circuit　　　　　　　　滤波电路
6. radio-frequency　　　　　　　　中频放大器
7. resonant circuits　　　　　　　射频
8. in accordance with　　　　　　方框图

Ⅱ. **Fill in the blank in each of the following sentences.**

1. The input signals to this radio are ＿＿＿＿＿＿＿radio waves.

2. The process by which the signal being transmitted is reproduced from the ＿＿＿＿＿ currents present at the receiver is called detection, or sometimes ＿＿＿＿＿.

3. The process of adjusting circuits to ＿＿＿＿＿ with the frequency of a desired signal is spoken of as tuning.

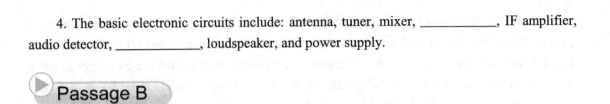

4. The basic electronic circuits include: antenna, tuner, mixer, _____, IF amplifier, audio detector, _____, loudspeaker, and power supply.

Passage B

Digital Television

Questions for passage discussion

What is digital television?
How many types can DTV be divided into? What are they?
What are the advantages of DTV?

Text

Over the past years, digital technology has rapidly changed the world we live in. It changes the way we communicate, the way we do business and the way we learn. Digital television (DTV) is normally used to encompass all digital television broadcasts and formats and the use of digital signaling to broadcast data. It is a new television service representing the most significant development in television technology since the advent of color television. DTV can provide movie theater quality pictures and sound, a wider screen, better color rendition, multiple video programming and other new services currently being developed. There are two types of digital television: standard definition (SDTV) and high definition (HDTV). Both offer images that are clearer, sharper and far more defined than analogue television. HDTV can provide the premium digital viewing experience. It can display four and half times more detail than analogue television. SDTV is a lesser quality picture than HDTV but significantly better than today's television.

1. SDTV

The ATSC approved a total of 12 formats that are collectively referred to as standard definition television. This was done in order to accommodate the wide variety of source material, and to enable easy conversion from a number of existing formats, and from the PC world, to digital broadcasting. The 12 SDTV formats are the result of all possible combinations of three resolutions with four frame rates. The resolutions are 704×480 with pixels compressed slightly yielding a 4:3 aspect ratio, 704×480 with pixels expanded slightly to yield a 16:9 aspect ratio and 640×480 with square pixels for an exact 4:3 aspect ratio. The frames are refreshed 60 times per second at a 2:1 interlace (yielding 30 complete frames per second), or refreshed progressively at 60, 30 or 24 frames per second.

2. HDTV

It is generally held that the term HDTV refers to any of the six broadcast formats that provide greater detail than the approximately 640×480 pixels in a good quality NTSC television picture. There are two groups of such formats: 1920×1080 pixels refreshed 60 times per second at a 2:1 interlace (yielding 30 complete frames per second), or refreshed progressively at either 30 or 24 frames per second; and 1280×720 pixels refreshed progressively at 60,30 or 24 frames per second. All of the HDTV formats use a 16:9 "widescreen" aspect ratio. The formats using 24 frames per second are designed to allow excellent reproduction of motion picture (movie studio) content.

The benefits of DTV are as follows.

1) Efficient utilization of bandwidth

At present, using analogue technology, a whole frequency channel is needed for carrying one television program. By using video compression technology, DTV enables several television programs to be digitally combined before they are carried on the same frequency channel. This will significantly improve spectrum efficiency, thus enabling the provision of wider programming choice within the same bandwidth.

2) Better picture and sound quality

Under the analogue environment, television signals are subject to interference by other signal sources such as power line, reflections from building, etc. The reception quality is therefore less than ideal. As digital signals are more robust than analogue ones, consumers would be able to get much better sound and picture quality through DTV. In addition, DTV enables the provision of high definition television which delivers cinema-quality pictures and CD-quality sound.

3) Innovative services

As DTV can transmit TV programs as well as data, viewers will be able to receive not only TV but also a variety of interactive, multi-media services through DTV. E-commerce on TV will be one of the many new commercial opportunities that the industry may explore.

New Words and Expressions

encompass	[in'kʌmpəs]	v.	包含，包括
represent	[ˌrepri'zent]	v.	代表，象征
rendition	[ren'diʃən]	n.	再现
color rendition			彩色再现
sharp	[ʃɑːp]	adj.	清晰的，清楚的
analogue	['ænəlɔg]	adj.	模拟
premium	['priːmiəm]	adj.	优质的，特级的
format	['fɔːmæt]	n.	格式
collectively	[kə'lektivli]	adv.	全体地，共同地
accommodate	[ə'kɔmədeit]	v.	适应
resolution	[ˌrezə'luːʃən]	n.	分辨率
aspect ratio			纵横比，屏幕高宽比
refresh	[ri'freʃ]	v.	刷新，更新

interlace	[ˌintəˈleis]	v.	交织，交错
spectrum	[ˈspektrəm]	n.	频谱
robust	[rəuˈbʌst]	n.	鲁棒性，稳健，坚固
innovative	[ˈinəuveitiv]	adj.	创新的

Notes

1. It changes the way we communicate, the way we do business and the way we learn.
它改变了人们的通信方式、商业贸易方式以及学习方式。

2. There are two types of digital television: standard definition (SDTV) and high definition (HDTV). 数字电视分为两类：标准清晰度电视和高清晰度电视。

3. ATSC(Advanced Television System Committee, 先进电视制式委员会)是美国数字电视地面传输标准，ATSC 广播频道的带宽为 6MHz，调制采用 8VSB，信源编码视频压缩采用 MPEG-2，音频压缩采用 AC-3 压缩标准。

Exercises

Ⅰ. **Answer the following questions.**

1. What is SDTV?

2. What is HDTV?

3. Which kind of fresh rate could we reproduce the motion picture?

4. What are the advantages of DTV?

Ⅱ. **Translate the following sentences into Chinese.**

1. DTV can provide movie theater quality pictures and sound, a wider screen, better color rendition, multiple video programming and other new services currently being developed.

2. HDTV can provide the premium digital viewing experience. It can display four and half times more detail than analogue television.

3. At present, using analogue technology, a whole frequency channel is needed for carrying one television program.

4. As DTV can transmit TV programs as well as data, viewers will be able to receive not only TV but also a variety of interactive, multi-media services through DTV.

5. This will significantly improve spectrum efficiency, thus enabling the provision of wider programming choice within the same bandwidth.

6. E-commerce on TV will be one of the many new commercial opportunities that the industry may explore.

> Reading

Mobile Communication

Questions for passage discussion

What is the cellular mobile telephone system?
What is the function of MSC?
What does the GSM stand for?

Text

Mobile telephone is one of the fastest growing and most demanded telecom applications ever. Today, it represents a large percentage of all new telephony subscriptions all around the world and its spectacular growth continues. In the long-term perspective, cellular radio using digital technology will become the universal way of communication for virtually everybody.

An automatic cellular mobile telephone system (CMTS) consists of three main components: mobile services switching center (MSC), radio base station (BS) and mobile station (MS) shown in Fig. 10.2.

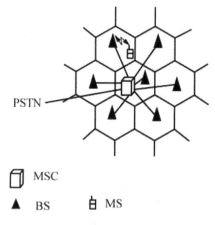

⬛ MSC

▲ BS   📱 MS

Fig. 10.2   Mobile Telephone

MSC constitutes an interface between the radio system and the public switching telephone network (PSTN). Calls to and from the mobile subscribers are switching by MSCs in CMTS. In order to obtain radio coverage of a given geographical area, a number of base stations, ranging from one (very exceptional case) up to a hundred or more, are normally required. Such a geographical area is called an MSC service area.

The base station contains channel units. Each channel unit is equipped with radio transmitter, radio receiver, and control unit. A control unit is used for such things as data communication with MSC and data signaling with mobile stations on the radio path. The majority of channel units are voice channel units. Such a voice channel unit is engaged in carrying one call at a time. Depending on how many simultaneous calls a base station is required to handle, the number of voice channel units in some base stations may be only a few, while in others up to a hundred or more. Each base station is connected to MSC by digital or analogue connections for speech and data communication.

The mobile station — a transportable, car mounted or pocket telephone, is the subscriber's equipment consisting of a radio transmitter and receiver, a logic unit for data signaling with the base station, and a telephone part with keys for dialing, microphone, etc.

When a call between a mobile subscriber and an ordinary subscriber has been set up, the speech is transmitted on the radio path between the mobile station and a voice channel unit of the base station situated close to the mobile station. Then follows, dedicated to this voice channel unit, voice line connection. Finally, the speech is switched in the MSC to the PSTN where the ordinary subscriber is to be found. Even for a call between any two mobile subscribers, the speech path will be set up in the MSC as well.

GSM as the second digital mobile standard expanded rapidly. GSM was referred to group special mobile, but it is now known on a world wide basis as global system for mobile communications. The European version of GSM operates in the 900MHz band, which is available in countries that are members of the European commission. While the 900MHz band in the United States was not available, so the 1900MHz band is used.

A third mobile access technology is CDMA. CDMA signals occur over an extended frequency band, referred to as broadband or spread spectrum communications. The key advantage associated with spreading a signal is that, from Shannon's Law, channel capacity can be maintained at a lower power level. Thus, CDMA supports low-power operations. Under CDMA, 1.23MHz of frequency spectrum accommodates one channel. According to some studies, CDMA can support 10 times the capacity of a TDMA system.

Exercises

Translate the following sentences into Chinese.

1. An automatic cellular mobile telephone system (CMTS) consists of three main components: mobile services switching center (MSC), radio base station (BS) and mobile station (MS) shown in Fig. 10.2.

2. Depending on how many simultaneous calls a base station is required to handle, the number of voice channel units in some base stations may be only a few, while in others up to a hundred or more.

3. Finally, the speech is switched in the MSC to the PSTN where the ordinary subscriber is to be found.

4. The European version of GSM operates in the 900MHz band, which is available in countries that are members of the European commission.

5. The key advantage associated with spreading a signal is that, from Shannon's Law, channel capacity can be maintained at a lower power level.

Translating Skills

名词性从句

名词性从句主要包括主语从句、宾语从句、表语从句和同位语句。一般由 that 引导，也可由 who、what、when、why、which、whom、whether、how 等引导。

1. 主语从句

【例 1】 What is more important is the great increase in circuit reliability.
更为重要的是，电路的可靠性显著提高了。
注：主语从句在很多情况下都可以放在句子后面，而用代词 it 作形式主语。
例如：
(1) It is+系动词+形容词(过去分词，名词)+that/what/how/whether
【例 2】 While technical applications are emerging for the hybrid architecture, it is unlikely that design teams would utilize this new capability unless it is also economically viable.
尽管从技术上讲可以(将 ASIC 与 FPGA 相结合)形成混合结构,但除非它在经济上合算,否则也不太可能获得设计人员的青睐。
(2) It appears, follows, seems, turns out, happens that…
【例 3】 It happens that the farad is inconveniently large as a unit and it is therefore customary to employ a submultiple as a working unit.
有时法拉作为一个单位太大而不便使用，因此，习惯上常采用法拉的约数作为实用单位。
【例 4】 In exampling radar problem it needs to be appreciated that a radar system will normally cover a very large volume of space.
在探讨雷达问题时，必须懂得雷达的覆盖空间很大。

2. 宾语从句

(1) 作动词的宾语。
【例 5】 This analysis leads us to conclude that technology and market trends have created a

need for the development of the hybrid ASIC / FPGA product.

分析表明，技术与市场发展趋势都需要研制混合 ASIC/FPGA 产品。

【例 6】 By carrying a small radio receiver called a radiopager, people can be contacted wherever they are.

携有小型无线电接收器(称为无线电 BP 机)的人，无论身在何处，都能联系上。

(2) 作介词的宾语。

【例 7】 Oscillators are different from amplifiers in that no input signal is required in the oscillators.

振荡器与放大器的区别在于，振荡器除了直流电源以外不需要输入信号。

【例 8】 MPEG-21 is looking to include an advanced tracking feature that would track and maintain a live record of where a user's content is situated and what restrictions , if any, are still in place on it.

MPEG-21 正想将先进的跟踪特性也纳入其中，该特性会实时记录用户内容的具体位置及可能存在的限制条件。

(3) 形式宾语 that 引导的宾语从句，若本身带有逻辑表语，常将其后置，而在前面使用形式宾语 it。

【例 9】 The effects we have just discussed make it apparent that here is a means of converting mechanical energy into electrical energy.

刚讨论的这些结果清楚地表明，这里有一种把机械能变为电能的方法。

3. 表语从句

【例 10】 One of the remarkable things about it is that the electromagnetic waves can move through great distances.

其显著特点之一就是电磁波能传播得很远。

【例 11】 This modulation is what the radio receiver utilizes to reproduce the radio program from the broadcasting station.

这种调制是收音机用以再现广播电台播送的无线电节目的一种手段。

【例 12】 What we are discussing is how a satellite can send information back to the earth.

我们正在讨论卫星怎样将信息发回地球。

【例 13】 The first decision that must be made is whether the data should be represented as a boundary or as a complete region.

首先要做的决定是应将数据表示成边界还是表示成一个完整的区域。

4. 同位语从句

(1) that 引导的同位语从句通常用来揭示主句中某个名词的内容。这样的名词有：fact、idea、doubt、conclusion、sense、condition 等。

【例 14】 This increases the risk that logic updates will be required, and therefore cost per chip will increase.

这增大了风险，即由于需要逻辑更新，每个芯片的成本增加。

【例 15】 The decoder performs the inverse operation to make the best decision based on the available signals, that a given message was indeed sent.

译码器完成相反的操作，即根据所得信号做出最佳判定，给定信息确实已发出。

【例 16】 This type of system is limited by the fact that there are not enough VHF frequencies available for large number of communications between individual users.

这种系统受到这样一个事实的限制，那就是，没有足够的可用 VHF 频率来满足个人用户之间的大量通信。

(2) whether、how、why 等引导的同位语从句。

【例 17】 The story how they invented this important device is quite interesting.

他们怎样发明这个重要装置的故事是十分有趣的。

Unit Eleven Data Communication

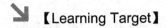 【Learning Target】

In this Unit, our target is to train your reading comprehension. Try to grasp the main idea of these passages and learn the speciality vocabularies.

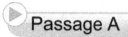

Data Communication

Questions for passage discussion

What is the digital information?
What is function of communications channel?

Text

Digital information is transmitted in the form of data signals over various types of telephone circuits. Data signals can travel on wire from one telephone pole to another, through underground cables, on the ocean floor in submarine facilities, and via communications satellites from continent to continent. Thus, in order to change the digital signal to a form, which is suitable for transmission, some type of data conversion equipment is required.

Data communications conveys the transmission of digital messages from devices external to the message source. "External" devices are generally thought of as being independently powered circuitry that exists beyond the chassis of a computer or other digital message source. As a rule, the maximum permissible transmission rate of a message is directly proportional to signal power and inversely proportional to channel noise. It is the aim of any communication system to provide the highest possible transmission rate at the lowest possible power and with the least possible noise.

In digital communication, the information is represented by individual data bits, which may be encapsulated into multibit message units. A byte, which consists of eight bits, is an example of a message unit that may be conveyed through a digital communications channel. A collection of bytes may itself be grouped into a frame or other higher-level message unit. Such multiple levels of encapsulation facilitate the handling of messages in a complex data communications network.

Any communications channel has a direction associated with it.

The message source is the transmitter, and the destination is the receiver. A channel whose direction of transmission is unchanging is referred to as a simplex channel. For example, a radio station is a simplex channel because it always transmits the signal to its listeners and never allows them to transmit back.

Most digital messages are vastly longer than just a few bits. Because it is neither practical nor economic to transfer all bits of a long message simultaneously, the message is broken into smaller parts and transmitted sequentially. Bit-serial transmission conveys a message one bit at a time through a channel. Each bit represents a part of the message. The individual bits are then reassembled at the destination to compose the message. In general, one channel will pass only one bit at a time (as shown in Fig. 11.1). Thus, bit-serial transmission is necessary in data communications if only a single channel is available. Bit-serial transmission is normally just called serial transmission and is the chosen communications method in many computer peripherals. Byte-serial transmission conveys eight bits at a time through eight parallel channels (as shown in Fig. 11.2). Although the raw transfer rate is eight times faster than in bit-serial transmission, eight channels are needed, and the cost may be as much as eight times higher to transmit the message. When distances are short, it may nonetheless be both feasible and economic to use parallel channels in return for high data rates. As an example, it is common practice to use a 16-bit-wide data bus to transfer data between a microprocessor and memory chip, this provides the equivalence of 16 parallel channels. On the other hand, when communicating with a timesharing system over a modem, only a single channel is available, and bit-serial transmission is required.

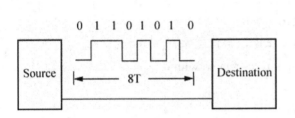

Fig. 11.1   Series transmission

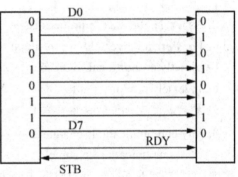

Fig. 11.2   Parallel transmission

New Words and Expressions

submarine	['sʌbməriːn]	adj.	海底的
chassis	['ʃæsi]	n.	机壳，机箱
proportional	[prəu'pɔːʃənəl]	adj.	成比例的，均衡的
encapsulate	[in'kæpsəleit]	v.	压缩
frame	[freim]	n.	帧
facilitate	[fə'siliteit]	v.	推动，促进
facility	[fə'siliti]	n.	工具
simplex	['simpleks]	adj.	单纯的，单一的
vastly	[vaːstli]	adv.	广大地，巨额地
simultaneously	[ˌsiməl'teiniəsli]	adv.	同时地
reassemble	[ˌriːə'sembl]	v.	重装，重组
compose	[kəm'pəuz]	v.	组成
serial	['siəriəl]	adj.	串行的
parallel	['pærəlel]	adj.	并行的

nonetheless	[ˌnʌnðə'les]	*adv.*	虽然如此，但是
feasible	['fiːzəbl]	*adj.*	切实可行的
microprocessor	[ˌmaikrəu'prəusesə]	*n.*	微处理器
equivalence	[i'kwivələns]	*n.*	同等，等价，等值
timesharing			分时(操作)

Notes

1. "External" devices are generally thought of as being independently powered circuitry that exists beyond the chassis of a computer or other digital message source.

be thought of …：被认为是……

independently powered circuitry 单独供电的电路

外围设备一般被认为是位于计算机机壳(机箱)外单独供电的电路或者是其他的数字信号源。

2. As a rule, the maximum permissible transmission rate of a message is directly proportional to signal power and inversely proportional to channel noise.

be directly proportional to   与……成正比

be inversely proportional to   与……成反比

通常，最大可允许的传输率与信号功率成正比，与信道噪声(功率)成反比。

3. Any communications channel has a direction associated with it.

it 指 communications channel。

任何通信信道都有一个与它有关的方向。

4. Although the raw transfer rate is eight times faster than in bit-serial transmission, eight channels are needed, and the cost may be as much as eight times higher to transmit the message.

as much as …：和……一样，高达……

尽管粗略看起来字节传送要比位传送快 8 倍，但它需要 8 个信道，因此费用也是位传送的 8 倍。

Exercises

Ⅰ. **Try to match the following columns.**

1. series transmission   分时系统
2. parallel transmission   数据总线
3. data communication   存储芯片
4. communication channel   串行传输
5. digital communication   并行传输
6. data bus   通信信道
7. memory chip   数据通信
8. timesharing system   数字通信

II. Fill in the blank in each of the following sentences.

1. In order to change the digital signal to a form, which is suitable for transmission, some type of _____ _____ equipment is required.

2. The maximum permissible transmission rate of a message is _____ proportional to signal power and _____ proportional to channel noise.

3. A byte, which consists of _____ bits, is an example of a message unit that may be conveyed through a digital communication channel.

4. _____ transmission conveys a message one bit at a time through a channel.

5. _____ transmission conveys eight bits at a time through eight parallel channels.

Passage B

Optical Fiber Communication Systems

Questions for passage discussion

What is advantage of optical fiber communication systems?
What is the different of optical fiber system and copper wire system?

Text

Today, the use of optical fiber systems to carry digitized video, voice and data is universal. In business and industry, optic fiber has become the standard for terrestrial transmission of telecommunication information. In military and defense, the need to deliver ever larger amounts of information at faster speeds is the impetus behind a wide range of retrofit and new fiber optic programs.

The technique applications of optical fiber communications have increased rapidly, since the first commercial installation of a fiber-optic system in 1977. Telephone companies began early on, replacing the old copper wire systems with optical fiber lines. Today's telephone companies use optical fiber throughout their system as the backbone architecture and as the long-distance connection between city phone systems. Cable television companies have also begun integrating fiber optics into their cable systems. The trunk lines that connect central offices have generally been replaced with optical fiber. In recent years it has become apparent that fiber optics are steadily replacing copper wire as an appropriate means of communication signal transmission. They span the long distances between local phone systems as well as providing the backbone for many network systems. Other system users include cable television services, university campuses, office buildings, industrial plants, and electric utility companies.

A fiber-optic system is similar to the copper wire system that fiber optics is replacing. The difference is that fiber optics uses light pulses to transmit information down fiber lines instead of using electronic pulses to transmit information down copper lines. At one end of the system is a transmitter. This is the place of origin for information coming on to fiber-optic lines. The transmitter accepts coded electronic pulse information coming from copper wire. It then processes and translates that information into equivalently coded light pulses. A light-emitting diode (LED) or an injection-laser diode (ILD) can be used for generating the light pulses. Using a lens, the light pulses are funneled into the fiber-optic medium where they transmit themselves down the line.

Fiber optics is the technology of using glass-based waveguides to transport information from one point to another in the form of light. Today's low-loss glass fiber optic cable offers almost unlimited bandwidth and unique advantages over all previously developed transmission media. The basic point-to-point fiber optic transmission system consists of three basic elements (see Fig. 11.3).

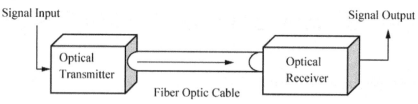

Fig. 11.3　Fiber optic transmission system

The optical transmitter: The transmitter converts an electrical analog or digital signal into a corresponding optical signal. The source of the optical signal can be either a light emitting diode, or a solid state laser diode. The most popular wavelengths of operation for optical transmitters are 850, 1300 or 1550 nanometer.

The fiber optic cable (as shown in Fig. 11.4): The cable consists of one or more glass fibers, which act as waveguides for the optical signal. Fiber optic cable is similar to electrical cable in its constructions, but provides special protection for the optical fiber within. For systems requiring transmission over distances of many kilometers, or where two or more fiber optic cables must be joined together, an optical splice is commonly used.

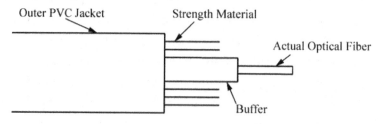

Fig. 11.4　A typical fiber optic cable

The optical receiver: The receiver converts the optical signal back into a replica of the original electrical signal. The detector of the optical signal is either a PIN-type photodiode or avalanche-type photodiode. "The basic purpose" of an optical receiver is to detect the received light incident on it and to convert it to an electrical signal containing the information impressed on the light at the transmitting end. The electronic information is then ready for input into electronic based communication devices, such as a computer, telephone or TV.

New Words and Expressions

optical	['ɔptikəl]	*adj.*	光学的
fiber	['faibə]	*n.*	纤维，光纤
impetus	['impitəs]	*n.*	动力，推动力
universal	[ˌjuːni'vəːsəl]	*adj.*	普遍的，通用的
terrestrial	[ti'restriəl]	*adj.*	陆地的
telecommunication			电信
retrofit	['retrəufit]	*v.*	改进，翻新
architecture	['ɑːkitektʃə]	*n.*	结构，体系结构
cable television			有线电视
integrate	['intigreit]	*v.*	集成
apparent	[ə'pærənt]	*adj.*	显然的，外观上的
light-emitting diode			发光二极管
injection-laser diode			注射式激光器二极管
funnel	['fʌnl]	*v.*	使集中
point-to-point			点对点
wavelength	['weivleŋθ]	*n.*	波长
nanometer			纳米
waveguide	['weivgaid]	*n.*	波导
splice	[splais]	*n.*	拼接，接头
replica	['replikə]	*n.*	复制品，副本
avalanche-type photodiode			雪崩光电二极管

Notes

1. In military and defense, the need to deliver ever larger amounts of information at faster speeds is the impetus behind a wide range of retrofit and new fiber optic programs.

在军事和防御领域，快速传递大量信息是大范围更新换代光纤计划的原动力。

2. Using a lens, the light pulses are funneled into the fiber-optic medium where they transmit themselves down the line.

采用透镜，将光脉冲集中到光纤介质，使光脉冲沿线路在光纤介质中传输。

3. The cable consists of one or more glass fibers, which act as waveguides for the optical signal.

光缆由一条或多条光纤构成，对光信号起到波导的作用。

4. Fiber optic cable is similar to electrical cable in its constructions, but provides special protection for the optical fiber within.

光缆在结构上类似于电缆，但在光缆内部提供有特殊的保护层。

Exercises

I. Answer the following questions.

1. Where is the optical fiber system used widely?

2. What are the components of the fiber optic system?

II. Translate the following sentences into Chinese.

1. Today's telephone companies use optical fiber throughout their system as the backbone architecture and as the long-distance connection between city phone systems.

2. The difference is that fiber-optics use light pulses to transmit information down fiber lines instead of using electronic pulses to transmit information down copper lines.

3. Today's low-loss glass fiber optic cable offers almost unlimited bandwidth and unique advantages over all previously developed transmission media.

4. The cable consists of one or more glass fibers, which act as waveguides for the optical signal. Fiber optic cable is similar to electrical cable in its constructions, but provides special protection for the optical fiber within.

Satellite Communication

Questions for passage discussion

What does the satellite system consist of?

Where is the satellite orbital position?

What is the most widely used frequency spectrum in a satellite system?

Text

Satellite access is a mature technology, and recent technological advancements have given it new life. Satellite communication has become a part of everyday life. An international telephone call is made as easily as a local call to a friend who lives down the block. The satellite television program brings the sights and sounds of the world into our homes each night.

A satellite system consists basically of a satellite in space which links many earth stations on the ground, as shown schematically in Fig. 11.5. The user generates the baseband signal which is routed to the earth station through the terrestrial network. The terrestrial network can be a telephone switch or a dedicated link to the earth station. At the earth station the baseband signal is processed and transmitted by a modulated radio frequency (RF) carrier to the satellite. The satellite can be thought of as a large repeater in space. It receives the modulated RF carries in its uplink (earth-to-space) frequency spectrum from all the earth station in the network, amplifies these carriers, and retransmits them back to earth station, processes the modulated RF carrier down to the baseband signal which is sent through the terrestrial network to the user.

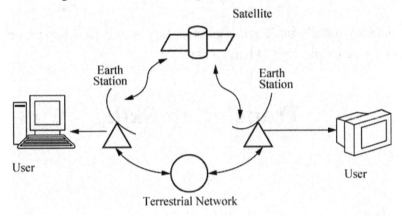

Fig. 11.5   Basic satellite system

Simply stated a satellite in a geostationary orbital position appears to be fixed over one potion of the earth. At an altitude of 22 300 miles above the equator, a satellite travels at the same speed at which the earth rotates, and its motion is synchronized with the earth's rotation. Even though the satellite is moving at an enormous rate of speed, it is stationary in the sky in relation to an observer on the earth. The primary value of a satellite in a geostationary orbit is its ability to communicate with ground stations in its coverage area 24 hours a day.

Most commercial communications satellites utilize a 500MHz bandwidth on the uplink and a 500MHz bandwidth on the downlink. The most widely used frequency spectrum is the 6/4GHz, with a uplink of 5.725 to 7.075 GHz and a downlink of 3.4 to 4.8 GHz. The 6/4GHz band for geostationary satellites is becoming overcrowded because it is also used by common carries for terrestrial microwave links. So 14/12GHz band and 30/20GHz band are used. The 14/12GHz band will be used extensively in the future and is not yet congested. But one problem exists—rain, which attenuates 14/12GHz signals much more than it does those at 6/4GHz. The frequency spectrum in the 30/20GHz band has also been set aside for commercial satellite communications. Because the equipment for the 30/20GHz band is still in the experimental stage and is expensive.

Exercises

Translate the following sentences into Chinese.

1. A satellite system consists basically of a satellite in space which links many earth stations on the ground, as shown schematically in Fig. 11.5.

电子信息专业英语

2. It receives the modulated RF carries in its uplink (earth-to-space) frequency spectrum from all the earth station in the network, amplifies these carriers, and retransmits them back to earth station, processes the modulated RF carrier down to the baseband signal which is sent through the terrestrial network to the user.

3. At an altitude of 22,300 miles above the equator, a satellite travels at the same speed at which the earth rotates, and its motion is synchronized with the earth's rotation.

4. The primary value of a satellite in a geostationary orbit is its ability to communicate with ground stations in its coverage area 24 hours a day.

Translating Skills

定 语 从 句

定语从句修饰句中的某一名词或代词，用在先行词之后。引导定语从句的关系词有 who、whom、whose、that、how、when、where、why 和 which。定语从句可以分为限制性定语从句和非限制性定语从句两种。

1. 限制性定语从句

限制性定语从句对所修饰的先行词起限制作用，在意义上与先行词密不可分，一般不可用逗号将其主句分隔。

【例1】 Once the signals are converted to light, they travel down the fiber until they reach a detector which changes the light signals back into electrical signals.

一旦信号变为光脉冲，就会沿光纤传输至检测器，该检测器将光信号变回为电信号。

【例2】 Sources are often described in terms of the frequency that they occupy.

信息源常用其所占用的频率来描述。

【例3】 The reader who is impatient to get on to digital systems should realize that many digital systems also require analog technology to function.

对于迫切想要了解数字系统的读者来说，应认识到许多数字系统也需要使用模拟技术。

【例4】 APON is a passive optical network where ATM is adopted to transmit broadband and narrowband cells via the SDH frame structure.

APON 是一种无源光纤网络，该网络采用 ATM 经 SDH 帧结构传输宽带和窄带信元。

注：当引导定语从句的先行词前有 all、any、no、like、much、very、first 等词，或先行词前为形容词最高级、序数词时，或先行词为 all、anything、nothing、everything 时，从句的引导词只能用 that。

【例5】This is one of the very few books at any level that presents a formula for finding any

154

voltage or current in the DC-excited RC(or RL)circuits that are so important in timers.

　　求解定时器中直流激励的 RC(或 RL)电路的电压或电流很重要，给出相应的公式的书很少，而本书即为其中之一。

　　【例6】　Noise signals are any electrical signals that interfere with the error-free reception of the message-bearing signal.

　　噪声信号可以是任何电信号，它会干扰载有信息信号的正确接收。

　　2．非限制性定语从句

　　非限制性定语从句仅对先行词进行解释或补充说明，有时含有原因、让步、时间、条件、结果等意思，从句要用逗号与主句分开，关系代词不能省略，通常用 which、who、when 等引导。

　　【例7】　Microwaves, which have a higher frequency than ordinary radio waves, are used routinely in sending thousands of telephone calls and television programs across long distances. (表示原因)

　　微波比一般无线电波频率更高，通常用它远距离传送大量长途电话和电视节目。

　　【例8】　For a radio wave in free space, the velocity is the same as that of light, which is approximately 3×10^8 meters per second.

　　自由空间中的无线电波，其传播速度与光速相同，约为 3×10^8 m/s。

　　3．介词+ which/whom/whose 从句

　　【例9】　First of all, let us introduce to you some of the circuits that are commonly found in radio-frequency systems and with which you may not be familiar. (familiar 与介词 with 为固定搭配)

　　首先介绍射频系统中一些常见的电路，也许你对这些电路并不熟悉。

　　【例10】　A magnet can cause an electric current in a wire near which it is moved. (which 指代 wire 从句中的主语，it 指代 magnet，根据全局含义确定介词 near)

　　磁铁在导线周围运动，导致导线中产生电流。

　　4．代词/名词+介词+which 从句

　　【例11】　Direct current is an electric current the charges of which move in one direction only.
　　直流电是电荷只向一个方向流动的电流。

　　【例12】　The analog world is full of relative numbers, tradeoffs, and approximations, all of which depend heavily on the basic semiconductor properties.

　　模拟领域充满了相对数、折中和近似值，所有这些在很大程度上取决于半导体的基本特性。

Unit Twelve   Computer Networks

In this Unit, our target is to train your reading comprehension. Try to grasp the main idea of these passages and learn the speciality vocabularies.

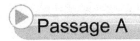

Computer Networks

Questions for passage discussion

What are the benefits of computer network?
What is the reference model of open system interconnection?

Text

Communication between distributed communities of computers is required for many reasons. At a national level, for example, computers located in different pats of the country use public communication services to exchange electronic messages (mail) and to transfer files of information from one computer to another. Similarly, at a local level within, say, a single building or establishment, distributed communities of computer-based workstations use local communication networks to access expensive shared resources—for example, printers, copiers, disks, tapes, etc. —that are also managed by computers. Clearly, as the range of computer communication networks proliferate, computer to computer communication will expand rapidly and ultimately dominate the field of distributed systems. A communication network is a series of points interconnected by communication lines, located at the points are computers, switching devices, and user terminals.

In general a computer network, as we know today, may be said to have gotten its start with the ARPANET development in the late 1960s and early 1970s. The initial ARPANET design had a definite structure of network architecture and introduced another key concept: protocol layering. Much of our present knowledge about network is a direct result of the ARPANET project.

The ISO, in the late 1970s, formulated a reference model to provide a common basis for the coordination of standards developments and to allow existing and evolving standards activities to be placed into perspective with one another. The ultimate aim was to allow an application process in any computer that supported the applicable standards to freely communicate with an application process in any other computer supporting the same standard, irrespective of its origin of manufacture. This model was termed the ISO reference model for open system interconnection (as shown in Fig. 12.1). It should be stressed, however, that this model is not concerned with specific applications of computer communication networks. Rather, it is concerned with the structuring of the communication software that is needed to provide a reliable, data transparent with the structuring of the communication software that is needed to provide a reliable, data transparent communication service (which is independent of any specific manufacturers equipment or conventions) to support a wide range of applications.

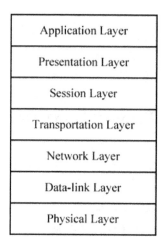

| Application Layer |
| Presentation Layer |
| Session Layer |
| Transportation Layer |
| Network Layer |
| Data-link Layer |
| Physical Layer |

Fig. 12.1　The model of OSI

A network is a series of points interconnected by communication lines, located at the points are computer, switching devices, and/or user terminals. A typical network includes the following components: host computers, nodes, terminal controllers, and terminals.

The two basic types of networks are local-area network (LAN) and wide-area network (WAN). A local-area network is two or more computers directly linked within a small area such as a room, building, or group of closely placed buildings. A wide-area network is two or more computers that are geographically dispersed and linked by communication facilities such as the telephone system or microwave relays.

The benefit of network is that it can transmit information rapidly and easily among widely separated people; people can share hardware and software resources on the network; a computer network can also provide high reliability by having alternative source of supply.

New Words and Expressions

community	[kə'mju:niti]	n.	公社，团体，共有，一致
exchange	[iks'tʃeindʒ]	v.	交换
access	['ækses]	n.	存取，接近，访问
proliferate	[prəu'lifəreit]	v.	增生，扩散
dominate	['dɔmineit]	v.	支配，占优势
terminal	['tə:minəl]	n.	终端
initial	[i'niʃəl]	adj.	最初的，初始的
definite	['definit]	adj.	明确的，一定的，有限的
protocol	['prəutəkɔl]	n.	协议
formulate	['fɔ:mjuleit]	v.	明确地表达，阐明
coordination	[kəu,ɔ:di'neiʃən]	n.	协调，协同，一致
evolve	[i'vɔlv]	v.	发展，进展，进化
perspective	[pə'spektiv]	n.	观点，看法，远景

reliable	[riˈlaiəbl]	*adj.*	可靠的，可信赖的
geographically	[dʒiəˈgræfikəli]	*adj.*	地理上的
facility	[fəˈsiliti]	*n.*	设备，工具
alternative	[ɔːlˈtəːnətiv]	*adj.*	可选择的，可替换的
distributed systems			分布式系统
application layer			应用层
presentation layer			表示层
session layer			会话层
transportation layer			传输层
network layer			网络层
data-link layer			数据链路层
physical layer			物理层
be termed			把……叫做

Notes

1. Similarly, at a local level within, say, a single building or establishment, distributed communities of computer-based workstations use local communication networks to access expensive shared resources—for example, printers, copiers, disks, tapes, etc. —that are also managed by computers.

say: 比方说，that 引导的定语从句修饰 resources。

2. The ultimate aim was to allow an application process in any computer that supported the applicable standards to freely communicate with an application process in any other computer supporting the same standard, irrespective of its origin of manufacture.

that 引导定语从句来修饰前面的 computer，supporting the same standard 动名词短语作定语修饰前面的 computer。

Exercises

Ⅰ. **Try to match the following columns.**

1. computer network	开放系统互连
2. open system interconnection	开关设备
3. local area network	参考模型
4. wide area network	欧姆定律
5. switching device	计算机网络
6. user terminals	分布式系统
7. distributed systems	广域网
8. reference model	局域网

Ⅱ. **Fill in the blank in each of the following sentences.**

1. As the range of computer communication networks proliferate, computer to computer communication will expand rapidly and ultimately dominate the field of _____.

2. The ISO, in the late 1970s, formulated a _____ _____ to provide a common basis for the coordination of standards developments.

3. This model was termed the ISO reference model for _____.

4. A network is a _____ of points interconnected by communication lines, located at the points are computer, switching devices, and/or user terminals.

5. A local area network is two or more computers directly linked within a small _____ such as a room, a building.

Passage B

Integrated Services Digital Network (ISDN)

Questions for passage discussion

What does ISDN stand for?
What are the services provided by ISDN?

Text

Imagine a network that would bring simultaneous voice and data applications to the home. A central computer could control telephone ringing, temperature, lighting on a room-by-room basis, and the operation of home appliances. This computer, in turn, could be controlled remotely by the user via the network. Other services might include call forwarding, call waiting, and special telephone ring signals, all tailored dynamically by the user depending upon the telephone number of the call party. Two-way television and easy access to data and video services could all be available. Banking, insurance and utility companies could design applications to take advantage of this network to provide better and more efficient services to the customer in the home.

While these scenarios may sound idealistic and futuristic, they are very real possibilities with the implementation of ISDN. ISDN, which stands for integrated services digital network, is a system of digital phone connections which has been available for over a decade. This system allows data to be transmitted simultaneously across the world using end-to-end digital connectivity (as shown in Fig.12.2). With ISDN, voice and data are carried by bearer channels (B channels) occupying a bandwidth of 64Kbps(bits per second). A data channel (D channel) handles signaling at 16Kbps or 64Kbps, depending on the service type.

There are two basic types of ISDN service: basic rate interface (BRI) and primary rate interface (PRI). BRI consists of two 64Kbps B channels and one 16Kbps D channels for a total of 144Kbps. This basic service is intended to meet the needs of most individual users.

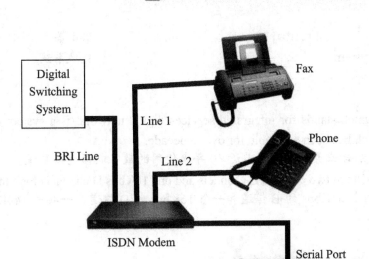

Fig. 12.2   ISDN system

PRI is intended for users with greater capacity requirements. Typically the channel structure is 23 B channels plus one 64Kbps D channel for a total of 1536Kbps. It is also possible to support multiple PRI lines with one 64Kbps D channel.

To access BRI service, it is necessary to subscribe to an ISDN phone line. Customers will also need special equipment to communicate with the phone company switch and with other ISDN devices. These devices include ISDN terminal adapters (sometimes called "ISDN Modem") and ISDN Routers.

The early phone network consisted of a pure analog system that connected telephone users directly by an interconnection of wires. This system was very inefficient, was very prone to breakdown and noise, and did not lend itself easily to long-distance connections. Beginning in the 1960s, the telephone system gradually began converting its internal connections to a packet-based, digital switching system. Today, nearly all voice switching in the U.S. is digital within the telephone network. Still, the final connection from the local central office to the customer equipment still largely is an analog line.

New Words and Expressions

ISDN			综合业务数字网
simultaneously	[ˌsiməlˈteiniəsli]	*adv.*	同时地
scenario	[siˈnɑːriəu]	*n.*	情节
idealistic	[aiˌdiəˈlistik]	*adj.*	空想的
futuristic	[ˌfjuːtʃəˈristik]	*adj.*	未来主义的
bearer	[ˈbɛərə]	*n.*	载体，承载
adapter	[əˈdæptə]	*n.*	适配器

| router | ['rautə] | | n. | 路由器 |
| switching system | | | | 交换系统 |

Notes

1. ISDN, which stands for integrated services digital network, is a system of digital phone connections which has been available for over a decade.

ISDN 代表综合业务数字网，是近 10 年来使用的数字电话连接系统。

2. BRI consists of two 64Kbps B channels and one 16Kbps D channels for a total of 144Kbps.

BRI 包括两个 64Kbps 的 B 信道和一个 16Kbps 的 D 信道，一共是 144Kbps。

Exercises

Ⅰ. **Answer the following questions.**

1. What is the PRI service?

2. How to access the BRI service?

Ⅱ. **Translate the following sentences into Chinese.**

1. This computer, in turn, could be controlled remotely by the user via the network.

2. ISDN, which stands for integrated services digital network, is a system of digital phone connections which has been available for over a decade.

3. BRI consists of two 64Kbps B channels and one 16Kbps D channels for a total of 144Kbps.

4. The early phone network consisted of a pure analog system that connected telephone users directly by an interconnection of wires.

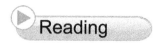

ATM

Questions for passage discussion

What does the term ATM stand for?

What are the benefits of using ATM system?

How many types of connection does ATM support?

Text

Asynchronous transfer mode (ATM) is an International Telecommunication Union

Telecommunication Standards Section (ITU-T) standard for cell relay wherein information for multiple service types, such as voice, video, or data, is conveyed in small, fixed-size cells. ATM networks are connection-oriented.

ATM is based on the efforts of the ITU-T broadband integrated services digital network (B-ISDN) standard. ATM is a cell-switching and multiplexing technology that combines the benefits of circuit switching (guaranteed capacity and constant transmission delay) with those of packet switching (flexibility and efficiency for intermittent traffic). It provides scalable bandwidth from a few megabits per second (Mbps) to many gigabits per second (Gbps). Because of its asynchronous nature, ATM is more efficient than synchronous technologies, such as time-division multiplexing (TDM).

With TDM, each user is assigned to a time slot, and no other user can send in that time slot. If a station has much data to send, it can send only when its time slot comes up, even if all other time slots are empty. However, if a station has nothing to transmit when its time slot comes up, the time slot is sent empty and is wasted. Because ATM is asynchronous, time slots are available on demand with information identifying the source of the transmission contained in the header of each ATM cell.

ATM's sophisticated bandwidth utilization capabilities enable providers to efficiently transport large, complex video packets without taxing a network (as shown in Fig.12.3).

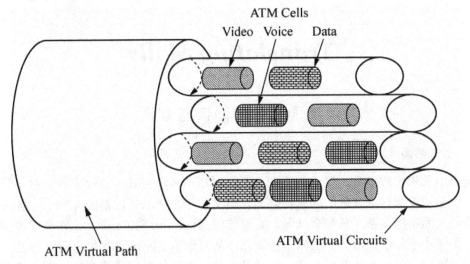

Fig.12.3   Asynchronous transfer system

ATM allocates bandwidth on demand by construction virtual channels and virtual paths between source and destination points on the ATM network boundaries. These channels are not dedicated physical connections, but are permanent virtual connections or switched virtual connections that are deconstructed when no longer needed.

ATM supports two types of connections: point-to-point and point-to-multipoint. Point-to-point connects two ATM end systems and can be unidirectional (one-way communication) or bi-directional (two-way communication). Multipoint connects a single-source end system (known as the root node) to multiple destination end systems (known as leaves). Such connections are unidirectional only. Root nodes can transmit to leaves, but leaves cannot transmit to the root or to each other on the same connection.

Exercises

Translate the following sentences into Chinese.

1. ATM networks are connection-oriented.

2. Because of its asynchronous nature, ATM is more efficient than synchronous technologies, such as time-division multiplexing (TDM).

3. If a station has much data to send, it can send only when its time slot comes up, even if all other time slots are empty.

4. ATM transfers information in short packets called "cells" with a fixed length of 48 bytes plus five header bytes.

5. ATM supports two types of connections: point-to-point and point-to-multipoint.

Translating Skills

英语长句的阅读与翻译

1. 长句的阅读

英语中长句比较多见，汉语句子则相反，以短小精炼见长，这代表着两种不同的思维方式，也是英汉两种语言之间的重要差异。英文句子之所以长，是因为句子中各种成分之间的修饰关系错综复杂，从句套从句，短语修饰短语，一环扣一环，让许多读者摸不着头脑，分不清主干，以致思维混乱抓不住重点，从而影响了阅读速度和阅读质量。

尽管英语长句中修饰关系复杂，但彼此之间的关系还是比较清晰的，有规律可循的：一个英语句子不管多么复杂冗长，只有一套主要的主谓结构，其他所有的成分都是围绕这个主要结构来修饰的。因此，遇到长句，最重要的就是确定句型结构，找出句子的主要结构，然后理顺各成分之间的关系。

1) 找出句子的主干结构

英语句子不管有多长，只有一套主干结构。找出句子的主干结构，就等于抓住了句子的主线，对句子要表达的主旨基本上就有了大致的理解。例如：

(1) Urging Americans to take responsibility for their health, Health and Human Services Secretary Tommy Thompson on Tuesday launched a $15 million program to try to encourage

communities to do more to prevent chronic diseases like heart disease, cancer and diabetes.

句的主干结构是 Health and Human Services Secretary Tommy Thompson launched a program，意思是"健康及人道服务部秘书汤米·汤普森发起了一项计划"，其他的现在分词短语和不定式短语都是作为状语修饰说明主干结构所表达的意思的。

参考译文：为了鼓励美国人承担起确保自己健康的责任，周二，健康及人道服务部秘书汤米·汤普森发起了一项耗资 1500 万美元的计划，大力鼓励社区在预防诸如心脏病、癌症及糖尿病上发挥更大作用。

(2) Ten days after the terrorist attack on the twin towers, structural engineers from the University at Buffalo and the Multidisciplinary Center for Earthquake Engineering Research headquartered at UB traveled to ground zero as part of a project funded by the National Science Foundation.

本句主干结构是 Structural engineers traveled to ground zero，意思是"结构工程师来到废墟现场"。句中还包括两个状语和数个定语。

参考译文：恐怖分子袭击世贸中心 10 天后，布法罗大学和总部设在 UB 的多学科中心地震研究所的建筑工程师来到了世贸中心的废墟现场，此行为国家科学基金会出资研究项目的一部分。

(3) While scientists are searching for the cause of the Columbia disaster, NASA is moving ahead with plans to develop a new craft that would replace shuttles on space station missions by 2012 and respond quickly to space station emergencies.

本句主干结构是 NASA is moving ahead with plans，意思是"国家航空航天局已经着手开发计划"。句中还有一个状语从句、一个定语从句及数个定语。

参考译文：当科学家们还在寻找哥伦比亚号灾难的原因时，国家航空航天局已经着手于新型飞行器的开发计划。这种飞行器将在 2012 年之前取代现有的穿梭机执行空间站任务，并且对紧急情况做出迅速反应。

2) 理顺修饰语之间的关系

一个句子只有一套主谓结构，却可以带有数个修饰语，如修饰名词的定语，修饰动词或全句的状语，包括时间状语、地点状语、比较状语、条件状语、程度状语，还有同位语等诸多修饰语。它们之间的关系纷繁交错，容易让读者乱了思路。因此，在阅读时，找出主干结构后，接着就需理顺它们之间的关系，注意不要把不同层次的修饰语张冠李戴，以免曲解句子意思。理顺关系的主要方法是对句子进行语法分析。例如：

(1) A survey of news stories in 1996 reveals that the anti-science tag has been attached to many other groups as well, from authorities who advocated the elimination of the last remaining stocks of smallpox virus to Republicans who advocated decreased funding for basic research.

本句的主干结构是 A survey reveals that …，that 后面跟着的从句作宾语；宾语从句的主谓结构是 the tag has been attached to groups，介词短语 from authorities … for basic research 用来补充说明 groups；介词短语中的两个 who 引导的从句分别修饰 authorities 和 Republicans。

参考译文：1996 年对新闻报道的调查披露反科学的标签也已贴在许多其他群体身上，从宣称消灭全部天花病毒的官员到鼓吹削减基础研究基金的共和党人。

(2) The main burden of assuring that the resources of the federal government are well

managed falls on relatively few of the five million men and women it employs.

本句主干结构是 The main burden falls on men and women，介词短语 of assuring …用来修饰主语 the main burden；介词短语中含有一个宾语从句 that the resources of the federal government are well managed；it employs 作为定语从句修饰 men and women。

参考译文：确保管理好联邦政府资源的重担落在了其雇用的 500 万雇员中的少数人身上。

(3) The American Institute of Biological Science, with more than 80 member societies and 250 000 members, has established an e-mail system enabling scientists and teachers in each state, and member societies, to keep each other informed about threats to the teaching of evolution.

本句主干结构是：The American Institute has established an e-mail system，介词短语 with more than 80 member societies and 250 000 members 作定语，修饰 the American Institute of Biological Science；现在分词短语 the American Institute of Biological Science 作定语，修饰 an e-mail system；不定式短语 to keep each other … the teaching of evolution 作目的状语。

参考译文：美国生物科学院拥有 80 多个成员社团和 250000 个成员，它建立了一个电子邮件系统使各州的科学家、教师和成员社团能互相联合，告知进化论教育面临的威胁。

3) 正确判断句子类型

除了以上说到的两种阅读长句的方法，正确判断句子类型也很重要，特别是句子属于特殊句型时，能够在最早时间确定句子类型，可以使读者理解思路保持清晰，容易抓住主干，对于提高阅读速度和阅读质量也很有帮助。例如：

(1) Certain it is that all essential processes of plant growth and development occur in water.
此句是倒装句，为了强调表语 certain，将其前置。正常语序为 It is certain …。
参考译文：植物发育生长的全部过程当然是在水中发生的。

(2) It is the neurohormone that controls our sleep and tells our body when to sleep and when to wake.
此句是强调句，强调句主要用于强调句中的某一成分，本句被强调的成分是主语 neurohormone。
参考译文：正是这种神经激素控制着我们的睡眠，告诉我们的身体什么时候睡觉什么时候醒。

(3) Heat can never be converted into a certain energy without something lost.
这是一个双重否定句，两个否定词为 never 和 without，双重否定实际表达了肯定的意思。
参考译文：热能每次转换成其他某种能量时，总是有些损耗。

2. 长句的翻译

英语中的长句比较多，通常是一句话中使用多个关联词，由此引出一个接一个的修饰成分，如定语从句、状语从句、同位语从句等，使句子变得错综复杂；而汉语比较喜欢使用短小简洁的句子，这两种语言习惯的差异给英语翻译带来了一定的困难。所以，翻译长句时应该做到：第一，要深入分析理解，保证自己对原文理解的正确性；第二，要组织好文字表达结构，力争正确译出原文的意思而不拘泥于原文的形式。

长句的翻译法主要有 3 种：分译法、逆序译法和顺序译法。

1）分译法

英语长句的翻译首选分译法。分译法就是把一个长句分译为几个汉语句子，把原文中与主句关系不十分密切的从句或修饰成分化为短句，分开译出。为使语气连贯，可以适当增加词语。例如：

(1) As has been said, manufacturing processes can be generally classified as unit production processes with small quantities being made each time and mass production processes with large numbers of identical items or products being produced.

前面说过，生产过程可以笼统地分为单件生产和批量生产。单件生产就是每次生产少量的工件；而批量生产就是生产大量规格相同的工件或产品。

(2) The loads a structure is subjected to are divided into dead loads，which include the weights of all the parts of the structure, and live loads, which are due to the weights of people, movable equipment, etc.

一个结构物受到的荷载可以分为净载和活载两种。净载包括该结构物各部分的重量。活载是由于人、可移动的设备等的重量所造成的。

2）顺序译法

顺序译法是指基本上按照英语原文的叙述层次和顺序把内容依次译成汉语，译文的顺序和原文顺序完全一样。例如：

(1) Clearly, if a solution is proposed as both logically correct and factually true, it must be verifiable by all qualified scientists, which means, at least, by all scientists working in the field.

很显然，假如一个解决办法在逻辑上正确又合乎事实，它还必须由所有合格的科学家鉴定，也就是说，至少要由在该部门的所有科学家鉴定。

(2) Nowadays, a most wonderful way of carrying messages to link the world together is to send an electronic signal or message from a station on the earth to a satellite traveling in space and then to make it come back to another earth station, which may be very far away from the sending station.

今天，传递信息把世界联系起来的一种十分巧妙的办法是：从地面站向在空间运转的卫星发射电子信号或信息，然后再让信号或信息返回到另一个地面站，这两个地面站之间可能距离十分遥远。

(3) In this way the distinction between heavy current electrical engineering and light current electrical engineering can be said to have disappeared, but we still have the conceptual difference in that in power engineering the primary concern is to transport energy between distant points in space; while with communication systems the primary objective is to convey, extract and process information, in which process considerable amounts of power may be consumed.

在这一方面，强电工程和弱电工程之间的区别可以说已经消失了，但是我们仍旧认为它们在概念上有所不同，因为电力工程的主要任务是在空间相距较远的各地之间输送能量，而通信系统的主要目的则是传递、提取和处理信息，在这个过程中可能会消耗相当大的电力。

3）逆序译法

一些英语句子的叙述顺序与汉语习惯不同或完全相反，这时，需要逆着原文顺序翻译。这种翻译几乎不可能完全保留原文语序，必须调整语序以符合汉语表达习惯。例如：

(1) One sign of how badly the seas have been overfished is that population of tuna have declined 94% since 1970.

自从 1970 年以来,金枪鱼的总存量递减了 94%,从中可以看出,对海洋渔场的狂捞滥捕已经到了什么程度。

(2) The method normally employed for free electrons to be produced in electron tubes is thermionic emission, in which advantage is taken of the fact that, if a solid body is heated sufficiently some of the electrons that it contains will escape from its surface into the surrounding space.

当将固体加热到足够温度时,它所含的电子就会有一部分离开固体表面而飞逸到周围的空间中去,这种现象称为热离子放射,通常,电子管就是利用这种现象产生自由电子的。

(3) The problem of possible genetic damage to human populations from radiation exposures, including those resulting from the fallout from testing of atomic weapons, has quite properly claimed much popular attention in recent years.

人类由于面临辐射威胁,其中包括原子武器试验产生的放射性散落物所造成的辐射威胁,很可能造成基因损伤,这一问题近年来已经引起人们的广泛重视。

Appendix

Appendix I Vocabulary and Phrases

a sequence of		一系列，一连串	8-PB
abbreviation	[ə,briːviˈeiʃən]	缩写，简写	1-PB
AC		交流	1-PA
access	[ˈækses]	存取，接近，访问	12-PA
accommodate	[əˈkɔmədeit]	容纳，提供空间；适应	5-PA
account for		说明……的原因，解释，对……负责	8-PB
accumulator	[əˈkjuːmjuleitə]	累加器	5-PA
accuracy	[ˈækjurəsi]	精确，准确	2-PB
achieve	[əˈtʃiːv]	实现，达到	3-PA
act on/upon		对……起作用，按照……而行动，作用于	8-PA
actuating signal		执行信号	8-PA
actuator	[ˈæktjueitə]	执行器，驱动器，调节器	8-PB
adapt to		变得习惯于……，使适应于，能应付……	8-PB
adapter	[əˈdæptə]	适配器	12-PB
adaptive	[əˈdæptiv]	适合的，适应的；自适应	8-PB
addition		加，加法	3-PA
addressable location		可寻址单元	5-PA
addressing mode		寻址方式	5-PA
AF		音频	10-PA
aircraft-piloting		飞机驾驶	8-PA
algebra	[ˈældʒibrə]	代数，代数学	3-PA
alloy	[ˈæləi,əˈlɔi]	合金	1-PA
alternating		交流，交变	1-PB
alternating-current (AC)		交流电流	7-PA
alternative	[ɔːlˈtəːnətiv]	可选择的，可替换的	12-PA

altitude	[ˈæltitjuːd]	高度，海拔	8-PB
aluminum	[əˈljuːminəm]	铝	6-R
amplification	[ˌæmplifiˈkeiʃən]	放大，扩大	10-PA
amplifier	[ˈæmplifaiə]	放大器	2-PB
amplitude	[ˈæmplitjuːd]	振幅，幅度	4-PB
analogous	[əˈnæləgəs]	相似的，类似的	8-R
analog-to-digit controller (ADC)		模数转换器	5-R
analogue	[ˈænəlɔg]	模拟，模拟电路	3-PA
AND gate		与门	3-PB
angular	[ˈæŋgjulə]	角度，用角度测量的	7-R
antenna	[ænˈtenə]	天线	10-PA
apart from		除……以外，除了	5-PA
apparatus	[ˌæpəˈreitəs]	仪器，设备，仪表，装置	1-PB
apparent	[əˈpærənt]	显然的，外观上的	11-PB
application layer		应用层	12-PA
application		应用	1-PB
appreciably	[əˈpriːʃiəbli]	明显地	5-R
apprehension	[ˌæpriˈhenʃən]	担心，忧虑	6-PA
approximation	[əˌprɔksiˈmeiʃən]	近似值	9-PB
architecture	[ˈɑːkitektʃə]	结构，构造，体系结构	5-PA
arithmetic	[əˈriθmətik, æriθˈmetik]	算术；算法，运算	5-PA
arithmetic logic unit (ALU)		算术逻辑单元	5-PA
armature	[ˈɑːmətjuə]	电枢	7-PB
arrows		箭头	2-PA
as little as		与……一样少，少则	6-R
as long as		只要，既然，如果	5-PA
aspect ratio		纵横比，屏幕高宽比	10-PB
assemble	[əˈsembl]	装配，组合，组装	7-R
assembly	[əˈsembli]	零件，部件，配件，总成	7-R
assembly line		装配线，生产流水线	6-PA
asynchronous	[eiˈsiŋkrənəs]	异步的	7-PA
attract	[əˈtrækt]	吸引	2-PB
attraction	[əˈtrækʃən]	吸引	4-PA
audio	[ˈɔːdiəu]	音频的	9-PA
aural	[ˈɔːrəl]	听觉的	9-PA
automate	[ˈɔːtəmeit]	使自动化，自动操作	6-PA
avalanche-type photodiode		雪崩光电二极管	11-PB
base		基极	2-PB
base on		根据……，以……为基础	8-R

baseband	['beisbænd]	基带	9-PA
basis	['beisis]	基础，要素	3-PA
battery	['bætəri]	电源	1-PB
be termed		把……称为	12-PA
bearer	['bɛərə]	载体，承载	12-PB
bearing	['bɛəriŋ]	轴承，支座	7-PB
behavior	[bi'heivjə]	运转状态，性能，行为	8-PB
billion		10 亿，大量的	2-PB
binary	['bainəri]	二进制的，二元的	3-PB
bipolar	[bai'pəulə]	有两极的，双极的	2-PB
bit addressable		位寻址	5-PA
blast furnace		鼓风炉	8-PB
block diagram		结构图，方框图	5-PA
boolean	[bulən]	布尔	3-PB
boring	['bɔ:riŋ]	镗削，镗孔	8-PB
boundary	['baundəri]	边界，界限，分界线	6-PB
brake	[breik]	制动器；刹(车)	8-PB
brushed machine		有刷电机	7-PA
buffer	['bʌfə]	缓冲，缓冲器	5-PA
cable television		有线电视	11-PB
calibrate	['kælibreit]	校准	4-PB
calibration	[,kæli'breiʃən]	刻度，标度，校准	4-PA
cam	[kæm]	凸轮	6-PA
capability	[,keipə'biləti]	能力，性能，功能，容量	6-PB
capacitance	[kə'pæsitəns]	电容	1-PA
capacitor	[kə'pæsitə]	电容器	1-PA
carbon	['kɑ:bən]	碳	7-PB
carrier	['kæriə]	载波	9-PA
categories	['kætigəriz]	类别	2-PB
cellular	['seljulə]	利用电台网通信的，蜂窝式无线通信系统的	2-PB
certification	[,sə:tifi'keiʃən]	认证，确认，鉴定	6-PB
channel		沟道	2-PB
characteristic	[,kærəktə'ristik]	特性	9-PA
charge	[tʃɑ:dʒ]	电荷	1-PA
chassis	['ʃæsi]	机壳，机箱	11-PA
chemical	['kemikəl]	化学，化学的	3-PA
chemical plant		化工厂	8-PB
civilian	[si'viljən]	民用的	2-PA

clamper	['klæmpə]	钳子	2-PA
classification		分类，类别	1-PB
closed-loop control system		闭环控制系统	8-PA
coil	[kɔil]	线圈	1-PA
coil energizing sequence		线圈激励序列	7-R
collectively	[kə'lektivli]	全体地，共同地	10-PB
collector		集电极	2-PB
color rendition		彩色再现	10-PB
combustion	[kəm'bʌstʃne]	燃烧，燃烧过程	3-PA
come down to		到达，归结为	6-PB
common		共有的，公共的	2-PB
common practice		司空见惯的事，惯例，习惯做法，常见的惯例	7-R
commonplace	['kɔmənpleis]	平凡的，普通的，平常的	8-PB
communication	[kə,mjuːni'keiʃne]	通信	3-PA
community	[kə'mjuːniti]	公社，团体，共有，一致	12-PA
commutator	['kɔmjuteitə]	整流子，换向器	7-PB
comparator	['kɔmpəreitə]	比较发生器	5-R
compatible	[kəm'pætəbl]	兼容的，相容的	6-PB
component	[kəm'pəunənt]	零件，部件，器件，元件	3-PA
compose	[kəm'pəuz]	组成	11-PA
composition	[,kɔmpə'ziʃne]	构成，成分	3-PA
compressor	[kəm'presə]	压缩机	6-R
comprise	[kəm'praiz]	包含，包括，由……组成	7-PB
concerned with		与……有关，关于，涉及	8-PB
condition		状态	2-PB
conducting		传导	2-PB
conductivity	[,kɔndʌk'tiviti]	导电性	2-PB
conductor	[kən'dʌktə]	导体	10-PA
conference		会议，年会	3-PA
confidential	[,kɔnfi'denʃəl]	秘密的，机密的	3-PA
configuration	[kən,figju'reiʃne]	构造，接法	2-PB
configure	[kən'figə]	使……成形，安装	5-R
configured as		配置为	5-PA
conjunction	[kən'dʒʌŋkʃne]	联合，结合	7-R
connecting		连接	2-PB
consist		包含，包括	2-PB
constant	['kɔnstənt]	恒定，不变，常量	1-PB
constraints		系统参数	3-PA

construct	[kən'strʌkt]	建筑，建设，构造	3-PA
consume	[kən'sju:m]	消耗	2-PB
consumer		消费者，顾客	3-PA
controlled variable		被控变量	8-PA
conventional	[kən'venʃənəl]	习惯的，传统的	2-PA
convergence	[kən'və:dʒəns]	收敛，会聚，集中	8-R
conversely		相反	2-PA
coordination	[kəu,ɔ:di'neiʃən]	协调，协同，一致	12-PA
counteract	[,kauntə'rækt]	抵消，反作用于	5-R
counterpart	['kauntə,pɑ:t]	对手，对方	6-PB
CPU (central processing unit)		中央处理单元	5-PA
crankshaft	['kræŋk,ʃɑ:ft]	机轴，转轴	3-PA
crash	[kræʃ]	崩溃，失效，停机	6-PA
critical		关键的，主要的	3-PA
critical resistance		临界电阻	1-PA
current	['kʌrənt]	电流	1-PB
customized	['kʌstəmaizd]	定制的，用户化的	6-PB
cutt speed		切削速度	8-PB
cycle	['saikl]	循环，周期	1-PB
cyclically	['saiklikəli]	周期性地，循环地	7-PB
cylindrical ceramic resistor		圆柱形陶瓷电阻	5-PB
damp	[dæmp]	减弱，抑制，使沮丧，使败兴	8-R
data compression		数据压缩	9-PB
data pointer register (DPTR)		数据指针寄存器	5-PA
data-link Layer		数据链路层	12-PA
DC		直流	1-PA
debate	[di'beit]	辩论，争论	6-PB
decoding	[,di:'kəudiŋ]	解码	9-PA
decoration	[,dekə'reiʃən]	装潢，装饰	2-PA
dedicated	['dedikeitid]	专用的，专门用途的	6-PA
defined		明确的，定义的	3-PA
definite	['definit]	明确的，一定的，有限的	12-PA
degradation	[,degrə'deiʃən]	衰减，衰弱	9-PA
deliver	[di'livə]	排放，供给，发出，提出	7-PB
demodulation	[di:,mɔdju'leiʃən]	解调	9-PA
demodulator	[di:'mɔdjuleitə]	解调器	9-PB
denote	[di'nəut]	代表，表示	8-R
depend upon		依赖，依靠，取决于	6-PB

derivative	[diˈrivətiv]	导数，微商	8-R
design		设计，计划	3-PA
designate	[ˈdezigneit]	指明	9-PA
desired value		期望值，预定值，期待值	8-PB
detector	[diˈtektə]	检波器	10-PA
deviation	[ˌdi:viˈeiʃən]	背离，偏离	8-PA
diagram	[ˈdaiəgræm]	框图	10-PA
diaphragm	[ˈdaiəfræm]	隔板，膜片	6-PA
digital		数字，数字电路	3-PA
digital-to-analog (D/A) converter		数-模转换器	5-PB
digit-to analog controller (DAC)		数模转换器	5-R
diode	[ˈdaiəud]	二极管	2-PA
direct		直流，直接	1-PB
direct addressing		直接寻址	5-PA
direct digital control (DDC)		直接数字控制	8-PB
direct digital controller (DDC)		直接数字控制器	5-R
direct-current		直流电流	7-PA
disciplines	[ˈdisiplins]	学术，学科	3-PA
discrete	[disˈkri:t]	离散的	9-PB
discretization	[disˈkri:taiˈzeiʃən]	离散化	9-PB
discriminate	[disˈkrimineit]	区别	10-PA
distinct	[disˈtiŋkt]	清晰的，明显的，清楚的，有区别的	6-PB
distortion	[disˈtɔ:ʃən]	失真	9-PA
distributed system		分布式系统	12-PA
disturbance	[diˈstə:bəns]	干扰，骚乱，扰动	5-R
divide	[diˈvaid]	分离，隔开	1-PB
division	[diˈviʒən]	分开，分割	4-PB
dome	[dəum]	拱形结构，圆屋顶	6-R
dominate	[ˈdɔmineit]	支配，占优势	12-PA
downtime	[ˈdauntaim]	停机时间，停工期	6-PB
drain	[drein]	漏极	2-PB
drill	[dril]	钻孔，打眼；钻头，钻床	8-PB
drive	[draiv]	驱动	3-PB
duplicate	[ˈdju:plikət, ˈdju:plikeit]	复制，重复，重做	8-PB
electric generator		发电机	7-PA
electric motor		电动机	7-PA
electrical machine		电机	7-PA
electrician	[ˌilekˈtriʃən]	电工，电气专家	6-PA

electrode	[i'lektrəud]	电极	2-PB
electrodynamic	[i͵lektrəudai'næmik]	电力学的，电动	4-PA
electrodynamic ammeter		电表	4-PA
electromagnet	[i͵lektrəu'mægnit]	电磁体，电磁铁	7-R
electromagnetic	[ilektrəumæg'netik]	电磁的	7-PA
electromechanical	[i͵lektrəumi'kænikəl]	机电的	6-PB
electronic circuits		电子电路	1-PA
electrostatic	[i͵lektrə'stætik]	静电学的	4-PA
electrostatic machine		静电机	7-PA
element	['elimənt]	原理，特性	2-PB
eliminate	[i'limineit]	消除，排除，除去	6-R
emf =electromotive force		电动势	7-PB
emitter	[i'mitə]	发射极	2-PB
enameled copper wire		漆包线	1-PA
encapsulate	[in'kæpsəleit]	压缩	11-PA
encoding	[in'kəudiŋ]	编码	9-PA
encompass	[in'kʌmpəs]	包含，包括	10-PB
ENOR gate		同或门	3-PB
entirely	[in'taiəli]	完全地，完整地	3-PA
EOR gate		异或门	3-PB
equation	[i'kweiʒən]	方程，方程式	3-PA
equivalence	[i'kwivələns]	同等，等价，等值	11-PA
equivalent	[i'kwivələnt]	相等的，相当的，当量	5-R
error signal		误差信号	8-PA
essential	[i'senʃəl]	必不可少的，本质的，实质的，基本的	8-R
establish	[i'stæbliʃ]	建立，成立	3-PA
ethylene drying facility		乙烯干燥装置	6-R
evaluate	[i'væljueit]	评估，评价，计算	8-PA
evolve	[i'vɔv]	演变，进化，发展	6-PA
exchange	[iks'tʃeindʒ]	交换	12-PA
execute	['eksikjuːt]	执行，实行	5-PA
expect	[iks'pekt]	期望	2-PA
extensive	[ik'stensiv]	广泛的，广阔的，大量的	3-PA
external memory		外部存储器	5-PA
extract	[ik'strækt, 'ekstrækt]	抽取，提取	7-PB
facet	['fæsit]	方面	9-PA
facilitate	[fə'siliteit]	推动，促进	11-PA
facility	[fə'siliti]	工具，设备	11-PA

fail-safe	['feilseif]	自动防故障装置的	7-R
familiar	[fə'miljə]	熟悉的，惯用的	8-R
faucet	['fɔːsit]	水龙头，旋塞	8-R
feasible	['fiːzəbl]	切实可行的	11-PA
feedback	['fiːdbæk]	反馈，反应	8-PA
felt material		毛毡；毛布；毡制品；油毛毡材料	7-PB
ferrite cores	['ferait]	铁氧体磁芯	1-PA
ferrite rod		铁磁棒	1-PA
ferromagnetic	['ferəumæg'netik]	铁磁的，铁磁体的	7-PA
fiber	['faibə]	纤维，光纤	11-PB
filter	[filtə]	过滤，滤波器	5-PB
filter circuits		滤波电路	1-PA
final control element		末级控制元件	8-PA
fit … in		装得下，放得进去	6-PA
flexibility	[fleksi'biliti]	弹性，适应性，柔韧性	6-PA
flexible	['fleksibl]	柔韧性，灵活的	5-PA
flow	[fləu]	流程，流量，流动；流动，涌流	8-PA
fluctuate	['flʌktjueit]	波动，起伏	8-PB
fluidize	['fluːidaiz]	使液化，流(态)化	6-R
flux	[flʌks]	磁通，(电，磁，光)通量	7-PB
format	['fɔːmæt]	格式	10-PB
formulate	['fɔːmjuleit]	明确地表达，阐明	12-PA
frame	[freim]	帧	11-PA
frequency	['frikwənsi]	频率	1-PA
full duplex		全双工，全双向的	5-PA
function	[fʌŋkʃən]	函数	3-PB
fundamental	[ˌfʌndə'mentəl]	基本的，必要的	2-PB
funnel	['fʌnl]	使集中	11-PB
futuristic	[ˌfjuːtʃə'ristik]	未来主义的	12-PB
gasoline	['gæsəliːn]	汽油，燃油	3-PA
gauge	[geidʒ]	规格，计量器，测量仪表	5-PB
generation	[ˌdʒenə'reiʃən]	产生	9-PA
generator	['dʒenəreitə]	发电机	7-PB
generic	[dʒi'nerik]	通用的，一般的	6-PB
geographically	[dʒiə'græfikəli]	地理上的	12-PA
glue	[gluː]	用胶水将物体粘合，粘牢，粘贴	7-PB

govern		统治，控制	2-PB
governor	[ˈgʌvənə]	调节器，控制器	8-R
grab	[græb]	抓，抓住	7-PA
graphite	[ˈgræfait]	石墨，石墨电极	7-PB
guarantee	[ˌgærənˈtiː]	保证，确保，使必然发生	8-R
hairspring	[ˈhɛəspriŋ]	细弹簧，游丝	4-PA
harmonic	[hɑːˈmɔnik]	谐波	4-PB
have the advantages of		有……的优点	6-PB
heat pump		热(力)泵；蒸汽泵	5-PB
heuristically	[hjuəˈristikəli]	启发式地，几乎都是	8-R
hierarchically	[ˌhaiəˈrɑːkikəli]	分等级地，分级体系地	8-R
hierarchy	[ˈhaiəˌrɑːki]	分级系统，分级结构，	
		数据层次	5-R
hold circuit		自保持电路	5-R
hole		空穴	2-PB
homopolar	[ˌhoməˈpəulə]	单极的，同极的	7-PA
humidity	[hjuːˈmidəti]	湿气，潮湿，湿度	8-PA
hybrid	[ˈhaibrid]	混合物，合成物	7-R
hydraulic	[haiˈdrɔːlik]	液压的	6-PA
hydraulic cylinder		液压缸	6-PA
idealistic	[aiˌdiəˈlistik]	空想的	12-PB
identify	[aiˈdentifai]	确定，打出，识别	8-PA
IF amplifier		中频放大器	10-PA
illustrate	[ˈiləstreit]	阐明	9-PB
imperfection	[ˌimpəˈfekʃən]	缺陷	9-PA
impetus	[ˈimpitəs]	动力，推动力	11-PB
implantable medical device		植入式医疗设备	5-PB
implement		实现，完成，履行	3-PA
implicitly	[imˈplisitli]	含蓄地，暗中地	9-PA
in addition to		除……之外，另外，加之	8-PA
in conjunction with		共同，与……一起，	
		与……共同	7-R
in operation		运转中，实施中，操作中	8-PB
in response to		对……的响应，	
		对……的反应	7-R
in the absence of		缺乏，不存在；缺乏……时，	
		在缺乏……的情况下	8-R
in the case of		在……情况下	6-PB
in the event that		如果，在……情况下	8-R

invent		发明	2-PA
inversion	[in'və:ʃən]	相反，反相	3-PB
inverter	[in'və:tə]	反相器	3-PB
involved	[in'vɔlvd]	有关的，复杂的	6-PA
ISDN		综合业务数字网	12-PB
junction	['dʒʌŋkʃən]	结点，会合点，	2-PB
juxtaposed	[,dʒʌkstə'pəuzd]	紧靠的	2-PA
keep track of		记住，留意	6-R
laboratory	[lə'bɔrətəri]	实验室	2-PB
ladder	['lædə]	梯形，阶梯，途径	6-PA
ladder logic		梯形图，梯形逻辑	6-PA
laminated	['læmineitid]	分层的，迭片的	7-PB
lamp	[læmp]	灯	2-PA
lateral	['lætərəl]	外侧的，侧面的，横向的	7-R
leveler	['levələ]	轧平机，校平器	6-R
levitation	[,levi'teiʃən]	轻轻浮起，悬浮	7-R
light-emitting diode		发光二极管	11-PB
limestone	['laimstəun]	石灰岩，石灰石	6-R
liquid level		液位	8-PB
logic gate		逻辑门	3-PB
loudspeaker	['laud'spi:kə]	扬声器	9-PA、10-PA
lubricant	['lu:brikənt]	润滑剂〔油〕；润滑的	7-PB
LVDT =linear variable differential transformer		线性可调差接变压器	5-PB
machine		机器，机械装置	3-PA
machinery	[mə'ʃi:nəri]	机械，机器	6-PA
Maglev Traction Motor		磁悬浮列车牵引电机	7-R
magnetic	[mæg'netik]	磁性的，有磁性的	7-R
magnetic field		磁场	7-PA
maintenance	['meintənəns]	维护，保持	4-PB
majority	[mə'dʒɔriti]	多数，大多数	1-PB
manipulate	[mə'nipjuleit]	操作，控制	6-PA
manipulated variable		控制变量	8-PA
manner		方法，方式	3-PA
manual	['mænjuəl]	手册	4-PB
mass	[mæs]	大规模的，大量的，许多的	8-PB
mathematical	[,mæθi'mætikəl]	数学，数学上的	3-PA
mechanical	[mi'kænikəl]	机械的，机器的	8-PB
mechanical energy		机械能	7-PA

mechanics	[miˈkæniks]	力学，机械学	8-R
mechanism	[ˈmekənizəm]	机构，机制，机械装置	8-R
medium	[ˈmiːdiəm]	介质，(存储)媒体	8-PB、9-PA
megawatt	[ˈmegəwɔt]	兆瓦	8-PB
metallic	[miˈtælik]	金属的；金属制的；含金属的	7-PB
metallurgic ally	[ˌmetəˈləːdʒikli]	冶金	2-PA
microcontroller	[ˌmaikrəukənˈtrəulə]	微控制器	5-PA
microprocessor	[ˌmaikrəuˈprəusesə]	微处理器	11-PA
military	[ˈmilitəri]	军用的	2-PA
mill	[mil]	磨，研磨	8-PB
milliammeter	[ˌmiliˈæmitə]	毫安表	4-PA
milliampere	[ˌmiliˈæmpɛə]	毫安	4-PA
missile-guidance		导弹制导	8-PA
mixer	[ˈmiksə]	混频器	10-PA
model		模仿，模拟	3-PA
modulate	[ˈmɔdjuleit]	调制	10-PA
modulation	[ˌmɔdjuˈleiʃən]	调制	9-PA
modulator	[ˈmɔdjuleitə]	调制器	9-PB
module	[ˈmɔdjuːl]	模数，模块	6-PA
mold	[məuld]	模子，模型	1-PA
multiplexer	[ˈmʌltipleksə]	多路复用器，多路转换器	5-PB
multiplier	[ˈmʌltiplaiə]	乘法器	4-PA
multitude	[ˈmʌltiˌtjuːd]	大量，众多	9-PA
NAND gate		与非门	3-PB
nanometer		纳米	11-PB
network layer		网络层	12-PA
noise	[nɔiz]	噪声	9-PA
nonetheless	[ˌnʌnðəˈles]	虽然如此，但是	11-PA
nonlinear	[nɔnˈliniə]	非线性	2-PA
nonlinearity	[ˌnɔnliniˈærəti]	非线性	5-R
non-recurring		非定期的，临时性的，一次性的	6-PB
NOR gate		或非门	3-PB
NOT gate		非门	3-PB
notation	[nəuˈteiʃən]	符号，标记	2-PA
N-type		N 型	2-PA
numeric control		数字控制	8-PB
obvious	[ˈɔbviəs]	明显的	4-PB

oddly	['ɔdli]	奇怪地	2-PA
offline	['ɔflain]	脱机的，离线的	6-PB
ohmmeter	['əum,miːtə]	欧姆表	2-PA
Ohm's law		欧姆定律	1-PA
on the basis of		以……为基础，根据……，	
		基于……	8-PA
one-way		单向的	2-PA
operation	[,ɔpə'reiʃən]	工作，运行，运算	2-PB
operational life		使用年限，使用寿命，	
		使用限期	6-PB
opposite	['ɔpəzit]	相反的	1-PB、2-PB
optical	['ɔptikəl]	光学的	11-PB
optimal	['ɔptiməl]	最佳的，最优的，	
		最理想的	8-R
optimum	['ɔptiməm]	最适宜的；最有利的，	
		最佳的	8-PB
OR gate		或门	3-PB
oscillation	[,ɔsi'leiʃən]	振荡，波动	8-R
oscillator	['ɔsileitə]	振荡器	2-PB
oscilloscope	[ɔ'siləuskəup]	示波器	4-PB
overkill	['əuvəkil, ,əuvə'kil]	过度的杀伤力	6-PB
overshoot	[,əuvə'ʃuːt, 'əuvəʃuːt]	过冲，超调，超越，超过	8-R
oxygen	['ɔksidʒən]	氧气	3-PA
package	['pækidʒ]	包装，封装	2-PB
parallel	['pærəlel]	并行，并联	1-PB
peak	[piːk]	峰值	2-PA
perform		执行，履行，运行	3-PA
performance	[pə'fɔːməns]	性能，表现	7-PA
periodically	[,piəri'ɔdikəli]	周期性地	1-PB
permanent	['pəːmənənt]	永久的	4-PA
permeability	[,pəːmiə'biliti]	渗透性	4-PA
permit	[pə'mit]	准许	2-PA
perspective	[pə'spektiv]	观点，看法，远景	12-PA
photic	['fəutik]	光	2-PA
physical	['fizikəl]	物理的	3-PA
physical layer		物理层	12-PA
pilot	['pailət]	指示器，调节器	6-PB
pin		管脚，引脚	5-PA
PM machine		永磁电机	7-PA

pneumatic	[njuːˈmætik]	气动的，气压的	6-PA
pneumatics	[njuːˈmætiks]	气动，气动装置，气动元件	8-R
point-to-point		点对点	11-PB
polarity	[pəuˈlærəti]	极性	1-PB
potential	[pəuˈtenʃəl]	电压，电势	2-PB
potentiometer	[pəˌtenʃiˈɔmitə]	电位计，分压器，电位器	5-PB
power rating		额定功率	1-PA
power supply		电源	6-PA
precision	[priˈsiʒən]	精确度，准确(性)	8-PB
predominant	[ˌpriˈdɔminənt]	占优势的，主导的	5-PA
predominantly	[ˌpriˈdɔminəntli]	显然地，显著地，占主导地位的	3-PA
prefix	[ˌpriːˈfiks,ˈpriːfiks]	前缀	1-PA
premium	[ˈpriːmiəm]	优质的，特级的	10-PB
prescribed	[prisˈkraibd]	规定的，法定的	8-PA
presentation layer		表示层	12-PA
preset	[priːˈset]	事先调整，预先安置，预先调试	8-PA
primarily	[ˈpraimərəli]	主要的，首先	3-PA
principle	[ˈprinsəpl]	原理	7-PA
priority	[praiˈɔrəti]	优先，优先级，优先权	5-PA
process stream		工艺流程，过程流	8-R
program counter (PC)		程序计数器	5-PA
program status word (PSW)		程序状态字	5-PA
programmable logic controller (PLC)		可编程逻辑控制器	6-PA
prohibit	[prəuˈhibit]	禁止	2-PA
proliferate	[prəuˈlifəreit]	增生扩散	12-PA
propel	prəuˈpel	推进；推动，驱动	7-R
property	[ˈprɔpəti]	性能，特点	3-PA
proportional	[prəuˈpɔːʃənəl]	比例的，成比例的	8-R
proportional to		与……成(正)比例	5-PB
proprietary	[prəuˈpraiətəri]	专用的，专有的	6-PA
protocol	[ˈprəutəkɔl]	协议	12-PA
provided		如果，假如	1-PB
p-type		P 型	2-PA
pulsating		波动的，脉动的	1-PB
punched card		穿孔卡片	8-PB
purge	[pəːdʒ]	清洗，净化	6-R
purpose		目的	2-PA

qualitatively	[ˈkwɔlitətivli]	定性地	2-PA
quantify	[ˈkwɔntifai]	确定数量，用数量表示	8-R
radically	[ˈrædikəli]	根本地，彻底地，完全地；	
		激进地，极端地	8-PB
radio-frequency		射频	10-PA
reaction rate		反应率，反应速率	5-PB
read only memory (ROM)		只读存储器	5-R
readout	[ˈriːdaut]	示值，读数	5-PB
reassemble	[ˌriːəˈsembl]	重装，重组	11-PA
receiver		接收器，接收机	1-PB
reciprocal	[riˈsiprəkəl]	倒数	1-PB
recombining		合并，汇合	1-PB
reconstruct	[ˌriːkənˈstrʌkt]	重建，重构	9-PB
recording		记录	3-PA
rectification		整流	2-PA
rectifier	[ˈrektifaiə]	整流，整流器	1-PB
rectify	[ˈrektifai]	调整，矫正	10-PA
redetermine	[ˌriːdiˈtəːmin]	重新决定，重新确定	8-PB
redundancy	[riˈdʌndənsi]	冗余	9-PB
refinery	[riˈfainəri]	提炼，精炼厂	8-PB
refresh	[riˈfreʃ]	刷新，更新	10-PB
register	[ˈredʒistə]	寄存器	5-PA
regulate	[ˈregjuleit]	控制，调节	1-PB
regulation	[ˌregjuˈleiʃən]	图表	2-PB
reject	[riˈdʒekt]	拒绝，抵制，丢弃	10-PA
relationship		关系	3-PA
relay	[ˈriːlei, riˈlei]	[电工]继电器	6-PA
reliable	[riˈlaiəbl]	可靠的，可信赖的	12-PA
reluctance	[riˈlʌktəns]	磁阻	7-PB
reluctance machine		磁阻电机	7-PA
rely on		依靠，依赖，信赖	5-PB
remote control		遥控，遥控器，遥控装置	5-PB
rendition	[renˈdiʃən]	再现	10-PB
repetitive	[riˈpetətiv]	重复的	8-PB
replica	[ˈreplikə]	复制品，副本	11-PB
represent	[ˌrepriˈzent]	代表，描述	3-PB
repulsion	[riˈpʌlʃən]	排斥	4-PA
researcher		研究人员	2-PB
resistance	[riˈzistəns]	电阻	1-PA

resistivity	[ˌriːzisˈtivəti, riˌz-]	电阻系数	1-PA
resistor	[riˈzistə]	电阻器	1-PA
resolution	[ˌrezəˈluːʃən]	分辨率	10-PB
resonant	[ˈrezənənt]	共振的，共鸣的	10-PA
respectively	[riˈspektivli]	分别地	3-PB
responding	[riˈspɔndiŋ]	响应	3-PB
response		反应	2-PB
responsiveness	[riˈspɔnsivnis]	响应性，反应性，应答性	8-R
retrofit	[ˈretrəufit]	改进，翻新	11-PB
reverse	[riˈvəːs]	反转，倒相	1-PB
revision	[riˈviʒən]	修改，校正	6-PA
revolution	[ˌrevəˈljuːʃne]	旋转，旋转周	7-R
robust	[rəuˈbʌst]	鲁棒性，稳健，坚固	10-PB
rogue	[rəug]	行为失常的，异常的	5-PB
roller	[ˈrəulə]	滚轮(轴，筒)，滚动	7-PB
root-mean-square		均方根	4-PB
rotate	[rəuˈteit, ˈrəut-,ˌrəuteit]	旋转，转动	3-PA
rotor	[ˈrəutə]	转子	7-PA
router	[ˈrautə]	路由器	12-PB
routine maintenance		例行保养	5-R
sandwich	[ˈsænwidʒ]	把……夹在……之间	2-PB
scale	[skeil]	刻度，进制	4-PB
scenario	[siˈnɑːriəu]	情况，情节	6-PB
schematic	[skiːˈmætik]	原理图	2-PA
schematically	[skiˈmætikəli]	示意地，原理性地	5-R
SCR abbr. = semiconductor control rectifier		晶闸管，可控硅	7-R
secure	[siˈkjuə]	拴牢；扣紧，固定	7-PB
selectivity	[silekˈtiviti]	选择性	10-PA
semiconductor	[ˌsemikənˈdʌktə]	半导体	2-PA
sensitive	[ˈsensitiv]	敏感的	8-R
sequential	[siˈkwenʃəl]	顺序的，相继的，连续的	8-R
serial	[ˈsiəriəl]	串行	11-PA
serial data transmission		串行数据传输	5-PA
series	[ˈsiəriːz]	串联	1-PB
servo amplifier		伺服放大器	7-R
servomechanism	[ˌsəːvəuˈmekənizəm]	伺服机构(系统)， 自动控制装置	8-PB
session layer		会话层	12-PA
shaft	[ʃɑːft]	轴，转轴	7-PB

sharp	[ʃɑːp]	清晰的，清楚的	10-PB
shift	[ʃift]	移动	9-PA
shrink	[ʃriŋk]	收缩，缩小	6-PB
significant	[sig'nifikənt]	重要的，大量的	4-PB
silicon	['silikən]	硅	2-PA
simplex	['simpleks]	单纯的，单一的	11-PA
simultaneously	[ˌsiməl'teiniəsli]	同时地，同步地	4-PB
sine	[sain]	正弦	4-PB
single chip microcomputer (SCM)		单片微型计算机	5-PA
sinusoidal wave		正弦波	9-PA
slave	[sleiv]	从属的	6-R
sleeve	[sliːv]	套筒，套管	7-PB
slip ring		滑动环；集电环	7-PB
solenoid	['səulənɔid]	[电]螺线管	6-PA
solid-state		使用电晶体的， 不用真空管的	2-PB
sophisticated	[sə'fistikeitid]	复杂的，高级的，尖端的， 精密的	6-PA
space-vehicle		宇宙飞船	8-PA
specialty vehicles		特种车辆，专用车	6-PB
spectrum	['spektrəm]	频谱	10-PB
spin	[spin]	旋转	7-PA
splice	[splais]	拼接，接头	11-PB
split ring		开口环，扣环	7-PB
spread over		分散，传开	6-PB
squirrel-cage induction motor		鼠笼式感应电机	7-R
squirrel-cage rotor		鼠笼式转子	7-PB
stability	[stə'biliti]	稳定(性)	8-R
stabilization	[ˌsteibilai'zeiʃən]	稳定性	8-PB
stack pointer (SP)		堆栈指针	5-PA
standstill	['stændstil]	停止，停顿，停止状态	7-R
stationary	['steiʃənəri]	不动的，静止的，固定的	7-PB
stator	['steitə]	定子，固定片	7-PA
stator assembly		定子总成	7-PB
steer	[stiə]	驾驶，掌舵；操纵； 控制；引导	8-PB
stick with		坚持，继续，坚持做	6-PB
strain	[strein]	拉紧张力，应变	5-PB
strain gauge		应变仪，变形测量器	5-PB

strategy	['strætidʒi]	策略，战略，行动计划	8-R
stress	[stres]	压力，应力	7-R
stretch wrapper		包装设备	6-R
submarine	['sʌbməri:n]	海底的	11-PA
subtract	[səb'trækt]	减去，减	5-R
subtraction	[səb'trækʃən]	减，减法	3-PA
succession	[sək'seʃən]	连续	9-PA
superconductor	[ˌsju:pəkən'dʌktə]	超导体	7-PA
supervise	['sju:pəvaiz]	监控，检测，操纵	5-R
suspend	[sə'spend]	悬浮，悬，挂，吊	7-R
sustain	[sə'stein]	维持，保持，承受，支持	7-R
switch	[switʃ]	开关	2-PA
switching system		交换系统	12-PB
symbol	['simbəl]	图表，符号	2-PA
synchronous	['siŋkrənəs]	同步的	7-PA
synchros = synchronous devices		同步设备	5-PB
synonymous	[si'nɔnəməs]	同义的，类义的	7-PA
synthesis	['sinθisis]	综合，合成	9-PB
tachogenerator	['tækə'dʒenəreitə]	测速发电机，测速传感器	5-R
tachometer	[tæ'kɔmitə]	转速表，转数计	5-R
tacho-voltage		转速电压	5-R
tailor	['teilə]	制作，改装，使合适	5-R
take up		占据，占用	5-PA
take the place of		代替	6-R
tandem	['tændəm]	串联式，双人的	1-PB
tank	[tæŋk]	(盛液体、气体的大容器)桶、箱、池、槽	8-PA
task	[tɑ:sk,tæsk]	工作，任务	3-PA
telecommunication		电信	11-PB
telegraph	['teligrɑ:f]	电报	9-PA
teleprinter	['teliˌprintə]	电传打字机	9-PA
teletype	['telitaip]	电传打字机，打字电报通信	5-R
temper	['tempə]	使缓和，使温和，减轻	8-R
tend to		易于，倾向于，有助于	8-PA
terminal	['tə:minl]	终端	12-PA
terminals		端子	2-PB
terrestrial	[ti'restriəl]	陆地的	11-PB
thermistor	[θə:'mistə]	热敏电阻，热元件	5-PB
thermodynamic	[ˌθə:məudai'næmik]	热力学的	3-PA

thermoelectric	[,θə:məui'lektrik]	热电的	5-PB
thought of as		将看做，视为	8-R
three-phase alternating current		三相交流电流	7-PA
timesharing		分时(操作)	11-PA
timing circuits		定时电路	1-PA
tooling	['tu:liŋ]	用刀具加工	8-PA
torque	[tɔ:k]	扭矩，转矩	4-PA
tote	[təut]	手提，拖拉，携带	6-R
trace out		描绘出，提出，追查	6-PA
trackside	['træksaid]	轨道旁的，轨道附近的	7-R
transducer	[trænz'dju:sə]	传感器，换能器，变换器	5-PB
transfer	[træns'fə:]	转移	7-PA
transformer	[træns'fɔ:mə]	变压，变压器	1-PB
transistor	[træn'sistə,-'zis-, trɑ:n-]	三极管	2-PB
transit	['trænsit]	运输，过境，中转	6-PB
transmission	[trænz'miʃən]	传播，传送	1-PB
transmitter	[trænz'mitə]	变送器，传导物，发射机	8-PA
transportation layer		传输层	12-PA
troubleshoot	['trʌblʃu:t]	故障检测	6-PB
truth table		真值表	3-PB
tuner	['tju:nə]	调谐器	10-PA
typically	['tipikəli]	代表性地，典型地；通常，一般	8-R
ubiquitous	[ju:'bikwitəs]	普遍存在的	1-PA
underlying	[,ʌndə'laiiŋ]	基础的，根本的	8-R
unfilter		未滤波的	1-PB
unipolar	[,ju:ni'pəulə]	单极的	7-R
unit		单位	1-PA
universal	[,ju:ni'və:səl]	普遍的，通用的	11-PB
up-counter		加法计数器	5-PA
upset	[ʌp'set, 'ʌpset]	打乱，扰乱，搅动	8-PA
utility		应用程序，功用	1-PB
utilization	[,ju:tilai'zeiʃən]	利用，使用	3-PA
utilize	['ju:tilaiz]	利用，应用	7-PA
valve	[vælv]	阀门	2-PA
variable	['vɛəriəbl]	变量	8-PA
variable-frequency controller		变频控制器	7-R
vast	[vɑ:st,væst]	巨大的，广大的	1-PB
vastly	[vɑ:stli]	广大地，巨额地	11-PA

velocity	[vi'lɔsəti]	速度	5-PB
versatile	['və:sətail]	通用的，万能的	5-PA
versus	['və:səs]	对，对抗，比较	6-PB
vertical	['və:tikəl]	垂直的	4-PB
virtually	['və:tʃuəli]	实际上，差不多，几乎	8-PB
viscosity	[vi'skɔsəti]	黏质，黏性	8-PA
viz	[viz]	即，就是	5-PA
voltage	['vəultidʒ]	电压	1-PA
volume		体积，容积	3-PA
waveform	['weivfɔ:m]	波形	9-PB
waveguide	['weivgaid]	波导	11-PB
wavelength	['weivleŋθ]	波长	11-PB
weld	[weld]	焊接	8-PB
winding	['waindiŋ]	线圈，绕组	7-PA
wired		连线，以线加强	2-PB

Appendix II Translation

第一单元　电子学基础知识

Passage A

电阻、电容和电感

电阻(图 1.1)是一种两端电子元件，根据欧姆定律 $V = IR$，它能在两端之间产生与通过它的电流成正比的电压。

电阻是电路和电子电路中的元件，在大部分电子设备中都会用到。实际的电阻和电阻线(由像镍、铬这样的大电阻系数的合金制成)一样，由多种化合物和薄膜制成。电阻器的主要特征有电阻、容许偏差、最大工作电压和额定功率。其他特性包括温度系数、噪声、感应系数及临界电阻。欧姆(符号是 Ω)是电阻的单位。在电学和电子学中常用的是千欧和兆欧。

电容器(图 1.2)可以储存电荷。电容器和电阻器用于定时电路中，因为电容器充满电荷需要时间。它们还充当电荷储存器，用于平滑直流电源。它们也用于滤波电路中，因为电容器容易通过交流(变化的)信号，而阻挡直流(不变的)信号。

电容是电容器储存电荷能力的度量尺度。电容量大意味着能储存更多的电荷。电容以法拉为单位计量，符号 F。然而 1F 很大，所以使用前缀来表示较小的电容值。3 个前缀，μ (微)、n(纳)和 p(皮)经常用到。

电感器(图 1.3)是通过将导线缠绕在合适的模子上构成线圈形成的。它的电特性称为感抗，单位是亨利，符号 H。1H 很大，所以使用 mH(毫亨)和 μH(微亨)，1000μH = 1mH，1000mH = 1H。铁磁芯和铁氧体磁芯增加感抗。电感器主要用于调谐电路中阻挡高频交流信号。它们容易通过直流信号，而阻挡交流信号，这一点与电容器相反。电感器在简单的项目(设备)中很少见，但无线电接收机的调谐线圈是一个例外。将漆包铜线缠绕在铁氧体棒上就形成一个电感器。

Passage B

直流电与交流电

只含有一个电源和一个负载的电路很容易分析，但是在实际应用中我们很少见到这种电路。一般情况下，我们见到的电路都是由两个以上的器件组合而成的。要连接两种以上的元器件，有两种基本方式：串联和并联。串联电路是一种由两个或两个以上元件首尾衔接或串在一起的电路。在这种电路中，电流在任何点上不再分开。与串联电路不同，并联电路的电流在构成一个闭合回路之前，有两个或两个以上的支路。

众所周知，两个电阻 R1、R2 串联，总电阻等于两者之和。另一方面，两电阻并联，总电阻等于两电阻倒数和的倒数。电容和电感的串并联与电阻的特点类似。

以上是电子学中的主要分类方法之一。不按电路中元器件的连接方法，而是按电路中的电流或信号分，电子电路一般被分为两类：直流电路和交流电路。

直流(DC)是一种流向不发生变化的电流(即极性保持不变)。它有可能是由电池或稳压电源供应的常量；也有可能是由未滤波的整流器供应的脉冲。这样的电路通常被称为直流电路。爱迪生安装的第一个应用系统就应用了直流技术。在爱迪生发明他的直流系统后不久，人们发现交流系统具有直流系统无法比拟的优越性。

电视机、收音机或任何其他的电器设备都是由交流电供电工作的。但是，什么是交流电呢？与直流电的方向不变不同，交流电的方向会周期性地变化，交流电简称 AC。如图 1.4 所示，在一个循环内，电流的幅度从 0 值开始变化，在 90 度时达到最大值，180 度时回到 0，270 度时达到最大的负值，360 度时又回到 0 值。每秒钟完成此类循环的个数被称为频率。在美国和世界上的很多其他地区，传输电能或给一般设备供电所用的频率都是 60Hz，而在中国用的频率是 50Hz。

交流被电广泛应用于大量的电路中，它可以被传输得很远，如果变化频率足够快，还可以进行无线传输；可以被变成各种电压值，并且应用变压器可以很容易地将其变大或变小，这些都是直流无法相比的。但是，在像照明和加热这些一般的应用电路中，既可以用直流也可以用交流。直流-交流转换器可以将直流输入变为交流输出，而且无任何衰减和增益，用它可以把直流变换为交流；运用由电阻、电容、电感组成的整流电路，也可以将交流变为直流。

Reading

集 成 电 路

1958 年，工作于得州仪器公司的杰克坎尔比、工作于仙童(飞兆)半导体公司的诺依斯和摩尔独立发明了一种极其重要的装置：集成电路，它将双极结型晶体管、金属氧化物半导体场效应管、电阻、电容以及它们之间的连接线整合到单一芯片上的一个功能电路中。

集成电路通常称为 IC 或者 chips。它们是在同一个承载结构(称为基质)上焊接在一个生产过程中制造的一些像三极管、二极管、电容、电阻这样的互相连接的电路元件形成的复杂电路，目的是实现信息(数据)转换过程中的特定功能。

在 20 世纪 60 年代早期，集成电路中大约包含 100 个器件，最小的大约为 25 μm。意识到通过使用更复杂的集成电路能大幅度地降低复杂电子系统的成本，工艺工程师们努力地增加芯片的尺寸，并减小器件的尺寸。现在最先进的集成电路中含有 1000 多万个器件，其大小只有 0.25 μm (人的头发直径大约为 25 μm)。器件小型化的趋势有望继续下去。除了器件数量增加外，集成电路尺寸也减小了，从而产生了更高性能的数字电路。所以，可以预期在电子学领域将会取得更大的进步。

集成电路的生产工艺可以分为两种类型：薄膜工艺和单块(分子)工艺。集成电路根据功能可分为两种：用于数字系统的集成电路和用于线性系统的集成电路。数字集成电路主要用于计算机、数字计数器、频率合成器和数字仪器中。模拟集成电路或者线性集成电路在一个连续范围内工作，其中包括运算放大器这样的装置。

这些进步要归功于物理电子学家、工艺工程师、电路设计员和系统设计员的协同工作。尽管本书主要讨论电路设计，但也为电子工业的工程师提供了有用的背景知识。

集成电路的发明是电子工业的一次伟大革命。有了这些技术，器件的尺寸、重量才能明显减小；更为重要的是，可以获得(实现)高稳定性、良好的功能特性、低成本及低能耗。集成电路已广泛应用于电子工业中。

第二单元　模　拟　电　路

Passage A

二　极　管

二极管是一种非线性电气设备，当电流通过它向一个方向移动时比向另一个方向移动容易得多，当前通常作为单向阀使用。尽管在现代电路设计中存在其他二极管技术，但最常见的是半导体二极管。半导体二极管的图表，如图 2.1 所示。

图 2.1　半导体二极管的原理图符号

在图 2.1 中，箭头指示的方向为电流流向。

将二极管置于一个简单的蓄电池灯回路中，它是否允许电流通过蓄电池灯要取决于所施加电压的极性(图 2.2)。

图 2.2(a)允许电流通过，二极管是正向偏置；图 2.2(b)禁止电流通过，二极管是反向偏置。

当电池的极性允许电子流过二极管时，二极管被认为是正向偏置。相反，当电池极性相反并且二极管阻挡电流通过时，二极管被认为是反向偏置。可以认为二极管像一个开关：当正向偏置时关闭，而当反向偏置时开放。奇怪的是，二极管符号的"箭头"指向与电子流的方向相反。这是因为二极管的图表是由工程师发明的，他们主要使用常规流符号表示电流像一股流动电荷从电压源的正极(+)流向负极(−)。这个惯例也适用于所有带有"箭头"符号的半导体。在传统流向中，箭头指向允许电流通过的方向，而阻止电流流向相反的方向。

制造半导体二极管的一种方法是创建一个包含 N 型材料毗邻 P 型材料的硅晶片。例如，在一个 N-沟道的 MOSFET，N 型漏极紧靠 P-沟道区域便形成了一个二极管。欧姆表可用于定性检查二极管的功能。通常应该有测量低电阻的方式和测量非常高的电阻的方式。为了达到这个目的而使用欧姆表时，应确保知道哪些测试导线是正极的，哪些是负极的！实际极性可能与所料的导线颜色所示的极性不一致，这取决于特定设计的计量表。

二极管普遍应用于军用和民用的电气设备中。例如，峰值检波器，夹紧器电路，电压乘法器和整改，这些都是二极管最流行的应用。现在二极管的一个类型是 LED(发光二极管)，它可以直接将电信号转化为光信号，因此普遍应用于人们日常生活中的照明、显示、信号和装饰中。

Passage B

三 极 管

三极管是一种类似于二极管的非线性半导体器件，通常作为放大器或电控开关使用。由于其反应速度快和精确度高，三极管可用于各种数字和模拟功能的实现中，包括放大、开关、稳压、信号调制和振荡器。三极管可独立成套，也可作为在一个非常小的面积内包含 10 亿或更多的晶体管构成的综合电路的一部分。因此，三极管逐渐成为控制计算机操作、移动电话和所有其他现代电子产品电路的基石。

三极管主要有两种类型：双极型三极管，又称为"双极结型三极管"(BJT)，和场效应三极管(FET)。第一种固态电子三极管是由研究人员威廉肖克利、约翰巴丁和沃尔特布拉坦于 1947 年 12 月在贝尔实验室制造出来的。而作为目前通用标准的"双极型三极管"是由威廉肖克利在 1950 年发明的。

双极结型三极管由 3 部分半导体材料组成。一类是所谓的 NPN 三极管，其中两个 N 型材料层中间夹着非常薄的 P 型材料层。两个 N 型材料层的 NPN 晶体管区域被称为发射极和集电极，而 P 型材料被称为基极。NPN 三极管的电路原理图如图 2.3 所示。

当作为放大元件使用时，基极和发射极的结点是在一个"正向偏置"(指挥)的地方，而基极和集电极的结点是"反向偏置"或不导电的。从基极到发射极电流的微小变化(输入信号)会引起从发射极进入基极的电子空穴(为 PNP 设备)或释放(为 NPN 设备)。具有吸引性电压的集电极引起大多数的电荷穿过集电极或被其收集，结果引起放大。

PNP 三极管和一个 NPN 三极管功能上的唯一差异是在操作时能否对结点准确偏置(极性)。对于任何给定的操作状态，每种类型三极管的电流方向和电压的极性必须相反。

有 3 种方式连接三极管，这取决于当时的用途。连接方式是根据同时具有输入和输出的电极分类的。它们被称为共基极构造、共发射极构造、共集电极构造。

虽然第一个三极管和硅芯片采用双极三极管，但是今天的大多数芯片都是 FET(场效应三极管)，它采用 CMOS 逻辑连接，以便消耗更少的能源。FET 有 3 个端子，即源极、漏极和栅极。源极和漏极之间的半导体区域称为沟道，其导电通道是由栅极终端的电位控制的。

Reading

放 大 器

像"门"这个抽象概念是构成大多数数字电路的基础一样，运算放大器是构成电子电路设计的基础。可以说运算放大器是模拟电子电路中最有用的独立设备。只需要外接很少几个元件，它就可以完成多种模拟信号的执行任务。它也相当便宜，大多数通用运放售价不足 1 美元/每个。现代工程设计还考虑到了耐久性，同时使用多个运算放大器，这样就可以在输出端承受直接短路而不造成危害。

运算放大器这个名字来源于很久以前的模拟计算机(1940—1960)，有了它，通过放大器捕捉后就可以把不同微分方程中的常数表示出来。因此，这些用特制真空管平衡对构造的放大器，必须要可靠、知名、有固定收益。由于三极管本身比真空管更依赖温度，所以起初人们认为要制造一个符合要求的三极管运算放大器是不可能的。但在 1964 年，人们发现通过在一个单一的硅芯片上构造平衡的三极管对并靠在一起，尽量减少热梯度，温度的问题是可以克服的。因此 709 诞生后快速取代了 703，然后是无处不在的 741。现在，运算放大器很少用于模拟计算机，而是已成为所有模拟电路的通用构建模块。运算放大器是一个多阶段双输入差分放大器，其被设计成一个几近理想的控制装置，具体地说就是一个电压控制的电压源。运算放大器的抽象描述如图 2.4 所示，由图可知它是一个 4 端口器件。这 4 个端口分别是输入端口、输出端口、一对电源端口。+VS 电压(例如，-15V)应用于正电源端口，而-VS 电压(例如，-15V)应用于负电源端口。输入电压(对照组)用于非反相和反相运算放大器的输入端并在输出端口出现。在抽象的运算放大器中，跨输入端口输入阻抗为无穷大，输出端阻抗为零。增益，或通过输入电压被放大的因素，也为无穷大。

运算放大器的符号和标准标签如图 2.4 所示。两个所需的外部电源已在图中明确显示，虽然显示它们不是惯例。除了适当的结点电压，5 个电流都已经标识，指示通用的地端子。在这种原始的电路中，电压 v_i 用来控制输出电压 v_o。让我们仔细研究这项控制功能，既找到了控制范围，以及控制成本，也就是说，v_i 端供给多少能量，就能控制多少数量的 v_o 终端的能量。为了解决第一个问题，这里设计了精确的电路，如图 2.5(a)所示，并测量输出电压 v_o，既作为时间的函数，又可作为 v_i 的函数，假设 v_i 是一些低频正弦波。结果显示在图 2.5(b)和图 2.5(c)中。注意电压轴的规模差异，这表明输出电压可能是输入电压的 300000 倍大。图 2.5 中 v_o 对应着 v_i 的区域，显然 v_o 与 v_i 线性相关，但超出这个范围太多，控制就变得无效，并且 v_o 保持为一个固定的电压，或饱和电压，大约是 12V 或-12V，这取决于 v_i 的极性。该曲线也随着相同运算放大器样品的不同而有所不同。

同一类型的不同设备可能有不同的特点。这些特点也可能取决于温度。

这些小电路在反馈工程学原理，尤其是负反馈中的作用的关键是，其中一对运算放大器的输出信号反馈到运算放大器的 v-输入端。它构成了几乎所有自动化控制流程的基础。用这个方法建立的运算放大器的实例有反相和非反相放大器、缓冲器、加法器、微分器和积分器。

运算放大器电路有时使用内置的正向反馈连接，其中一对运算放大器的部分输出信号反馈到运算放大器的 v^+ 输入端。这种运算放大器电路的实例包括振荡器和比较器。

第三单元　数　字　电　路

Passage A

电子电路设计历来有两个主要领域：模拟和数字。第二单元已经介绍了模拟电路。而在这个单元中将讨论有关数字电路的知识。数字电路是发展最快的学科之一。而数字电路的广泛使用也促进了集成电路的发展。因此，一些消费电子产品正变得越来越智能化，体积越来越小。例如，MP3 几乎完全取代了录制音频的模拟设备。液晶电视的发明取代了 CRT 电视。3G 可以应用于视频会议等。而这一切都依赖于数字和集成电路技术。

但是，什么是数字电路和数字系统？它们由什么组成呢？所有类型的机器，包括计算机，都是在已经设计好的方式下准确地完成任务的。有些机器部件从本质上说是纯粹的物理性，因为它们的组成和行为是由化学、热力学和物理特性严格控制的。例如，发动机的就是把由汽油和氧气燃烧时释放的能量转化成曲轴的旋转的。还有些机器实际上只是运算，因为它们的设计主要是遵循由人规定的参数来实现一系列逻辑功能的，而不是物理学的法则。红绿灯的工作就主要是由人定义的，而不遵循自然物理学法则。数字逻辑和算术是构建这类系统的关键组件，而此系统就是由数字电路组成的数字系统。

所有的数字系统都是建立在数字逻辑设计上的，布尔代数是数字逻辑设计的数学基础，并且建立了一种把任务规则数字化的方法。

布尔逻辑(数字逻辑)是数学的一个分支，它是 19 世纪由名为乔治·布尔的英国数学家发现的。其基本原理是用代数方程为逻辑关系建立模型。布尔代数应用了逻辑运算，包括 AND、OR 和 NOT，而不是用加法和减法等算术运算。而所有这些都由逻辑门电路实现，它们是数字电路的基本组成部分。

逻辑门是一个由数个输入端和一个输出端(一般情况下)构成的电子元件。和逻辑运算对应，有 3 种主要的逻辑门：AND 门、OR 门以及 NOT 门。输入和输出，一般是两种状态之一：逻辑 0 或逻辑 1，它有两个枚举值：true 和 false。这些逻辑值由电压(例如，逻辑 0 为 0V，而逻辑 1 为 3.3V)或电流表示。逻辑门自动执行逻辑运算，把所有的输入端作为条件，得出输出端。当然，数字门电路本质上是模拟器件，但为简单起见，往往忽视他们的模拟特性。

与模拟系统相比，数字系统具有许多优点。例如，它具有很强的抗干扰性，保密性能好。此外，模拟电路具有的高传输率、高信道利用率和小的网络延迟也是模拟电路无法比拟的。

Passage B

逻 辑 门

在数字电子系统中，信息用二进制位表示。一个二进制位可以表示 0 或 1。布尔函数实际上由电子门来实现。

门电路的输入由电压驱动，通常 0V 代表逻辑 0，5V 代表逻辑 1。门电路输出电压也有两个值，0V 代表逻辑 0，5V 代表逻辑 1。除了某些特殊情况，通常一个逻辑门只有一个输出。注意门电路需要电源供电。在加载的输入和输出响应之间总有时间延迟。真值表用来显示逻辑门函数。用逻辑门可以构造数字系统。这些逻辑门包括与门、或门、非门、与非门、或非门、同或门、异或门。它们的基本运算可以由辅助的真值表来描述。以下给出了这些逻辑门的说明。

与门(图 3.1)：仅当所有输入都是高电平时输出为高电平。点用于表示与运算，如 A·B。记住这个点有时可以省略，如 AB。

或门(图 3.2)：如果有一个或多个输入为高电平，则输出为高电平。+ 用于表示或运算。

非门(图 3.3)：非门产生与输入信号相反的输出信号。它也称为反相器。如果输入变量为 A，其反相输出为非 A，可以用 A'或在 A 上加一条横线表示。

与非门(图 3.4)：与非门等于在与门之后接一个非门。如果任意一个输入都是低电平，与非门的输出是高电平。与非门的符号是在与门后面加一个小圆圈接到输出端，这个小圆圈表示反相。

或非门(图 3.5)：或非门等于一个或门紧接一个非门。如果任意一个输入都是高电平，或非门的输出是低电平。或非门的符号是在或门的后面加一个小圆圈接到输出端，这个小圆圈表示反相。

异或门(图 3.6)：如果某一个输入(不是两个输入同时)为高电平，异或门的输出为高电平。符号⊕用于表示异或运算。

同或门(图 3.7)：同或门与异或门功能相反。如果某一个输入(不是两个输入同时)为高电平，异或门的输出为低电平。

Reading

存 储 器

内存由数字电路构成，和其他器件一样，它是构成计算机的基本组件，因为它被用于临时存储微处理器正在处理的数据和指令。随着大规模集成电路的发展，内存的容量变得越来越大，而存储速度也变得越来越快。人们用的内存主要有两种：ROM 和 RAM。接下来讨论一下两者的不同之处。

随机存储器或称为 RAM，也被称为主存、内存或主存储器，是人们常说的计算机存储器。用户可以购买不同规格的内存：256MB、512MB、1GB、2GB 和 4GB 的。通常它被简单地称为内存，其实计算机中还有其他类型的内存。它是使用最广的一种类型，由一组芯片构成，其存储单元由控制部件中的地址表管理。

顾名思义，RAM 中的内容可以很容易地以任意顺序(随机地)读出(或称访问)，而不用考虑顺序问题。RAM 始终靠电流进行操作；而且，如果电源关闭或中断，RAM 会很快丢失人们辛辛苦苦存入的内容。因此人们把 RAM 称为易失性或非永久性的存储器。

一个标准的内存条或单元，又长又薄，像一把直尺。内存单元的底部有一个或多个缺口，用于指示正确的安装，并且有很多内衬，通常是些镀金片。内存安装在计算机主板的内存卡槽上。找到内存卡槽两边的小链条，内存就可以很容易地固定在卡槽中。内存条和内存卡槽需要匹配，所以，在购买或安装之前要检查主板制造商的信息。

另一种内存是只读存储器或称为 ROM，主要用来永久性地存储程序或者数据。这些数据和程序是做在 ROM 芯片中或者说通过硬连线实现的。如在微型计算机中就有内置 ROM 芯片(有时称为 ROM BIOS，即 ROM 基本输入/输出系统)，该芯片用来存储一些关键的程序，如计算机的启动或引导程序。一旦数据被写到 ROM 芯片上，就不能通过正常的方法删除或修改。对于大多数 ROM 来说，修改数据的唯一方法就是修改实际电路。ROM 的读取速度比 RAM 慢，因此如果需要快速处理，则将 ROM 中的内容传送到 RAM 中。

和主存(RAM)不同的是，ROM 可以在计算机断电的情况下保存数据，这是因为 ROM 是非易失性的而 RAM 是易失性的。有各种各样的 ROM，如 EPROM(可擦除 ROM)和 EEPROM(电擦除 ROM)。EPROM 和 EEPROM 可以用特殊的方法修改数据。因为紫外线可以清除 EPROM 中的信息，因此出现了"闪存"这个词。

第四单元　常　用　仪　器

Passage A

模拟仪器及其使用

1. 直流电流与电压的永磁可动线圈式仪表

基本原理是带有指示器的可动线圈在特别设计的永久磁场中旋转，从而移动系统的角度响应值恒定，而仪表刻度不随场值的变化而改变。为量度高于 20mA 的电流值，即引起用于导入、导出移动线圈的游丝过热的电流，我们使用带有并联毫安计的分流器。毫安计的刻度按分流器及仪表总电流划分。要量度电压，仪表通过的电流必须小一些。因此，一系列用于 0.1～10mA 的电流全刻度偏差的电阻器和乘法器得以使用。

2. 交流电流与电压的动铁式仪表

在此类仪表中，要被测量的电流或电压用于激活一个固定线圈，其场内放置一个带弹簧与指针的高导磁性钢制移动叶片。叶片的运动总是增加其通量，因此由电磁体和叶片磁场反应生成的力矩会增加该连续的自感。该力矩与线圈电流的平方成正比，相应的刻度能读取其量值。这类仪表也称为吸引型仪表。另一类称为排斥型。排斥型动铁式仪表也很常用。

3. 测量电流与电压的电动式仪表

此类仪表通常选择用于精度测量及商用实验室测量，基本原理是较重的固定线圈与较轻的活动线圈之间的力场反应。每一线圈的电流与被测量的电流或电压成正比，而且场间反应所提供的力矩与被测量的电流和电压的平方成比例。对相对较低的电流进行测量时，必须将固定的与移动的线圈串联起来以传送整个电流。较强电流的测量则使用并联线圈结构。除少部分电表中的电流外，所有被测量电流均通过与合适电阻器串联的固定线圈传送。同样，与电阻器串联的移动线圈要与固定线圈及其电阻器并联。

在电动式伏特计中，固定和移动的线圈要串联起来传送整个电流。一个合适的乘法器则决定电压的范围。

4. 测量超低(50V)、超高直流、交流电压的静电伏特计

在此类仪表中，电场对带电电极的作用产生偏转力矩。该力矩总是很小。若构造合理，此类仪表同样可以测定直流或交流电压值，因此被用来用直流值刻度校正其他交流仪表的刻度值。

Passage B

示 波 器

　　在需要观测电信号准确波形时通常使用示波器。除了显示信号的振幅，示波器还能显示失真测量频率，两个动作的时间间隔(如脉冲宽度或脉冲上升时间)，以及两个相关信号的相对间隔。一些现代数字示波器能分析和显示一个独立事件的频谱。专用示波器，也称为频谱分析仪，具有高敏感的输入，可以显示的光谱范围高达 GHz。

　　示波器可以显示电路中变化电压(或电流)的精确波形。用它测量电压(或电流)既有优点，也有缺点。 最明显的优点是示波器在测量电压(或电流)波形的幅度时，能同时显示波形、频率和相位。而用万用表或电子电压表只能显示波形幅度。而且，大多数电表是根据正弦波来校准的。当被测信号含有大量谐波时，校准便不精确了。而用示波器，电压是根据显示的含有许多谐波的波形测得的。

　　使用示波器测量电压(或电流)的主要缺点是分辨率问题。简单而便宜的万用表或电子电压表的刻度比示波器更容易读。在大多数情况下，示波器的垂直刻度用于测量电压(或电流)，每一小刻度代表一定的电压值(或电流值)。当电压很高时，示波器的刻度难以细分。

　　示波器屏幕的电压振幅可以通过峰-峰值所占垂直格数乘上所设定的 volts/cm 控制旋钮来确定。例如，假如振幅是 4cm，控制旋钮设置在 1V/cm，则峰-峰值为 4V。通常峰-峰值需要转换成有效值，因为大多数电子维修和故障手册所给的电压大多是有效值。

　　总而言之，如果只想知道电压(或电流)波形的幅度，就使用仪表，因为它读数简便。而当波形特性和幅度同样重要时，则使用示波器。

Reading

数字万用表

　　万用表是非常有用的测量仪器。通过操作万用表上的切换开关，可以方便快捷地将其设置为电压表、安培表或欧姆表。每种类型的仪表都有几种挡位选择(称为量程)，还可以选择交流和直流。有些万用表还有其他一些功能，如测量晶体管、电容和频率范围等。

　　万用表有两种类型：数字型和模拟型。模拟万用表用指针指示，数字万用表用液晶屏显示。

　　模拟万用表通常有一个功能和量程选择开关。它有一个极性转换开关以便转换测试引线。表针上有一个用于机械调零的螺钉，在测量电阻时为补偿电池电量减弱，它具有零位调节控制功能。通过转换测试引线或极性开关，模拟万用表能读出正、负电压。数字万用表的显示器上通常有一个自动的极性指示标志。

　　所有的数字仪表都用电池提供显示所需的能量，所以实际上它们并不使用来自被测电路的能量，这就意味着在直流电压测试范围内具有 $1\,M\Omega$ 或更大，通常为 $10\,M\Omega$ 的电阻(通常称为输入阻抗)，因而它们不大会影响被测电路。

　　为确保正确读数，仪表必须正确连接到电路中。电压表要跨接(并联)在电路或被测元件两端。在测量电流时，断开电路，将电流表串联到电路中或被测量部分。当测量电路元件的电阻时，必须移除电路电源将仪表和被测元件并联起来。

1. 用万用表测量电压和电流

(1) 根据预期的读数范围选择大一级的量程。

(2) 连接仪表，确保万用表的表笔以正确的方式形成回路。如果接反了，对于数字表可能是安全的，对于模拟表则可能造成损坏。

(3) 如果读数超出刻度范围，则立即断开，选择更高一级的量程。

万用笔使用不当容易损坏，可采取以下预防措施。

(1) 在调节量程前，保持万用表处于断开状态。

(2) 在测量前检查量程设置。

(3) 绝不能把万用表设置在电流挡(除非实际要测量电流)。因为万用表的电阻较小，所以在电流挡时最容易损坏。

2. 用万用表测量电阻

数字万用表的另一个有用的功能是欧姆表。欧姆表是测量电阻的仪表，如果电路没有电阻，则欧姆表的读数为 0，如果电路断开，则欧姆表的读数为无穷大。

第五单元　　基于计算机的控制系统

Passage A

单片机简介

单片微型计算机，也称为微控制器，是一种将大多数必需的资源都放在一个集成电路上的计算机。微控制器的主要系列是 8 位机，比如 AT80C51 和 TMS370，因为对需要微控制器完成的绝大多数任务来说，这已成为通用的字长。

8051 系列有大量器件可用，它们的区别在于以下几方面：存储器类型及容量、计数器/定时器数量、串行接口的类型、输入/输出端口个数等。80C51 有 3 种不同的封装类型，基本上都是 40 引脚，具有如图 5.1 所示的体系结构。

1. CPU

CPU 是微处理器的大脑，它读取用户的程序并根据存储在那里的每条指令执行预期的任务。它的主要部件是 8 位算术逻辑单元(ALU)、累加器、少量的寄存器，如 B 寄存器、堆栈指针(SP)、程序状态字(PSW)及 16 位寄存器，如程序计数器(PC)和数据指针寄存器(DPTR)。

2. 内部 RAM

80C51 有 128 字节的片内 RAM，以及一些特殊功能寄存器(SFR)。包含特殊功能寄存器空间在内，它一共提供 256 个可寻址单元，但是通过将存储空间分割成 3 个区，即低端128 字节、高端 128 字节和特殊功能寄存器空间，内部 RAM 的寻址方式可容纳 384 字节。

低 128 字节可使用直接和间接寻址方式访问。高 128 个字节只可用直接寻址方式访问，在这一空间中地址以 0H 或 8H 结尾的单元也可位寻址。

3. 内部 ROM

提供微控制器内部 ROM 是为了使控制程序可以常驻片内。如果控制程序可用 4KB 的 ROM 容纳，那么就不需要外部程序存储器。但是，如果控制程序需要更大的存储容量，外部存储器最大可增加到 64KB。

4. 输入/输出端口

80C51 的 I/O 端口结构极为灵活，并且是多功能的。该器件有构成 4 个 8 位并行端口(P0、P1、P2 和 P3)的 32 个输入/输出引脚。每个引脚可在软件控制下进行输入或输出。即使在同一个端口内部，不同引脚可以相互独立地进行输入或输出，或者同一个引脚可在不同时间分别进行输入或输出。P0、P2 和 P3 的所有引脚除了执行常规输入/输出功能外，还可用于完成许多不同的任务。

5. 定时器/计数器

80C51 有两个 16 位的定时器/计数器寄存器，称为定时器 0 和定时器 1。定时器 0 和定时器 1 是加法计数器，可通过编程实现对内部时钟脉冲进行计数(定时器)，或者对外部脉冲计数(计数器)。每个计数器被分成两个 8 位寄存器以提供定时器的低字节与高字节，即 TL0、TH0 和 TL1、TH1。

6. 串行接口

80C51 有一个片内串行口，使器件与外部电路之间可以进行串行数据通信。串行口是全双工的，所以它可以同时收发数据。串行口在接收模式还可以缓冲，因此在第一个数据字节从寄存器读走之前，它就可以接收第 2 个数据字节。

7. 中断

无论在计算机程序运行的哪一时刻，都可以通过软件技术或使用称为中断的硬件信号强制微控制器对外部情况做出响应。软件技术牵涉到检查标志或端口引脚的状态，要占用宝贵的处理器时间，而中断信号只在必要时停止主程序执行。

80C51 提供 6 个中断源。只要不是正在为同级或更高优先级的中断服务，一个中断就会得到服务。如果正在为较低优先级的中断提供服务，将会被停止，而转去为新的、高优先级的中断服务。当新的中断服务完成后，才会继续完成已停止的低优先级中断服务。

Passage B

微型计算机控制系统

工业过程可以用微型计算机或模拟控制器进行控制。在这类系统中使用了各种不同类型的传感器，如电位计、应变仪、线性可调差接变压器或者同步设备。被测参数，如位置、温度、压力、流速或密度，通常用电压来反映。

纯模拟系统的限制在于只能完成有限的数据处理，以及发现有必要改变数据处理的类型但难以实现。如果需要提供模拟信号的数字读数，就会产生额外的费用，因为需要为每个这样的读数使用模/数转换器。

将数字微型计算机引入这样的系统，在很大程度上扩大了信号处理的范围，在有些情况下，可以进行快速分析以确定不能直接测量的一些特性。它也提供一种处理控制信号的简单方法。更大的好处是，微型计算机能调整表示测量值的电压，找出不正常的读数，并且滤除信号中存在的有害的噪声。

使用数字微型计算机的典型控制系统可以说明常规的联机数字控制，其中模拟传感器产生与被测参数成比例的电压。由于微型计算机每次只能接收一个测量信号，所以进入 A/D 转换器转换之前，要按次序提取传感器的信号。输入数据由微型计算机在存储程序的控制下进行处理。提供给各种控制设备、进行过程控制的数字信号首先以指定顺序从微型计算机输出。每个输出信号都由数字/模拟(D/A)转换器转换成模拟信号，然后以模拟信号的形式由输出多路器分配到相应控制单元。在多数控制系统中，还要有一些位于微型计算机与控制过程之间的直接数字信号线，用于传送只需要开关动作的信息。

测量仪器系统使用与控制系统相同的模式，只是它们没有由微型计算机到控制过程的输出信号，也没有控制设备。一般来说，只有在测量仪器系统需要采集大量的数据、数据处理很复杂或者费时很长并且可能需要脱机使用微型计算机时，才会将微型计算机加入到仪表中。很明显，这样的系统有相当多的优点，它可以收集需要的测量值、进行处理，并以需要的形式提供数据，尤其是，通过给微型计算机输入新程序，很容易改变数据处理方式。

一个最常用的被控量是温度，用于对房间进行加热和制冷，或者用于控制化学或生物过程的反应速度。当使用燃料燃烧或电阻加热时，控制工程师能有效地控制加热，但必须依靠散热来制冷。相反，热泵或珀尔帖热电设备既能加热又能有效地制冷。

图 5.2 给出了一个常用的基于微型计算机的温度控制系统的原理图。热敏电阻和电桥提供电压，使用 A/D 转换器进行转换，并由微型计算机程序读取。控制程序向 D/A 转换器写入一个数值，将转换器的输出信号放大以驱动烤箱的电阻。热敏电阻用于检测温度，圆柱陶瓷电阻用于加热。

微型计算机还广泛用于自动控制产品和设备，如汽车发动机控制系统、植入式医疗器械、遥控器、电动工具和玩具等。

Reading

微控制器在数控系统中的应用

微控制器广泛应用于数控系统中。简单地说，对受控变量(如温度、位置等)进行监视，并从参考信号中减去监视该变量的传感器的输出值。从比较器输出的差分信号是误差值，称为驱动信号，用做对过程的输入。典型的系统结构如图 5.3 所示。

微控制器可用于这一系统中，称之为直接数字控制(DDC)。电机转速是被控变量，转速表用做传感器，产生与速度成正比的电压。比较器是一种电子装置，如果转速由于某种原因降低了，则驱动信号为正，使放大器给电机提供更大的电流，增大电机转矩，从而提高转速。如果转速太高，则驱动信号为负，电机转矩减小、转速变慢。很明显，当转速表输出电压大致等于参考电压时，运转速度将趋于稳定，所以转速与电位计的位置成正比。外加负载可使电机减速，但这会导致驱动信号增大，使电机产生更大的转矩来抵消外部负载的影响。输出轴可能要提供数千瓦的功率，它的转速可以只通过旋转参考电位器来控制。

使用微控制器所得到的好处有：(1)对有害干扰进行调控；(2)用低功率参考信号间接控制可能是大功率的设备；(3)减少非线性的不良影响。

这种系统的表现形式多种多样，在许多情况下比较器要复杂得多。它通常称为控制器，在其中可以使用微控制器，称为直接数字控制器(DDC)，虽然使用了复杂得多的数字控制方案。

每过一定时间间隔对传感器的输出进行采样，采样时间要非常接近，以使输出信号在两次采样之间不会有明显变化。这种信息由模拟-数字转换器转换成二进制形式，并由微控制器存储。程序使用输入微控制器中的读数，并从参考值中减去此值，产生对过程反馈信号的等效数字量。这个数字量由计算机输出，送到数字-模拟转换器(DAC)，产生一个成比例的电压，并保持不变直到复位为止(保持电路)。然后再次对传感器输出进行采样，处理采样值，DAC复位保持电路，如此继续下去。

控制程序使用的参考信号可以是一个固定的数值(设置点)，但也可通过一个电传打字机重新设置来改变。它也可以是从另一台计算机传来的数字参考信号。大型系统中的层次体系越来越常见，由一个中央计算机监控许多微控制器的控制功能。参考信号本身可以不断变化，微控制器可以轻松地处理这种情况，这是数字控制的一个优点。

尽管使用专门定制的控制器将程序存储在只读存储器(ROM)中来控制如前所述的单个系统是可行的，但有效的方式是用一台微控制器去控制，比如说50个闭合回路。对传感器输出进行采样、处理，并用其设置保持电路的状态，提供适当的过程输入信号。由于微控制器速度很快，这一过程可能只需要到下次采样之前 1/100 的时间。因此，多个过程输出"多路复用"接入微控制器，并对应地使用联动多路分配器为保持电路提供信号。用这种方式，微控制器被分时复用，在重复控制第一个回路之前，能控制50个左右的独立回路。

微控制器控制常用于过程工业中，如化工厂、炼油厂、钢铁厂及复杂的机械系统，如雷达系统、跟踪望远镜、飞机控制系统等。

第六单元　PLC 基础

Passage A

PLC 概述

可编程逻辑控制器，或可编程控制器，简称 PLC，是工业专用装置，用于连接和控制模拟和数字设备。PLC 也是一种特殊的计算机装置，应用于实际过程的自动化，比如控制工厂装配线上的机械等。可编程逻辑控制器一般使用微处理器。程序通常可用来进行复杂的顺序控制，并由工程师编写。程序存储在有备用电池的随机存储器或者电可擦除可编程只读存储器(EEPROM)中。

PLC 以多种形状和尺寸出现。它们可以小到能装到衬衣口袋里，而比较复杂的控制系统则需要大型的 PLC 机柜。通常较小的 PLC 设计有固定的 I/O 点。

所有 PLC 的基本结构如图 6.1 所示。

由图 6.1 可见，PLC 有 5 个主要部件：中央处理单元(CPU)、程序存储器、数据存储器、输出设备和输入设备。

CPU 专门用于运行一个程序，监测一系列不同输入，并对输出进行逻辑操作以实现所需要的控制。它们要有灵活的编程方式，还具有比传统控制系统更可靠(没有程序崩溃或机械故障)、更紧凑、更经济的优点。程序存储器用于存储逻辑控制序列的指令。开关状态、联锁状态、以前的数据值和其他运行数据存储在数据存储器中。

与其他计算机比较，最主要的区别是 PLC 有专门的输入/输出装置。这些装置将 PLC 与传感器和执行机构相连接。PLC 能读取限位开关、温度指示器和复杂定位系统的位置信息。有些甚至使用机器视觉。在执行方面，PLC 能驱动任何一种电机、气压或液压缸、薄膜装置、磁性继电器或螺线管。输入/输出装置可以内建在简单的 PLC 中，或者 PLC 有插入其中的外部 I/O 模块与专用的计算机网络相连。老式自动化系统要使用几百或几千个继电器和凸轮定时器，于是人们发明了 PLC 是要用做较便宜的替代品。通常，通过对一台 PLC 编程可替代数千个继电器。最初可编程控制器用在汽车制造业中，通过对软件的修改可以取代硬连线控制面板的重新连线。

PLC 经过多年的发展，其功能已经包括典型的继电器控制、复杂的运动控制、过程控制、分布控制系统和复杂的网络连接。

最早的 PLC 采用简单的梯形图来描述形成逻辑电路的决策，梯形图源自于电气连线图。使用梯形图，电气技师们很容易找出电路原理图的问题。选择梯形图主要是为了降低现有技术人员的理解难度。

如今，已经证明 PLC 非常可靠，但是可编程计算机仍然有很长的路要走。依照国际电工委员会的 61131-3 标准，现在 PLC 可以使用结构化的编程语言和逻辑基本运算来进行编程。

某些可编程控制器可使用一种图形编程符号，称为顺序功能图表。

然而，应该注意的是，PLC 价格不再非常昂贵(经常是数千美元)，而成为通用解决方案的一种典型产品。现代功能完善的 PLC 只要数百美元。实现机械自动化还有其他的方法，比如定制的基于微控制器的设计，但是这两者之间有一些差别：PLC 包含直接操作外部大功率负载需要的所有部件，而微控制器还需要电子工程师设计电源、输入/输出模块等。同时基于微控制器的设计不具备 PLC 现场可编程的灵活性，那也正是在生产线上运用 PLC 的原因。

Passage B

PLC 与其他控制形式的对比

尽管 PLC 广泛应用于工业控制中，但它并不是过程控制的唯一选择。坚持只用基本继电器可能也有好处，这取决于具体的应用。然而另一方面，计算机也是一种可以采用的方式。PLC 与微控制器的争论已经持续了很长时间。更经常的情况是，虽然这个问题并不归结为一个"非此即彼"的情况，但包含了技术融合。

1. PLC 与继电器

当开始为 PLC 编程时，PLC 是否比仅用继电器控制更为必要这一问题仍然要考虑。多年来随着 PLC 价格降低，体积缩小，并且性能提高，这个问题已经几乎没有什么争议，但

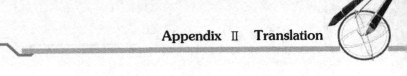

设计者还是要自问 PLC 是否真正对他们的应用有突出的优势。有些问题应该要提出。

(1) 将来是否需要扩展？

PLC 可以很容易地在插槽中加入一个新的模块，或者加入扩展底座。

(2) 是否需要高可靠性？

PLC 被认为比单个部件更可靠。

(3) 是否要考虑停机时间问题？

对继电器系统进行改变或故障检测意味着系统必须进入脱机状态。PLC 的修改一般能在线进行，而没有停机时间。

(4) 是否需要增加功能或输出？

PLC 会比他们的机械对手更快。

(5) 是否需要进行数据采集和通信？

只能使用 PLC 或计算机。

2. PLC 与专用控制器

专用控制器是一个专门用于进行参数控制的装置，比如 PID 控制器测量温度用于加热控制。它们的优点是所有部件一体式封装，一般带有显示器和按钮。在简单的应用中使用很好。今天的 PLC 可以从价格方面和功能上与这些控制器进行竞争，特别是如果需要一个以上的控制器时。PLC 还能提供更高的灵活性，因为它们能通过编程来处理各种不同的情况。

3. PLC 与微控制器

PLC 很适用于一定范围的自动化任务。这些任务一般是工业生产过程，自动化系统的开发和维护费用要高于自动化系统的总成本，在系统的使用年限内需要对其进行改造。PLC 含有与工业指示器和控制器相匹配的输入和输出装置；几乎不需要进行电气设计，设计问题集中在对所需操作顺序的表述上。PLC 应用一般是高度定制化的系统，所以成套的 PLC 费用要比专门定制的控制器设计要低。相反，在产品大批量生产的情况下，定制控制系统更经济，因为器件成本更低，可以优先选取这种方案而不用一般的解决方案，而且一次性工程费用被分配到成千或上百万件产品上。

对大批量或非常简单的固定自动化任务会使用不同的技术。例如，用户洗碗机会使用一个量产成本只有几美元的机电凸轮定时器进行控制。

基于微控制器的设计适用于要生产几百或几千件产品的情况，所以开发费用(包括电源设计、输入/输出硬件和必要的测试和认证)可以分散到多件商品上，适用于最终用户不需要修改控制的情况。汽车应用就是一个例子，每年要生产几百万件，最终用户几乎不修改这些控制器的程序设计。然而，一些专用车辆，比如运输汽车从经济上考虑使用 PLC，而不用定制设计控制，因为产量小，开发费用不合算。

非常复杂的过程控制，如在化工行业中使用的，可能需要一些超出高性能 PLC 功能的算法和性能。速度极高或非常精确的控制可能也需要定制解决方案，如飞机飞行控制。

PLC 可以包括单变量反馈模拟控制环路的逻辑系统，一个"比例-积分-微分"或 PID 控制器。例如，PID 环路可用于控制生产过程的温度。以前 PLC 一般只配置几个模拟控制回路；在需要几百或几千个回路控制过程的情况下会使用分布式控制系统。随着 PLC 功能的增强，DCS 与 PLC 应用之间的界限已经变得不明显了。

Reading

PLC 的应用

可编程逻辑控制器是一种数字操作装置，它使用可编程存储器作为内部存储器，用于存储实现特定功能，以控制机器和流程的指令，如逻辑、顺序、定时、计数和算术运算功能。随着电子元器件变得更小、更可靠，PLC 变得速度更快、功能更强、能够控制更多个输入和输出。20 世纪 70 年代晚期有人研制出了高速局域通信网络，使大型的过程或机器可由几个较小的控制器控制。

20 世纪 80 年代出现了更快、功能更强大的 PLC；带有扩展指令集和 16 位运算能力，而不是 8 位，而且进行浮点计算而不是整数计算。PLC 的体积缩小到单张卡片就可以完成原来需要使用整个机柜完成的工作。小型及超小型 PLC 也出现在通常少则需要 6 个继电器的应用中。

最近在不同品牌的 PLC 和个人计算机及主机之间的通信方面已经得到了发展。现在对操作员接口设备的选择也在不断增加，它可以添加到 PLC 中，而无须由 PLC 直接控制。现在有些 PLC 带有可用于模拟和专门输入/输出模块的计算机模块。

PLC 应用在任何领域。在文档轧平机、包装设备、包装机和装配线、电力分配系统和制炼厂中都能找到它们。随着小型自含式 PLC 的出现，现在普通电工对先前使用继电器逻辑实现的小型应用进行设计、安装和编程是很容易的。

下面列出 PLC 在工业中的一些实际应用，并对每一控制系统作进行简要说明。

锅炉控制：单独的 PLC 用于化工厂的 4 个锅炉中的每一个控制清洗过程、指示灯关闭、火焰安全检查、所有互锁和安全关闭检查、主燃烧器点火、温度及阀门从天然气转到燃油。对 PLC 编程使其成为能源管理系统，以获取最大效率和安全性。

压缩机站控制：使用多个压缩机的压缩机站由 PLC 控制，由它进行起动和关闭顺序及所有安全联锁控制。

乙烯干燥设备：在乙烯干燥设备中，潮湿的气体首先从盐丘中清除出来，然后烘干并注入到主管道，用两个 PLC 来控制整个操作过程。一个 PLC 用于控制加热器燃烧及关闭系统。第二个 PLC 用于控制干燥器单元中的干燥和再生循环。两个 PLC 都作为从器件，并连接到位于中央操作控制室的主 PLC 上。主 PLC 控制关闭顺序，也监测一些关键过程变量。

自动焊接：PLC 已成功地应用到汽车工业中的自动焊接机控制上。在汽车车体中使用铝是为了减轻重量，但这产生了一个负荷分配问题，因为焊铝比焊钢每条焊缝要消耗更多的电流。为了消除这一问题，基于优先级规则的分时自动焊接机利用了 PLC 的数据处理和算术运算能力。

煤流化过程：将 PLC 安装在流化床上以确定给定数量的煤产生的能量。碎煤和石灰石的混合物通过喷嘴吹到加热床上，监测燃烧速率与温度。PLC 控制阀门的动作顺序，替代了继电器控制系统。可编程控制器的模拟操作功能使喷射阀受控于动作顺序控制系统。通过 CRT 也可以对控制设备进行监控。

材料处理：在由 PLC 控制的存储/检索系统中，运送斗中零件在整个系统中装载、传送。控制器跟踪运送斗。操作员的控制台使零件能得以快速装载或卸载。打印机提供库存打印输出，比如存储巷号、分配给每巷的零件和巷中的零件数量。

第七单元　电　　机

Passage A

电　机　简　介

电机是一种能够根据法拉第电磁感应定律实现能量转换或传递的电磁设备。根据传统的定义，电机是电动机或发电机的代名词，而它们都是电能-机械能转换器：将电力转换为机械动力 (即电动机) 或将机械动力转换为电力 (即发电机)。机械动力中的运动可以是旋转运动或直线运动。虽然变压器不包含任何运动的部件，但它们也被包括在电机家族中，因为它们利用了电磁感应现象。

1. 电机简要历史

电机已存在多年了。自从多年前首次使用以来，电机的应用已得到迅速扩展。目前，电机的应用仍在不断快速增长。

与电机运转有关的多数早期发现是关于直流系统的。不久以后交流发电和配电也得到普遍应用。目前，几乎所有的电力系统都生成和分配三相交变电流。变压器使交流发电机发出的电压得以提高，而使电流相应减小，这就能够以减小的电流值进行远距离配电，从而减少了电力的损失，并提高了系统效率。

在家用电器、工业和商业应用中，使用电机驱动机器和精密设备的情况增多了。现在许多机器和自动化工业设备都需要精确的控制，因此从主要用于铁路列车的早期直流电机开始，电机设计和复杂性已经发生了改变。

复杂运输系统也对电机的应用产生了一定的影响。汽车和其他的地面运输方式使用电动机起动，将发电机用于电池充电系统。最近电动汽车的发展已经成为了重点。

2. 电机的分类

当对电机(电动机和发电机)分类时，从电能向机械能转换的物理原理开始比较合理。

电机可以是同步的，意思是定子线圈所建的磁场与转子等速度旋转；或者是异步的，意思是两者有速度差别。永磁电机和磁阻电机总是同步的。有转子绕组的有刷电机，当转子用直流或用与定子同频率的交流供电时为同步，而当定子和转子以不同频率的交流供电时为异步。感应电机通常是异步的，但如果在转子绕组中有超导体，也可以同步的。

考虑到这些，将普通电机正确归类如下。

1) 电磁转子电机

电磁转子电机在转子中有某种电流，建立了与定子绕组相互作用的磁场。转子电流可以是永久磁场(永磁电机)的内部电流，通过电刷供给转子的电流(有刷电机)，或者由变化的磁场在闭合转子绕组内产生的电流(感应电机)。

2) 阻电机(步进电机)

磁阻电机(磁阻电动机)在转子中没有绕组，只有将铁磁性材料做成一定形状，使在定子中的"电磁铁"可以"抓住"转子的齿并将其移动一点。然后关掉这个电磁铁，而打开另一组电磁铁，使定子进一步移动。这种电机又名步进电机，它适用于低速和准确的位置控制。可以在磁阻电机的定子中使用永久磁场以提高性能。

3) 静电电机(静电电动机)

在静电电机(静电电动机)中，扭矩是通过转子和定子中的电荷相互吸引或排斥产生的。

4) 单极电机

单极电机(单极电动机)是真正的直流电机，它通过电刷给旋转的轮子提供电流。将轮子插入磁场，当电流穿过磁场，从轮子的边缘到中心流动时就会产生转矩。

Passage B

电机基本结构

所有电机都包含耦合电路和磁电路，用于将电能转换为机械能或将机械能转换为电能。电机一词往往用来描述用于工业驱动的机器，而不管它是否作为电动机将电能转换为机械运动，或者是否作为发电机由机械能转换为电能。

旋转电机用于实现机用于电能量转换。这种能量转换过程通常需要在机电设备中存在两个重要的功能部件：产生磁通密度的磁场绕组和感应出工作电动势的电枢绕组。

在旋转电机中，通过使绕组在磁场中机械旋转，使磁场经过绕组，或者设计磁路使其磁阻随转子的旋转而改变，就会在绕组或一组线圈中产生电压。使用其中的任何一种方式，与特定线圈相关联的磁通就会周期性改变，并且会产生随时间变化的电压。

发电机用于将机械能转换成电能，而电动机用于将输入电能转换为机械能输出。发电机和电动机具有多种机器所共有的基本结构特点。各种机器尽管结构相似，但功能不同。原动机给发电机提供旋转运动，这是机械能输入。导线与发电机的磁场之间相对运动会产生电能输出。电动机有供给绕组的电能和通过电磁相互作用产生机械能或转矩的磁场。

大多数旋转电机的结构都有些类似。大多数电机都有一个固定的部件，称为定子，和一组旋转导体，称为转子。定子包括一个轭架或机架，起支撑作用，并作为电机中产生的磁通的金属路径。

1. 场磁极和绕组

旋转电机有场磁极，它是定子总成的一部分。场磁极由多层钢板构成，固定在机架上。它们在靠近转子的部分通常是弯曲的，目的是为磁通量提供一个低磁阻路径。场绕组或场线圈位于场磁极周围。场线圈是电磁铁，它与转子形成电磁场相互作用，在电机中产生电压或转矩。

2. 转子构造

在电机研究中，需要理解由电动机或发电机的旋转部分产生的电磁场，这一部分称为电枢或转子。有些类型的电机使用固体金属转子，称为鼠笼式转子。

3. 滑环，开口环(扣环)和电刷

为将电能提供给旋转装置，如电枢，必须以一定的方式接通滑刷。滑动电刷通过滑环或扣环接通。滑环是由用绝缘材料做的圆筒构成的，两个分开的固体金属环贴在上面。由碳和石墨制成的滑动电刷就贴在金属环上，这样即可在旋转过程中从滑环施加或提取电能。扣环换向器类似于滑环，只是将固体金属环分成两个或多个独立的部分。一般来说，滑环用于交流电动机和发电机，而直流电机采用扣环换向器装置。换向器的间隙或开口要保持最小，以减少电刷火花。

4. 电机其他部分

在旋转电机结构中还有其他几个部分。其中包括转子轴，在一组轴承之间旋转。轴承可以是球形、滚珠或套筒式。轴承油封，一般由黏结材料制成，用来润滑轴承周围，并保持清洁。转子芯一般由叠层钢片构成，以便在磁极间提供低磁阻路径，并减少涡流。内部和外部的电气连接提供了，供给或提取电能的一种方式。

Reading

特 种 电 机

在许多特殊应用中，广泛使用一些特殊的电机，通常称为专用电机。这里是一些常见的例子。

1. 集成式启动发电机

用于轻型混合动力电动汽车中的电子控制集成式起动发电机，将汽车起动机和发电机组合到一个电机中。常规的起动机是一个低速、大电流的直流电机，而发电机是三相变速交流电机。

2. 磁悬浮列车牵引电机

直线式感应电机的原理可用于驱动高速磁悬浮列车，它悬浮在由列车下面路基中的电磁铁所产生的磁场上。轨道旁一组单独的制导磁铁用于控制列车相对于轨道的横向位置。因此，磁悬浮列车使用电磁力完成3种不同的任务：悬浮、导向和驱动列车。

3. 齿轮电机

普通工业电机一般不适合作为低速应用的直接驱动。而且，让中、低功率的电机工作于低速状态是一种浪费。齿轮电机能用于这些应用。这种装置由高速电机和齿轮减速器组成，它们组装成一个整体。齿轮的硬齿能承受巨大的压力，可确保该部件使用寿命长。

齿轮电机在农业、工厂等领域中被广泛地用于塔吊、升降机、建筑机械这样的一些独立机械上。

4. 制动电机

机械制动器经常与电机联合使用，以取代电动制动电路，或都使用电动制动电路。这些部件由电机和制动器构成，并组装成一个完整的部件。制动器可能用来制动电机及其负载，或者只用来提供保持转矩，注意到这一点很重要。只用于保持的制动器如果用于使负载停转，它很快就会损坏。一般情况是制动器只使用保持功能，特别是对无刷伺服电机而言。

制动电机可以设计有故障保护装置。如果电源中断，那么制动器自动起作用。

5. 转矩电机

转矩电机由三相鼠笼式感应电机的基本设计发展而来。它们不是为得到一定的输出而设计的，而是为了得到最大转矩，它们可以在静止状态和/或低速运行状态(当用固定频率的电源供电时)提供最大转矩。

6. 步进电机

一种特殊的直流电机，称为步进电机，是永磁或变磁阻直流电机，它有如下性能特点：它能向两个方面转动，以精确的角度增量运动，在零转速时有保持转矩，能用数字电路控制。将数字脉冲加到电气驱动电路上，它会以准确的角度增量运动，称为步进。用脉冲的个数和速度控制机轴的位置和速度。在通常情况下生产每转一周需要 12、24、72、144、180 和 200 步的步进电机，每步可使转轴产生 30°、15°、5°、2.5°、2° 和 1.8° 的角度增量。

步进电机要么是双极性电机，需要两个电源或可交换极性电源，要么是单极性电机，只需要一个电源。它们使用直流电源供电，并需要数字电路产生使电机转动的线圈激励序列。步进电机产生的功率一般低于 735W，所以只能用于低功率位置控制应用中。

7. 伺服电机

伺服电机可以是交流或直流电机。早期的伺服电机一般是直流电机，因为多年来控制大电流的唯一方式是使用晶闸管。随着晶体管能够控制大电流和对大电流进行高频开关，交流伺服电机用得就更多了。早期的伺服电机专门设计用于伺服放大器。现在这种电机是为可能使用伺服放大器或变频控制器的应用设计的，也就是说，电机可用于一个应用的伺服系统中，或者用于另一个应用的变频驱动中。有些公司也将未使用步进电机的闭环系统称为伺服系统，所以可以将与速度控制器连接的简单交流感应电机称为伺服电机。

第八单元　自　动　控　制

Passage A

自动控制系统简介

自动控制在工程和科学的发展中起着极其重要的作用。除了在宇宙飞船、导弹制导和飞机驾驶系统等方面极为重要外，自动控制已经成为现代生产及工业过程中重要而不可缺少的组成部分。例如，在过程工业中压力、温度、湿度、黏度和流量的控制，制造业中零部件的加工、处理、装配这些工业操作以及其他许多行业中，自动控制都是不可或缺的。

自动控制系统是一个预先设定的闭环控制系统，它有两个相关的过程变量：被控量和控制量。被控量是需要保持在指定值或在指定范围内的过程变量。例如，在水池水位控制系统中，储水池的水位是被控量。控制量受控制系统控制，使被控量能保持在指定值或指定范围内的过程变量。在前例中，水注入池中的速度便是控制量。

1. 自动控制系统的功能

在任何自动控制系统中都有 4 个基本功能：测量、比较、计算、修正。在上述例子的水池水位控制系统中，水位变送器用来测量水池中的水位，并将表示水位高低的信号传递给水位控制装置，在那里控制器将该信号与所指定的信号进行比较，然后水位控制装置计算出供水阀要打开多少能减小实际水位和指定水位之间的差距。

2. 自动控制的基本组成

执行自动控制系统的功能需要有 3 种基本元件：测量元件、误差检测元件和末端控制元件。这些元件之间的联系以及它们所执行的功能如图 8.1 所示。测量元件通过传送和计算被控量，执行测量的功能。误差检测元件先将被控量的值与期待值进行比较，如果实际值和期待值间有偏差便给出一个误差信号。末端控制元件通过纠正系统的控制量对所给的误差信号做出响应。

3. 反馈控制

反馈控制是当扰动出现时尽量减小系统输出量与参考输入量(或任意变化的期望状态)之间偏差的一种操作，并且其工作基于这种偏差。

图 8.2 所示的是反馈控制系统的基本组成。

反馈元件用来确定反馈信号和被控输出之间的关系。参考点是一个外部信号，将其加到控制系统的相加点，使控制设备产生指定动作。这个信号反映了被控量的期待值，也称为"设定值"。被控输出量是受控设备的数值或状态，它代表被控量。反馈信号传送到相加点并且在此与输入的参考信号进行代数相加以得到控制信号。控制信号表示控制环的控制动作，其值等于参考输入信号和反馈信号的代数和。该信号也称为"误差信号"。控制量是对其进行控制，使设备输出(被控量)保持期待值的过程变量。而扰动量是系统不需要的输入信号，它将扰乱设备的控制输出值。

4. 反馈控制系统

反馈控制系统是通过比较输出与参考输入之间的偏差，并以此作为控制手段，来保持它们之间的既定关系的系统。

Passage B

自动控制的应用

虽然自动控制的范围几乎没有限制，但这里将只讨论现代工业中很常见的例子。

1) 伺服系统

伺服系统在自动控制中很常见。伺服系统，或简称为"伺服"，是被控变量为机械位置或运动的闭环控制系统。设计伺服系统时要使输出对输出命令的变化做出快速、精确的反应，这样可以将伺服机构看成一个流装置。

伺服系统的另一种形式通常称为速率或速度伺服系统，控制输出的变化率或速度。

2) 过程控制

过程控制是用于生产过程中的变量控制的一个术语。化工厂、炼油厂、食品加工厂、鼓风炉和钢厂是自动控制应用于生产过程的例子。过程控制与使变量，如温度、压力、流量、液位、黏度、密度和成分，保持在期待值有关。

当前过程控制中的大量工作都涉及扩展数字计算机的应用，以提供对过程变量的直接数字控制。在直接数字控制中，计算机直接根据设定值和过程变量的测量值计算控制变量的值。计算机的决策应用于过程中的数字执行机构上。由于计算机重复了模拟控制器的动作，所以这些常规控制器便不再需要了。

3) 发电

电力行业主要与能源转换与分配有关。发电量可能超过几百兆瓦的大型现代发电厂需要复杂的控制系统来处理许多变量之间的相互关系，提供最佳电力生产(状态)。发电控制有 100 个受控于计算机的控制变量。

自动控制还延伸应用到电力分配中。电力系统通常由若干发电厂组成。当负载需求波动时，需要控制电力生产和传输，以使系统运行费用达到最低。另外，多数大型电力系统相互连接，要控制系统之间的电力流动。

4) 数字控制

有许多生产操作必须在重复的基础上高精度进行，如镗、钻、铣、焊。数字控制是使用重定位指令，称为程序，去控制这种操作序列的系统。完成指定操作的指令被编码，并存储在穿孔纸带、磁带或者穿孔卡片这样的媒体上。这些指令一般以数字形式存储，所以称之为数字控制。指令确定要使用什么刀具，采用何种方式(比如切削速度)，刀具运动路径(位置、方向、速度等)。

5) 运输

为了给现代城市地区提供大规模运输系统，需要大型、复杂的控制系统。现在很多自动运输系统都有每隔几分钟一班的高速列车。自动控制对于保持连续不断的列车流是必需的，并提供舒适的加速和到站刹车性能。

飞机飞行控制是运输领域中的另一个重要应用。由于系统参数范围大及控制之间相互作用，已经证明这是最复杂的一个控制应用。实际上飞机控制系统经常是有适应能力的，也就是说，操作应自适应于周围环境。例如，由于飞机的行为在低海拔和高海拔时可能有根本的不同，所以必须将控制系统修改为海拔高度的函数。

船舶驾驶和滚动稳定性控制与飞行控制相似，但通常需要高得多的功率，并需要较低速的响应。

Reading

PID 控制器简介

比例-积分-微分(PID)控制算法已经成功应用了 50 多年。容易理解，它是一种健壮的算法，不管过程设备的动态特性如何变化，都能提供优秀的控制性能。

PID 控制算法包含 3 个独立的参数，因此有时也称之为三项控制：比例、积分和微商值，用 P、I、D 表示。比例值确定对当前偏差的作用，积分值确定基于最近误差和的作用，微商值确定基于偏差变化率的作用。这 3 种作用的加权和用于通过控制元素来调整过程，比如控制阀的位置或者加热元件的供电。因此，这些值可以从时间的角度解释：比例值取决于当前偏差，积分值取决于以前偏差的累积，微商值是基于当前变化率对未来偏差的预测。

PID 控制器是一个通用控制环反馈装置(控制器)，广泛地应用于工业控制系统里，PID 是最常用的反馈控制器。在对基本过程缺乏了解的情况下，PID 控制器是最好的控制器。

有些应用可能只需要使用一种或两种方式提供适当的系统控制，这时将 PID 控制器称为 PI、PD、P 或 I 控制器。PI 控制器是特别常见的，因为微商作用对测量噪声非常敏感，并且没有积分值，会由于控制作用使系统达不到其目标值。

关于控制回路的一个大家熟悉的例子是当调整热、冷水龙头阀门，使水龙头出水保持在所需温度时采取的行动。这里一般涉及两个过程流的混合：热水和冷水。人可以通过摸一下水来感知或测量水的温度。根据这一反馈，他们执行控制动作——调节热水和冷水阀门，直到过程温度稳定在所需值上。

检测水温与测量过程值或过程变量值类似。需要的温度值称为设定点。过程的输入(水阀门位置)称为控制变量。测量温度与设定值之间的差称为误差，它定量表示水是太热或是太冷，以及热多少或冷多少。

测得温度并算出误差后，控制器决定何时改变水龙头位置及改变多少。当控制器刚打开阀门时，如果想要温水，它们会将热水阀门稍微打开一点；如果需要很热的水，会将热水阀门全加开。这是简单比例控制的例子。如果热水不能很快到位，控制器会试图通过将热水阀门随时间推移开得越来越大来加速这一过程。这是积分控制的例子。只用比例和积分控制方式，在有些系统中水温会在热和冷之间振荡。

为了实现逐步收敛到期望值，可能需要使用控制器抑制预计要出现的振荡。因此，为了弥补这一影响，控制器可能会选择缓和它们的调整，这可以看做是微分控制方法。

PID 控制器经历了许多技术上的改变，从力学和气动技术，经过电子管、三极管和集成电路，到微处理器。微处理器对 PID 控制器产生了巨大的影响。实际上现在所有的 PID 控制器都是以微处理器为基础的。这就为有可能提供额外功能，如自动调整、增益设定及连续适应。

第九单元　通信系统

Passage A

通信系统

今天，通信在人们的生活中几乎无处不在：人们手中的电话，家中的收音机、电视机，办公室和家用的连接到因特网上的计算机和报纸，这些都能提供来自全球各地的即时信息。

从最基本的意义上来讲，通信本身包含了从一点到另一点的一系列过程的传输，如下所述。

(1) 信息源的产生：语音、音乐、图像或计算机数据。

(2) 用某个精确的物理量描述信源信号，可用系列符号表示，如电的、声的或视频的。

(3) 将这些物理量符号以适合于物理媒介传输的形式进行编码。

(4) 编码的物理量传输到要求的目的地。

(5) 原始信号的解码与还原。

(6) 原始信号的再生,伴有一定的质量上的衰减,这种衰减是由系统的一些缺陷造成的。

一般的通信系统包括下列组成部分(如图 9.1 所示)。

(1) 信源。信源用来产生消息,可以是写的或说的文字,或是某种形式的数据。

(2) 发信机。发信机把消息转变为信号,信号形式要适合在通信信道中传送。

(3) 通信信道。通信信道是用于从发信机传送信号到接收机的媒质。信道可以是无线电或者是直接的有线连接。

(4) 接收机。接收机可以看做是与发信机相反的设备。它把接收到的信号转变成消息,并把消息传给终端,这个终端可以是一台扬声器、电传打字机或一个计算机数据库。

所有通信信道的一个不好的特征是在信号上都叠加了噪声。这种人们不希望存在的噪声会引起电话中的声音失真,或者电报报文或数据中的差错。

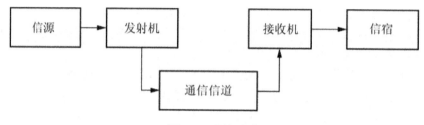

图 9.1　通信系统

通信系统的目的是通过通信信道传输包含信息的信号。这种包含信息的信号称为基带信号。基带指信源原始信号的频带。为了恰当地使用通信信道传输,需要把基带频率成分迁移到其他的频率范围内,在传输完成后相应地将基带频率成分再迁移回来。例如,一个无线电系统的基带信号频率通常在语音频率范围,30kHz 及以上。为使系统有效地工作需要采用一种频带迁移方法。一种方法是采用调制技术,用调制波来改变载波的某个参数。当谈及连续载波调制时,常用的载波形式是正弦波。基带信号称为调制波形。调制在通信系统的发射端完成。在系统的接收端恢复出需要的原始基带信号,这一过程称为解调,是与调制相反的过程。

Passage B

数字通信技术

在一些应用中要传送的信息本身就是数字的,如英文文字、计算机数据等。这种信源称为离散(数字)信源。

在数字通信系统中,发送端和接收端的功能必须扩展,在发送端包含消息信号的离散化功能,在接收端包含信号综合或信号插补功能。附加功能包括去除冗余和为信道编解码。

图 9.2 所示为数字通信系统的功能框图和基本单元。信源的输出可以是模拟信号如音频、视频信号,也可以是数字信号,如计算机输出,时间上是离散的,输出有限个字符。在数字传输系统中,通常信源将消息转变为二进位的序列。理想的是用尽可能少的二进制

位来表示信源输出。换句话说，信源的输出或多或少含有冗余，要寻求一种有效的表示方法。将模拟或者数字信源有效地转换为二进位序列的过程称为信源编码或者数据压缩。

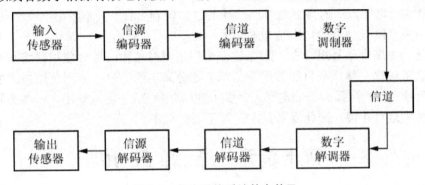

图 9.2 数字通信系统基本单元

由信源编码器输出的表示信息的二进位序列被输入到信道编码器。信道编码器的作用是以一种可控的方式，在二进制的信息序列中引入一些冗余，这些冗余在接收机中用来克服传输中遇到的噪声和干扰。由信道编码器输出的二进制序列被输入到数字调制器。数字调制器作为与通信信道的接口。因为实际中的所有通信信道都可以传输电信号(波形)，数字调制器的主要用途是把二进制信息序列映射成信号波形。

在数字通信系统的接收端，由数字解调器处理不可靠信道传输的波形，把每个波形转变为代表被传输数据估计值的单一数字。利用传输数据中的冗余，解码器尝试把损耗的位置填补起来。当传输的信息没有冗余时，解码器必须判定给定时间间隔内的波形代表哪个符号。另一方面，当传输的信息含有离散信道编码器产生的冗余时，解调器的输出要输入到信道解码器中来重构原始信息序列。

最后一步，当需要产生模拟输出时，源解码器结合源编码方法，接收信道解码器的输出，来重构原始信号。由于存在信道解码差错和可能的失真，源解码器的输出信号是原始信号的近似值。原始信号和这个重构信号的差异或者差异的函数作为衡量数字通信系统失真的度量标准。

Reading

模 拟 通 信

任何一个通信系统的目标都是将信息(语音、视频、数据)通过媒介或信道从信源端发送到接收机。传输的信道可以是有线通信(电话、有线电视)中的电线或者是无线通信(商用收音机和电视，无线电话)中的自由空间。发射机发射辐射功率通过天线向自由空间中广播信源信息。接收端通过天线接收这些功率并输入到接收机中。由于信息信号占有相似的频带(基频)，只有借助时域或频域复用技术才能通过一条信道传输这些信号。

幅度调制和频率调制是两种实现频域复用的模拟技术，在商业无线电广播系统中被广泛应用，分别是调幅广播和调频广播。可以使用调制技术将基带信号迁移到频谱中不同的高频位置。频谱迁移中使用的另一信号称为载波信号。调制的另一优点是，借助载波将低频基带信号转变到适合于在自由空间中传输的高频信号。

最通用的调制方法是改变 $A \cdot \cos(\omega t + \theta)$ 的载波，其中 θ 是任意的常数，A 为波形峰值振幅，ω 是载波频率。调制方法是使振幅 A 成为信息信号 $f(t)$ 的函数或者增加一个基于 $f(t)$ 的余弦波相位。这些方法的特点是对连续载波进行调制。由于载波频率远高于基波 $f(t)$ 的最大频率，所以连续波调制的输出是带通信号。

复用是指将多个信号组合在一起通过一个信道同时传输。频分复用是将每个信号调制到不同的载波频率，然后在目的端用一组滤波器分离出原信号。应用复用技术的有遥感勘测数据、调频立体声广播和长途电话。至少 1800 路语音信号可以复用在一条直径小于 1cm 的同轴电缆上进行传输，因此复用技术提高了通信效率。

第十单元　通信应用

Passage A

收音机电路

现代收音机的框图如图 10.1 所示。收音机的输入信号是振幅调制无线电波。基本电路包括天线、调谐器、混频器、本地振荡器、中频放大器、音频检波器、音频放大器、扬声器和电源。

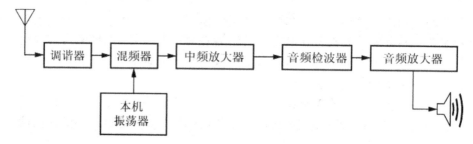

图 10.1　收音机的框图

辐射能量的任何天线系统都能够吸收传输的无线电波能量。由于通过接收天线波导的每个电波具有各自的电压，这样接收设备要具备将所需要的信号从其他干扰信号中分离出来的能力。根据发射站的不同频率使用谐振电路完成信号的分离，谐振电路可以区别特定的频率。需要指出通过天线电路与某一特定频率谐振，可以从该频率信号吸取能量。这样可以在一定程度上分离出信号。进一步可以选择在接收端调整本地调谐电路抑制所有的其他加性信号。区分不同的频率成分称为选择性，调整电路到谐振频率的过程称为调谐。

尽管可以接收到数千千米之外无线电信号，但是要获得满意的接收效果还要将天线接收的信号放大。在检测之前对射频电流进行放大的方法称为射频放大，在检测之后对整形电流进行放大的方法称为音频放大。接收微弱信号时采用信号放大方法可以获得较满意的音频响应。

从射频信号中重现被传输的原始信号的过程称为检波或解调。如果有用信号的发射是通过改变信号的振幅(即调幅)完成的，则检波就是通过对射频电流进行整流完成的。整流电流随着原始调制信号而变化，从而重现原始有用信号，这样，已调波被整流而产生的电流可以看成随原始信号幅度变化的平均值电流。

接收机电路由多级组成。每级由晶体管与提供工作电压、电流和信号电压、电流的元件相连组成，每级都有输入回路，让信号进入；也都有输出回路，让信号(通常是放大后的信号)输出。当一级接一级时，第一级的输出回路将信号馈送给第二级，信号经过主机放大，直到足以驱动扬声器发声。

Passage B

数 字 电 视

在过去的岁月里，数字技术使人们生存的世界发生了巨大的变化。它改变了人们的通信方式、商业贸易方式以及学习的方式。数字电视通常包含所有的数字电视广播和格式，以及使用数字信号传递数据。它是彩色电视问世以来电视技术的重大发展。数字电视可以提供影院质量的图像和声音，宽屏幕，更好的色彩再现，多个视频节目和正在开发的新服务。数字电视有两种：标准清晰度电视和高清晰度电视。这两种数字电视的画面都比模拟电视更清晰。高清电视呈现特级的数字视觉体验，其清晰度是模拟电视的 4.5 倍。标清电视的图像质量低于高清电视，但比目前的模拟电视好得多。

1. 标清电视

先进电视制式委员会批准了总计 12 种格式的标准清晰度电视，这样做是为了使从计算机到数字广播领域中各种广泛的素材易于在已有的格式之间转换。由 3 种分辨率和 4 种帧频进行组合得到这 12 种格式。这三种分辨率分别是屏幕长宽比为 4:3 的 704×480 分辨率，长宽比为 16:9 的 704×480 分辨率，和正方形像素长宽比为 4:3 的 640×480 分辨率。4 种帧频为隔行扫描的 60 次每秒，逐行扫描的 60、30、24 帧每秒。

2. 高清电视

普遍认为，高清电视是指具有高质量 NTSC 图像、分辨率大于 640×480 像素的 6 种广播格式。这 6 种格式又分为两组：一组是 1920×1080 像素，刷新频率为隔行扫描 60 帧每秒，逐行扫描 60、30、24 帧每秒；另一组是 1280×720 像素，刷新频率为逐行扫描 60、30、24 帧每秒。所有的高清电视格式都使用宽屏的 16:9 长宽比。24 帧每秒的格式适于再现运动内容的图像。

数字电视的优点如下。

1) 高效利用带宽

目前，使用模拟技术传送一路电视节目需要占用整个频道，而采用视频压缩技术，数字电视能够将多个电视节目在调制到同一频道上之前先进行数字化融合，这样可以在很大程度上提高频谱利用率，从而在相同的带宽内提供更多的节目供用户选择。

2) 图像和声音质量更好

在模拟环境中，电视信号会受到来自其他信号源的干扰，比如电力线、建筑物的反射等，因此接收质量要低于理想情况。由于数字信号比模拟信号稳定，用户能接收到更优质的声音和图像。此外，数字电视还能支持高清晰度电视，而高清电视可以传送影院效果的图像及 CD 质量的声音。

3) 创新的服务

由于 DTV 可以传送电视节目，也可以传送数据，观众不仅能接收电视节目，还能通过它享受各种交互式、多媒体服务。电视上的电子商务将会成为工业探究的许多新的商业契机之一。

Reading

移 动 通 信

移动电话是发展最迅速、需求最高的电信应用之一。现今，它在全球所有新签署的电话用户协议中占有很大的份额，而且还在以惊人的速度持续增长。从长远角度来看，利用数字技术的蜂窝无线电将成为几乎每一个人的全球通信方式。

蜂窝移动电话系统由 3 个主要部分构成：移动业务交换中心、无线基站以其移动台，如图 10.2 所示。

移动业务交换中心构成了无线电系统与公共电话交换网之间的界面。呼入和呼出移动用户均由 CMTS 中的 MSC 来完成切换。为了获得给定地域的无线覆盖范围，通常需要一个(非常例外的情况)、百个甚至更多的基站，这一地域称为蜂窝移动电话的一个服务区。

基站中含有信道单元。每一个信道单元都配有无线电发射机、无线电接收机及控制单元。控制单元用于与交换中心进行数据通信以及在无线链路上与移动台进行数据信号的发送。大多数信道单元是音频信道单元。这种音频信道单元用于一次传送一个呼叫。一些基站中的音频信道单元的数量可能很少，而其他基站中的数目却可以达到上百个或是更多，这取决于基站所需要处理的同步呼叫的多少。每个基站都通过数字的和模拟的连接线连接到移动交换中心，以完成语音或数据通信。

便于携带的、可以车载或袖珍电话的移动台是一个用户端设备，它由无线电发射机及接收机、用于与基站发送数据信号的逻辑单元以及配有拨号键盘和话筒的电话等组成。当移动用户与普通固话用户之间建立呼叫之后，语音就会经无线通道在移动台和靠近移动台的基站音频信道单元间进行传输。接下来，利用专用于这种音频线路单元的音频线来连接。最后，语音信号在 MSC 中可建立与 PSTN 网中的普通固话用户的切换，甚至对于任意两个移动用户语音通路也可以在 MSC 中建立。

GSM 作为第二代数字通信标准发展迅速，GSM 原指特殊移动组，现在在世界范围内指全球通。

第三种移动接入技术是码分多址。码分多址信号产生在一个拓展的频带上，称为宽带或扩频通信。由香农定理可知，扩展信号频带的主要优点是信道容量可以保持在一个低功率水平。因此，码分多址技术支持低功率操作。在码分多址中，$1.23MH_2$ 带宽可以容纳一个信道。根据研究，码分多址系统的容量是时分复用系统的十倍。

第十一单元　数据通信

Passage A

数　据　通　信

　　数据信息以数字信号的形式在各种电话信道上传输，数据信号可以通过导线从一根电线杆传送到另一根电线杆；可经由地下电缆传送；通过微波设备从一个山头传送到另一个山头；可以穿过海底电缆，通过通信卫星，从一个大陆(洲)传到另一个大陆(洲)。为了把数字化及其信号变换为适合在上述设备中传输的信号形式，需要使用某种类型的数据转换设备。

　　数据通信是把数字信息从外围设备传输到信号源的。外围设备一般被认为是位于计算机机壳外单独供电的电路或者是其他的数字信号源。通常，最大可允许的传输率与信号功率成正比，与信道噪声成反比。任何通信系统的目标就是以最低功率损耗，最小噪声的状态下，获得最高传输率。

　　在数字通信信道中，信号是以单独的数据位的形式存在的，这些数据位被压缩成多位信息单元。每个字节由 8 个比特(位)组成，它们可以看成是在数字通信信道中传送的一个信息单元。收集到的字节能自身构成一个帧或其他高级的信息单元。这样的多级压缩技术有助于对复杂数据通信网络中心进行处理。

　　任何通信信道都有一个与它有关的方向。

　　信号源是一个发射机，信宿就是一个接收机。信号传输方向不变的信道被称为单工信道。无线电台就是单工信道，因为其总是把信号发射给听众，而不会从听众那里发射回来。

　　半双工信道是一种方向可以改变的单向物理信道。消息在半双工信道中能双向传送，但不能同时双向传送。使用对讲机时，一方讲话，另一方接听；停一下后，再由另一方讲话，先前一方接听。

　　全双工信道允许双方同时传送消息，它由两个单工信道组成，即连接在相同点之间的前向信道和反向信道。如果只对前向信道的信息流量进行控制，那么反向信道的传输速率就要低一些。电话就是最好的例子。

　　大多数数字消息都不仅仅是几个数据位。因为同时传送所有的长消息既不经济也不实用，所以消息被分成更小的部分，然后传送出去。串行位传送是一次传送一位数据。每一位都代表消息的一部分。然后每个单独的位在信宿再重新组合成消息。一般来讲，一个信道一次只能通过一位(图 11.1)。因此如果数据通信中只有一个信道，就必须是串行位传送。串行位传送通常简称为串行通信，许多外围设备都选择这种通信方式。串行字节传输是在 8 个并行信道中一次传送 8 位数据(图 11.2)。尽管粗略看起来字节传送要比位传送快 8 倍，但它需要 8 个信道，因此费用也是位传送的 8 倍。当传输距离很短时，要想得到高传输率，使用并行信道是可行的，而且也经济。举例来说，在微处理器和存储芯片间的数据传送采用 16 位数据总线，这就是说要有 16 个并行信道。另一方面，当通信系统是一个通过调制解调器连接的分时操作系统时，因为只有一个信道，那就必须经串位传送了。

Passage B

光 纤 传 输

今天，人们使用光纤系统承载数字化的视频、语音和数据是很普遍的。在商用和工业领域，光纤已成为地面传输标准。在军事和防御领域，快速传递大量信息是大范围更新换代光纤计划的原动力。

光纤通信技术的应用，自 1977 年光纤系统首次商用安装以来迅速增多，电话公司很早就开始用光纤链路取代旧的铜线系统。今天的许多电话公司在他们的系统中全面使用光纤作为干线结构和进行城市电话系统之间的长距离连接。有线电视公司也开始集成光纤到他们的有线系统中。连接中心交换局的长途线路已经被光缆所取代。近年来，作为一种通信信号传输的适当手段，光纤稳步替代铜线是显而易见的，这些光缆在本地电话系统之间跨越很长的距离并为许多网络系统提供干线连接。其他系统用户包括有线电视服务，大学校园、办公楼、工业工厂和电气公司。

光纤系统类似于由光纤替代的铜线系统。两者之间的区别是，光纤使用光脉冲沿光线路传输信息，以替代使用电子脉冲沿电缆传送信息。在系统的一端是一个发射机，是信息到光纤线路的起始点。发射机接收的电子脉冲编码信息来自铜线。然后将信息处理并转换成等效的编码光脉冲。使用发光二极管(LED)或注射式激光二极管产生光脉冲，同时采用透镜，将光脉冲集中到光纤介质，使光脉冲沿线路在光纤介质中传输。

光纤是一种采用玻璃作为波导，以光的形式将信息从一端传输到另一端的技术，今天的低损耗玻璃光纤相对于早期发展的传输介质，几乎不受带宽限制并具有独一无二的优势，点到点的光纤传输系统由 3 个基本部分构成：产生光信号的光发送机、携带光信号的光缆和接收光信号的光接收机，如图 11.3 所示。

光发射机：光发射机用于将电模拟信号或数字信号转换为相应的光信号，光信号源既可以是光发射二极管，也可以是固态激光二极管。光传输最常采用的工作波长是 850nm、1300nm 或 1550nm。

光缆(图 11.4)：光缆由一条或多条光纤构成，对光信号起到波导的作用。光缆在结构上类似于电缆，但在光缆内部提供有特殊的保护层。系统需要在数千千米的距离上传输，就必须用电缆接头将两条或多条光缆连接在一起。

光接收机：光接收机用于将光信号转换回原始信号。光信号检测器既可以是 PIN 型光电二极管，也可以是雪崩光电二极管。光接收机的"基本目的"是检测接收到的入射光并将其转换成含有信息的电信号，该信息在发送端被施加在光波上面，然后将准备好的电信息输入到通信电子设备，如计算机、电话或电视中。

Reading

卫 星 通 信

卫星接入是一种成熟的技术，最近的技术发展又带给它新的生命。卫星通信逐渐成为日常生活的一部分。打一个国际电话就像给住在同一街区的朋友打本地电话一样简单。卫星电视节目每天晚上都将全世界的画面和声音带进人们的家中。

卫星系统基本上由一个空中卫星与空中卫星链接的众多卫星地面站组成，如图 11.5 所示。 由用户生成基带信号，基带信号通过地面网传送到地面站，地面网可以是电话交换局或是到地面站的专用链路。在地面站基带信号经过处理后由已调制的射频载波信号传送到卫星上，卫星可以看成是一个大的空间中继站，它以上行频率(地对空)接收从网中所有地面站传送来的已调波信号，并加以放大，未避免干扰再以下行频率(空对地)重新发送回地面站。接收地面站将已调波信号加以处理后还原出基带信号，并将其通过地面网送到用户端。

简单地讲，在一个与地面相对静止的轨道位置上的卫星对地球的一部分地区表现为固定的，在赤道上空 22300 千米的高度上，卫星与地球以同样的角速度运行，即它的运转与地球自转是同步的。尽管卫星是以很高的速度运行的，对于一个地球上的观察者而言，它总是停留在天空中的同一个位置上。一个位于与地面相对静止的轨道上的卫星的主要作用在于它可以一天 24 小时与它覆盖的地面通信。

大多数商业通信卫星上行线路和下行线路都使用 500MHz 带宽。最广泛使用的频段为 6/4GHz，其上行频率为 5.725～7.075GHz，下行频率为 3.4～4.8GHz。6/4GHz 频段对同步卫星来说正变得越来越拥挤，因为它也被地面微波链路的公共载波使用。14/12GHz 频段和 30/20GHz 频段也被使用。14/12GHz 频段还不拥挤，未来将被广泛使用。但该频段存在一个问题，即雨天对信号的衰减较 6/4GHz 频段大得多。30/20GHz 频段已经留出供商用卫星通信使用，但 30/20GHz 频段的设备仍在实验阶段，并且价格昂贵。

第十二单元　计算机网络

Passage A

计算机网络

由于多种原因，分布于不同地区的计算机之间需要进行通信，例如，在全国范围内，位于不同地区的计算机使用公共通信服务设施来交换电子信息(邮件)及从一台计算机传递文件信息到另一台。类似地，在局域范围内，比如说在单独的大楼或建筑内，分散的计算机工作站可以利用局域网共享昂贵的资源，如打印机、复印机、磁盘、磁带等，这些都可由计算机管理。很显然，随着计算机通信范围的扩大，计算机对计算机的通信将迅速增加，而且最终将主导整个计算机分散系统领域。通信网是由通信线路互相连接在一起而形成的一系列网点，位于网点上的是计算机、转接设备和用户终端。

一般来讲，人们今天所说的计算机网络，可以说是从 20 世纪 60 年代末 70 年代初 ARPANET 的产生开始的。起初 ARPANET 的设计就具有确切的网络结构，并提出了一个关键的概念：协议分层。现在关于网络的大部分知识都是 ARPANET 工程的直接结果。

国际标准化组织 ISO 在 20 世纪 70 年代后期提出了一个参考模型，该模型为协调标准的开发提供了一个公共依据，并且使得现有的和发展中的标准工作相互协调，其最终目标是使支持这些可用标准的任何计算机能与支持相同标准的其他计算机在一个应用程序上随意通信，而不管使用何种计算机，这一模型称为 ISO 开放系统互连参考模型(如图 12.1 所示)。需要强调的是，该模型与计算机通信网络专用程序无关。然而，为支持更大范围的应用，它只与需要提供可靠的、数据透明的通信业务的通信软件结构有关，而与任何厂家的设备和规范无关。

网络是由通信线路互相连接在一起的一系列网点，位于网点上的是计算机、转接设备与/或用户终端。一个典型的网络包括以下部件：主计算机、网点、终端控制器和终端。

网络的两种基本类型是局域网和广域网。局域网是一个小范围内，如一个房间、一座大楼，或一组相距较近的建筑物内的两台或多台计算机直接连接起来构成的。广域网是在地理位置上分散的两台或多台计算机通过诸如电话系统或微波中继等通信设施连接在一起构成的。

网络的优点是它能够在相距很远的人们之间快速便捷地传递信息；人们可以在网络上共享软硬件资源；由于具有可选资源，计算机网络的可靠性也很高。

Passage B

<h1 style="text-align:center">综合业务数字网</h1>

设想一个网路，它可以将同步的声音及数据应用带入家庭，一台中央计算机可控制室内的电话铃声、温度、照明和家用电器的操作。该计算机可以由用户通过网络依次摇控。其他服务还包括呼叫转移、呼叫等待及特定电话铃声信号，所有这些均可根据呼叫方的电话号码由用户动态地确定。双方交互电视、方便的数据存取及视频服务均可以实现。银行业、保险和公共事业公司可以设计利用这一网络为待在家中的客户提供更有效的服务的应用。

虽然这些情节听起来可能很理想化，很遥远，但用 ISDN 来实现是切实可行的。ISDN 代表综合业务数字网，是近 10 年来使用的数字电话连接系统。该系统使用端到端的数字连接在全世界范围同时进行数据传输(图 12.2)。在 ISDN 中，语音和数据都在占 64Kbps 的载波信道(又称为 B 信道)中传输。数据信道(又称为 D 信道)以 16Kbps 或 64Kbps 的速率处理信令。

有两种基本的 ISDN 服务类型：基本速率接口(BRI)和主速率接口(PRI)。BRI 包括两个 64Kbps 的 B 信道和一个 16Kbps 的 D 信道，一共是 144Kbps，这主要是为了满足大多数个人用户需求的基本业务。

PRI 是为了满足用户更大容量的需求而设计的，典型的信道结构是 23 个 B 信道加一个 64Kbps 的 D 信道，一共是 1536Kbps。也可以以一个 64Kbps 的 D 信道支持多个 PRI 线路。

要使用 BRI 业务，就必须预定 ISDN 电话线。用户还需要与电话公司交换机及其他 ISDN 设备通信的专用设备。这些设备包括 ISDN 终端适配器(有时也叫做 ISDN 调制解调器)和 ISDN 路由器。

最早的电话网络是由把用户用电话线连接起来的纯模拟系统组成的。这种系统效率低，噪声大，并且容易崩溃，且不利于实现长距离连接。从 20 世纪 60 年代开始电话系统的内部连接慢慢地向基于分组的数字交换系统转变。如今，美国电话网络中的所有语音交换都已经数字化了，但是最后的连接——从电话局端到用户电话设备大部分仍然是模拟线路。

Reading

ATM 异步传输模式

异步传输模式是国际电信联盟-电信标准部门为信元中继创建的标准。信元中继中的信息可以是多种业务类型的，如语音、视频或数据，它们都将转换成一个个小的固定大小的信元。ATM 网络是面向连接的。

ATM 是在 ITU-T 的宽带综合业务数字网(B-ISDN)标准的基础上发展起来的。ATM 是一种信元交换多路复用技术，它综合了电路交换(保证容量和固定传输时延)和分组交换(间断传输的灵活和高效)的优点。它能提供每秒几兆比特到每秒几吉比特的可变带宽。由于异步传输的特点，ATM 比同步技术如时分多路复用(TDM)更高效。

在 TDM 中，每个用户被分配一个时隙，别人不能在该时隙发送信息，如果某处有许多信息要发送，它只能等到它自己的时隙到来时再发，即使别的时隙空闲时也不能使用。然而，若某处在它的时隙到来时没有信息需要发送，则该时隙为空，白白地浪费了。而 ATM 是异步的，在每个信元头都包含传输源的信息标识，所有的时隙都可以随意使用。

异步传输模式在源节点和目的节点间构造虚信道和虚通道，根据需求分配带宽。这些信道是临时的虚连接，或无用户使用的交换虚连接，而不是专用的物理连接。

ATM 提供两种连接类型：点对点和点对多点。点对点连接的两个 ATM 终端系统可以是单向通信，也可以是双向通信。点对多点方式连接一个单一源终端系统(称为根结点)和多个目的终端系统(称为叶结点)，这种连接只能是单向通信。根结点可以给叶结点发送信息，但叶结点不能给根结点发送信息，即不能在一个连接中相互通信。

参 考 文 献

[1] 高艳萍. 电子信息专业英语[M]. 北京：中国电力出版社，2007.

[2] 冯新宇. 电子技术专业英语教程[M]. 北京：电子工业出版社，2009.

[3] 刘小芹，刘骋. 电子与通信技术专业英语[M]. 2 版. 北京：人民邮电出版社，2008.

[4] 江华圣. 电信技术专业英语[M]. 武汉：武汉大学出版社，2007.

[5] 丁宁. 电子信息技术专业英语[M]. 北京：机械工业出版社，2007.

[6] 任治刚. 电子信息工程专业英语教程[M]. 2 版. 北京：电子工业出版社，2008.

[7] 杨泽清. 电子信息专业英语[M]. 2 版. 北京：机械工业出版社，2009.

[8] 李霞. 电子与通信专业英语[M]. 北京：电子工业出版社，2005.

[9] 刘晓莉，苏雪，邓青. 机电一体化及数控专业英语[M]. 北京：人民邮电出版社，2008.

[10] 江华圣. 电工电子专业英语[M]. 北京：人民邮电出版社，2006.

[11] 綦战朝. 机电专业英语[M]. 北京：清华大学出版社，2007.

[12] 温丹丽. 电子信息类专业英语[M]. 北京：机械工业出版社，2009.

[13] 朱晓玲. 机电工程专业英语[M]. 北京：机械工业出版社，2007.

[14] 李久胜，马洪飞，陈洪钧，刘汉奎. 电气自动化专业英语[M]. 哈尔滨：哈尔滨工业大学出版社，2000.

[15] Theodore Wildi. Electrical Machines, Drives, and Power Systems(影印版)[M]. 北京：科学出版社，2002.

[16] Tony R. Kuphaldt. Lessons In Electric Circuits[J]. Semiconductors, 2007,3.

[17] Steven Holzner. Physics For Dummies[M]. Indiana: Wiley Publishing, Inc., 2006.

[18] Anant Agarwal, Jeffrey H. Lang. Agarwal and Lang Foundations of Analog and Digital Electronic Circuits[M]. Denise E. M. Penrose.2005.

[19] John Hindmarsh Alasdair Renfrew. Electrical Machines and Drive Systems[M]. 1997.

[20] A.E.Fitzgerald, Charles Kingsley, Stephen D. Umans. Electric Machinery[M]. Sixth Edition. Publisher: Mc-Graw-Hill Higher Education, 2002.

[21] Dino Zorbas. Electric Machines, Principles, Applications, and Control Schematics[M]. Publisher: West Publishing Company, 1989.

[22] Gray C. B.. Electrical machines and drive systems[M]. Publisher: Essex, England: Longman Scientific & Technical; New York: Wiley, 1989.

[23] Charles I Hubert. Electric Machines, Theory, Operation, Application, Adjustment and Control[M]. Publisher: Macmillan Publishing Company, 1991.

[24] http://www.ee.surrey.ac.uk/Projects/Labview/gatesfunc/index.html.

[25] http://www.automation.com/resources-tools.

[26] http://www.labvolt.com/products/automation-and-robotics/programmable-logic-controllers-plc.

[27] http://www.plcdev.com/plcs_versus_other_types_of_controls.

[28] http://www.mpoweruk.com/motorsspecial.htm.

[29] http://blog.csdn.net/llyy0107/archive/2009/06/05/4245454.aspx.

北京大学出版社高职高专机电系列教材

序号	书号	书名	编著者	定价	出版日期
1	978-7-301-10464-2	工程力学	余学进	18.00	2006.1
2	978-7-301-10371-9	液压传动与气动技术	曹建东	28.00	2006.1
3	978-7-301-11566-4	电路分析与仿真教程与实训	刘辉珞	20.00	2007.2
4	978-7-5038-4863-6	汽车专业英语	王欲进	26.00	2007.8
5	978-7-5038-4864-3	汽车底盘电控系统原理与维修	闵思鹏	30.00	2007.8
6	978-7-5038-4868-1	AutoCAD 机械绘图基础教程与实训	欧阳全会	28.00	2007.8
7	978-7-5038-4866-7	数控技术应用基础	宋建武	22.00	2007.8
8	978-7-5038-4937-4	数控机床	黄应勇	26.00	2007.8
9	978-7-301-13258-6	塑模设计与制造	晏志华	38.00	2007.8
10	978-7-301-12182-5	电工电子技术	李艳新	29.00	2007.8
11	978-7-301-12181-8	自动控制原理与应用	梁南丁	23.00	2007.8
12	978-7-301-12180-1	单片机开发应用技术	李国兴	21.00	2007.8
13	978-7-301-12173-3	模拟电子技术	张 琳	26.00	2007.8
14	978-7-301-09529-5	电路电工基础与实训	李春彪	31.00	2007.8
15	978-7-5038-4861-2	公差配合与测量技术	南秀蓉	23.00	2007.9
16	978-7-5038-4865-0	CAD/CAM 数控编程与实训(CAXA 版)	刘玉春	27.00	2007.9
17	978-7-5038-4862-9	工程力学	高 原	28.00	2007.9
18	978-7-5038-4869-8	设备状态监测与故障诊断技术	林英志	22.00	2007.9
19	978-7-301-12392-8	电工与电子技术基础	卢菊洪	28.00	2007.9
20	978-7-5038-4867-4	汽车发动机构造与维修	蔡兴旺	50.00(1CD)	2008.1
21	978-7-301-13260-9	机械制图	徐 萍	32.00	2008.1
22	978-7-301-13263-0	机械制图习题集	吴景淑	40.00	2008.1
23	978-7-301-13264-7	工程材料与成型工艺	杨红玉	35.00	2008.1
24	978-7-301-13262-3	实用数控编程与操作	钱东东	32.00	2008.1
25	978-7-301-13261-6	微机原理及接口技术(数控专业)	程 艳	32.00	2008.1
26	978-7-301-12386-7	高频电子线路	李福勤	20.00	2008.1
27	978-7-301-13383-5	机械专业英语图解教程	朱派龙	22.00	2008.3
28	978-7-301-12384-3	电路分析基础	徐 锋	22.00	2008.5
29	978-7-301-13572-3	模拟电子技术及应用	刁修睦	28.00	2008.6
30	978-7-301-13575-4	数字电子技术及应用	何首贤	28.00	2008.6
31	978-7-301-13574-7	机械制造基础	徐从清	32.00	2008.7
32	978-7-301-13657-7	汽车机械基础	邰 茜	40.00	2008.8
33	978-7-301-13655-3	工程制图	马立克	32.00	2008.8
34	978-7-301-13654-6	工程制图习题集	马立克	25.00	2008.8
35	978-7-301-13573-0	机械设计基础	朱凤芹	32.00	2008.8
36	978-7-301-13582-2	液压与气压传动	袁 广	24.00	2008.8
37	978-7-301-13662-1	机械制造技术	宁广庆	42.00	2008.8
38	978-7-301-13661-4	汽车电控技术	祁翠琴	39.00	2008.8
39	978-7-301-13658-4	汽车发动机电控系统原理与维修	张吉国	25.00	2008.8
40	978-7-301-13653-9	工程力学	武昭晖	25.00	2008.8
41	978-7-301-14139-7	汽车空调原理及维修	林 钢	26.00	2008.8
42	978-7-301-13652-2	金工实训	柴增田	22.00	2009.1
43	978-7-301-14656-9	实用电路基础	张 虹	28.00	2009.1
44	978-7-301-14655-2	模拟电子技术原理与应用	张 虹	26.00	2009.1
45	978-7-301-14453-4	EDA 技术与 VHDL	宋振辉	28.00	2009.2
46	978-7-301-14470-1	数控编程与操作	刘瑞已	29.00	2009.3
47	978-7-301-14469-5	可编程控制器原理及应用(三菱机型)	张玉华	24.00	2009.3
48	978-7-301-12385-0	微机原理及接口技术	王用伦	29.00	2009.4
49	978-7-301-12390-4	电力电子技术	梁南丁	29.00	2009.4
50	978-7-301-12383-6	电气控制与PLC(西门子系列)	李 伟	26.00	2009.6
51	978-7-301-13651-5	金属工艺学	柴增田	27.00	2009.6
52	978-7-301-12389-8	电机与拖动	梁南丁	32.00	2009.7
53	978-7-301-12391-1	数字电子技术	房永刚	24.00	2009.7
54	978-7-301-13659-1	CAD/CAM 实体造型教程与实训(Pro/ENGINEER 版)	诸小丽	38.00	2009.7
55	978-7-301-15378-9	汽车底盘构造与维修	刘东亚	34.00	2009.7

序号	书号	书名	编著者	定价	出版日期
56	978-7-301-13656-0	机械设计基础	时忠明	25.00	2009.8
57	978-7-301-12387-4	电子线路 CAD	殷庆纵	28.00	2009.8
58	978-7-301-12382-9	电气控制及 PLC 应用(三菱系列)	华满香	24.00	2009.9
59	978-7-301-15692-6	机械制图	吴百中	26.00	2009.9
60	978-7-301-15676-6	机械制图习题集	吴百中	26.00	2009.9
61	978-7-301-16898-1	单片机设计应用与仿真	陆旭明	26.00	2010.2
62	978-7-301-15578-3	汽车文化	刘 锐	28.00	2009.8
63	978-7-301-15742-8	汽车使用	刘彦成	26.00	2009.9
64	978-7-301-16919-3	汽车检测与诊断技术	娄 云	35.00	2010.2
65	978-7-301-17122-6	AutoCAD 机械绘图项目教程	张海鹏	36.00	2010.5
66	978-7-301-17079-3	汽车营销实务	夏志华	25.00	2010.6
67	978-7-301-17148-6	普通机床零件加工	杨雪青	26.00	2010.6
68	978-7-301-16830-1	维修电工技能与实训	陈学平	37.00	2010.7
69	978-7-301-13660-7	汽车构造(上册)——发动机构造	罗灯明	30.00	2010.8
70	978-7-301-17398-5	数控加工技术项目教程	李东君	48.00	2010.8
71	978-7-301-17573-6	AutoCAD 机械绘图基础教程	王长忠	32.00	2010.8
72	978-7-301-17324-4	电机控制与应用	魏润仙	34.00	2010.8
73	978-7-301-17557-6	CAD/CAM 数控编程项目教程(UG 版)	慕 灿	45.00	2010.8
74	978-7-301-17609-2	液压传动	龚肖新	22.00	2010.8
75	978-7-301-17569-9	电工电子技术项目教程	杨德明	32.00	2010.8
76	978-7-301-17679-5	机械零件数控加工	李 文	38.00	2010.8
77	978-7-301-17608-2	机械加工工艺编制	于爱武	45.00	2010.8
78	978-7-301-17696-2	模拟电子技术	蒋 然	35.00	2010.8
79	978-7-301-17707-5	零件加工信息分析	谢 蕾	46.00	2010.8
80	978-7-301-17712-9	电子技术应用项目式教程	王志伟	32.00	2010.8
81	978-7-301-17730-3	电力电子技术	崔 红	23.00	2010.9
82	978-7-301-17711-2	汽车专业英语图解教程	侯锁军	22.00	2010.9
83	978-7-301-17821-8	汽车机械基础项目化教学标准教程	傅华娟	40.00	2010.10
84	978-7-301-17532-3	汽车构造(下册)——底盘构造	罗灯明	28.00	2010.10
85	978-7-301-17877-5	电子信息专业英语	高金玉	26.00	2010.10

电子书(PDF 版)、电子课件和相关教学资源下载地址：http://www.pup6.com/ebook.htm，欢迎下载。

欢迎免费索取样书，请填写并通过 E-mail 提交教师调查表，下载地址：http://www.pup6.com/down/教师信息调查表 excel 版.xls，欢迎订购。

欢迎投稿，并通过 E-mail 提交个人信息卡，下载地址：http://www.pup6.com/down/zhuyizhexinxika.rar。

联系方式：010-62750667，laiqingbeida@126.com，linzhangbo@126.com，欢迎来电来信。